" '...the life of the ship and it [hidden] curate answer. It's the navi[hidden] says Peter Ifland, Ph.D., Co[hidden] USNR (Retired).

"Where are we?" Well, yes. We're sitting here safe and dry in the Science Museum at the University of Coimbra. But the question has a different urgency when the ship is approaching a rocky coast and the life of the ship and its crew depends on a fast and accurate answer. It's the navigator's job to provide the answer."

—Peter Ifland, Lecture at the University of Coimbra, Portugal, October 2000.

"Over the years, Peter Ifland has built an immensely important collection of navigation instruments, equal to the standard of any large maritime museum in the world."

—Willem Morzer Bruyns, Senior Curator, Scheepvaart Museum, Amsterdam, The Netherlands, on Dr. Ifland's donation of his collection of navigation instruments to The Mariner's Museum, 1998.

"[Peter Ifland's gift of his navigation instrument collection] is certain to become an essential research resource that will light the path of understanding of the navigational arts through the ages. The Museum's collection will become a lodestone for all interested in celestial navigation."

—Stuart Talbot, Chairman (1998) of the Scientific Instrument Society, London.

On Peter Ifland's *Taking the Stars: Celestial Navigation from Argonauts to Astronauts*. Newport News: The Mariners' Museum, 1998.

"Peter Ifland has produced a wonderfully readable and remarkably thorough account of the history of sextants and other instruments of celestial navigation."

—Deborah Jean Warner, Curator, Physical Sciences,
National Museum of American History, Smithsonian Institution.

"Dr. Ifland's evidence and information is presented on three levels through superbly detailed photographs of the instruments, via documentary history of their development, and in lucid and comprehensive instructions for the practical use of each instrument."

—Allan Chapman, Wadham College, Oxford.

"*Taking the Stars* will likely impress, inform, and delight historians and mariners for as long as the fascinating tools it documents. It must be the definitive treatise on instruments used for celestial navigation, tracing their history from the earliest Chinese and Arabic systems for determining the altitude of the sun in home waters, right through to the complex averaging and recording aviation octants developed during World War II and, yes, even the little bubble sextant used on the *Gemini IV* space flights."

—Ben Ellison, *Maritime Life and Traditions*, No. 9, 2000.

"...a tremendous addition to nautical history... The experienced navigator will gain new insight and the novice will undoubtedly be awed by the beauty of the instruments and Ifland's lucid explanation of the process of navigation by the stars."

—Twain Braden, *Ocean Navigator.*

Line of Position Navigation

Sumner and Saint-Hilaire, The Two Pillars of Modern Celestial Navigation

The iron hulled *Pommern* under full sail. (National Museums & Galleries of Northern Ireland, Ulster Folk and Transportation Museum.)

Line of Position Navigation

SUMNER AND SAINT-HILAIRE,
THE TWO PILLARS OF MODERN
CELESTIAL NAVIGATION

by Michel Vanvaerenbergh
and Peter Ifland

Unlimited Publishing
Bloomington, Indiana

Distributing Publisher:
Unlimited Publishing LLC
Bloomington, Indiana

http://www.unlimitedpublishing.com

Contributing Publisher:
Peter Ifland

Cover images:

The French Ironclad *Magenta* at Cherbourg for the British Channel Fleet's visit of August 1865 (detail). Used with the kind permission of Mr. Mark Myers, RSMA, P/ASMA, Cornwall, United Kingdom.

Chart of the South Atlantic, "Berchaus, Chart of the World, Gotha Jestes, Perthes,1882", with permission of the Bibliothéque Royal de Belgique, Brussels.

Unlimited Publishing LLC provides worldwide book design, printing, marketing and distribution services for professional writers and small to mid-size presses, serving as distributing publisher. Sole responsibility for the content of each work rests with the author(s) and/or contributing publisher(s). The opinions expressed herein may not be interpreted in any way as representing those of Unlimited Publishing, nor any of its affiliates.

First Edition.

Copies of this book and others
are available to order online at:

http://www.unlimitedpublishing.com/authors

ISBN 1-58832-068-5

Unlimited Publishing
Bloomington, Indiana

Acknowledgements

THE AUTHORS gratefully wish to acknowledge the critical contribution to the preparation of this publication by the following institutions:

Museé national de la Marine, Palais de Chaillot, Paris, for copies of several articles by Marcq Saint-Hilaire in the *Revue Maritime et Coloniale* and for biographical material on Admiral Saint-Hilaire.

Service historique de la Marine, Château de Vincennes, Armées, France for biographical material on Admiral Saint-Hilaire and copies of a number of publications from the 1870's related to navigation techniques of that era.

Harvard University Collection of Historic Scientific Instruments and the Harvard Archives for biographical information on Captain Sumner.

Contents

Acknowledgements • *vii*

Introduction • *xi*

Chapter 1 *The State of the Navigator's Art at the Beginning of the Nineteenth Century* • 1

Chapter 2 *Captain Thomas H. Sumner and His Line of Position Method* • 9

Chapter 3 *Marcq Saint-Hilaire and His "Intercept" Method* • 17

Chapter 4 *Sumner's and Saint-Hilaire's Methods in the Twentieth Century* • 23

Bibliography • 30

Appendix A *A New and Accurate Method of Finding a Ship's Position at Sea*, by Captain Thomas H. Sumner, 1843, Reprinted • [A-*i*], [A-1]–[A-88]

Appendix B Part 1 *Note on the Determination of Position*, by Marcq Saint-Hilaire, Captain of Frigates, 1873, • [B1-*i*], [B1-41]-[B1-58]

Appendix B Part 2 *Calculation of the Observed Position*, by Marcq Saint-Hilaire, Captain of Frigates, 1875, • [B2-341]–[B2-376]

Appendix C *Technical Notes* • [C-1]

Introduction

AN EXPERIENCED NAVIGATOR can step out on deck, sight three celestial bodies with a sextant, note the time of each observation, step back into the wheel-house, do the arithmetic of sight reduction, and plot a tight fix on the chart, all within about five minutes.

It was not always so quick and easy to find one's way by the stars. We owe a succession of brilliant, insightful people spanning a millennium for the remarkable capability we now have. Astronomers provide us with almanacs that accurately predict the position of the sun, the stars, the planets and of our erratic moon for years into the future. Clock makers now count the oscillations of cesium atoms, average the values from a number of different locations and transmit time signals to us by satellite. Instrument makers give us sextants that are light, stable over a wide range of temperatures, with drum-micrometers that are easy to read to one-tenth of a minute. Our charts are accurate and reliable with all the navigation aids and potential hazards clearly marked. In addition, the mathematics of sight reduction has been simplified, even computerized, to the point of sixth grade arithmetic.

For all of these dazzling modern developments, we owe two practicing navigators of the nineteenth century for the fundamental concepts of celestial navigation that we use today: Captain Thomas Hubbard Sumner for his Line of Position method and Lieutenant, later Admiral, Marcq Saint-Hilaire of the French Navy for his Intercept method. The purpose of this book is to describe the basic concept of celestial navigation that each invented and subsequently published. A reprint of the First Edition of Captain Sumner's book of 1843 (Appendix A) and a translation of the key articles by Lieutenant Marcq Saint-Hilaire from the mid 1870's (Appendix B) will make these landmark publications more broadly available. Finally, a brief review of the modification of sight reduction methods and almanac presentations that made Sumner's and Marcq Saint-Hilaire's methods ultimately so universally popular and practical will bring the story up to date.

Appreciation of the conceptual contributions of Captain Sumner and Lieutenant Saint-Hilaire is particularly appropriate at this time. The advent of the Global Positioning System, (GPS), has all but completely re-placed celestial navigation. The celestial bodies used for GPS are man-made satellites instead of the sun, moon and stars. With the recent release of un-degraded signals for civilian use, positions accurate to three meters, available instantaneously, is routine. Computer programs continuously display positions on exquisitely detailed digital charts along with all the related information a navigator could hope for. To the extent that celestial is taught and used at all, it is as a backup, just in case the GPS system should fail.

Chapter 1

The State of the Navigator's Art
at the Beginning of the Nineteenth Century

ALL OF THE TOOLS a navigator needed to establish his position were well developed by the early 1800's. Chronometers were dependable enough and beginning to become affordable. Sextants and octants were accurate and easy to use. The first edition of Bowditch in 1802 corrected most of the thousands of errors in previously published navigation tables. Charts became progressively more accurate as the capability to determine longitude improved.

Latitude was easy to determine by any one of several methods. The straightforward approach was to measure the altitude of the sun at the moment it passed through the meridian at Local Apparent Noon (LAN). The only other piece of information needed, the sun's declination for that day, was readily available from tables in the Nautical Almanacs, the ephemerides or in the standard navigational texts. [1,2,3]

Example:[2, p 152] October 17th, 1805, in longitude by estimation 51W, the meridian altitude of the sun's lower limb was 28°40', the observer being north of the sun; height of the eye 14 feet. Required the latitude of the place of observation?

Observed alt. sun's lower limb	28° 40'S	Sun's declination 17th Oct	9°12'S
Semidiameter	+16'	Correction for Longitude	+3'
Dip, refraction	-5'	Reduced declination	9° 15'S
True altitude sun's center	28° 51'	Sun's Zenith distance	61° 9'N
		Latitude	51° 54'N

This method could be applied equally well with the fixed stars, the planets and the moon using the data on declination, with suitable corrections, from the Nautical Almanac.

It was not always possible to observe a celestial body at the meridian. In this case, latitude could be determined by making two observations of the altitude of a celestial body, knowing the elapsed time in the interval between the two observations measured by a sandglass or a watch. Pedro Nunes first proposed this method in 1537[4] as a graphical solution on a globe. The method was expanded by Hues in 1594[5] and greatly improved by Douwes[6] with the publication of tables giving the trigonometric values for the factors in the computation of the sun's meridian altitude.

Example[1, p160] Being at sea in latitude 46°30' north by account, when the sun's declination was 11°17'N at 10h.2m. in the forenoon, the sun's corrected central altitude was 46°55' and at 11h.27m. in the forenoon, his correct central altitude was 54°9'. Required the true latitude, and the true time of the day when the greater altitude was taken?

	Times	Altitudes	Natural sines			
	h m s			Latitude by account	46°30' Sec	0.16219
2nd Obs,	11 27 00	54° 9'	81055*	Declination	11°17' Sec	0.00848
1st Obs	10 2 00	46° 55'	73036*	Log Ratio		0.17067
Elapsed time	1 25 00	Diff Natural Sines	8019	Log Diff Natural Sines		3.90412
½ Elapsed time	0 42 30		h m s	Log ½ Elapsed time		0.73429
		Middle time**	1 15 10	Log middle Time		4.80908
		½ Elapsed time	0 42 30	The corresponding Log Rising is**		3.00608
		2nd Obs. from Noon	0 32 40	Subtract log ratio Secant*		0.17067

Natural Number 685 corresponding to log 2.83541

Natural sine of the greatest altitude 81055 90°00'

Natural sine of Sun's meridian altitude 81740 equal to 54°50'

Sun's zenith distance 35°10'N

Sun's declination is 11°17'N

Latitude is 46°27'N

*From included tables of logarithmic and trigonometric functions.

** "Middle Time" is the difference between the time of occurrence of half the elapsed time between the two observations and noon. *** "Log Rising" is the correction applied to the natural sine of the greatest altitude to obtain the natural sine of the meridian altitude, derived from the time from noon of the observation of the greatest altitude.

For many years the nautical almanacs provided projections of the time of solar and lunar eclipses, the occultation of one of the fixed stars by the moon and the time of eclipses of the satellites of Jupiter (when a satellite enters Jupiter's shadow) and occultation (when a satellite passes behind Jupiter). Any of these predictable celestial events could be used to determine the time at the prime meridian. This value could then be compared with the local apparent time to deduce longitude. However, eclipses occurred infrequently and it was difficult to make most of the other observations at sea. Thus, they proved much more useful to land-based surveyors and mapmakers.

An emerging method of finding longitude in the early 1800's was "Longitude by Chronometer". This method depended on calculating the angle between the observer's meridian and the meridian of the star by solving the classical **PZX** spherical triangle where **P** is the celestial pole, either North or South; **Z** is the observer's zenith, the point directly over-head; and **X** is the position of the celestial body, usually the sun. The calculation of the angle at **P**, known as the Local Hour Angle (LHA), is made using three known values: the declination of the celestial body read from the nautical almanac for the time and date of the observation, the altitude of the celestial body as measured with an octant or sextant with appropriate corrections, and the dead reckoning latitude.

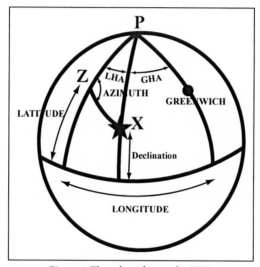

Figure 1. The celestial triangle, **PZX**.

The equation is:

$$\cos P^* = \frac{\cos \mathbf{XZ}\,[90 - \text{altitude}] \pm \cos \mathbf{PZ}\,[90 - \text{latitude}] \times \cos \mathbf{PX}\,[90 - \text{declination}]}{\sin \mathbf{PZ}\,[90 - \text{latitude}] \times \sin \mathbf{PX}\,[90 - \text{declination}]}$$

*Notations in[ ] indicate how the value is derived using the known factors in the triangle.

The ship's chronometer gives the mean time at the prime meridian when the sun sight was taken or the time of the observation needed to enter the Nautical Almanac to find the right ascension of a celestial body other than the sun. For a sun sight, the local hour angle, **P** from the above equation, was then added to (if the sun was east of the observer's meridian) or subtracted from (if the sun was west of the observer's meridian) the chronometer's mean time to get longitude. Similarly, the angle **P** was added to or subtracted from any other celestial body's right ascension to obtain longitude.

The following example was referred to as "Bowditch's third method" for determining apparent time that could then be compared to chronometer time to get longitude. This is the method Captain Sumner used in his calculations to derive a line of position:

Example[1, p173] Suppose on the 10th of October 1804, sea account, at 8^h21^mA.M. by watch, in the latitude 51°30'N, longitude 52°E of Greenwich per account, the altitude of the sun's lower limb, by fore observation was 13°32', and the correction for Semidiameter and dip 12 miles; required the apparent time of the observation?

						90° 0'
					Latitude	51°30'N
Colatitude	38°30' N		Cosecant	0.20585	Colatitude	38°30'N
Declination	6°34' S		Secant	0.00286		
Difference Meridian Altitude	31°56'	Natural sine	52893			
☉'s corrected Altitude	13°40'	Natural sine	23627			
		Difference	29266	log = 4.46636		
				4.67507	Corresponding to	
			which in the column of rising is 3hr 52' 51"			
			subtracted from 12hr	12		
			gives True Apparent Time	8hr 7' 9" [which		
			compared to Chronometer Time gives Longitude.]			

[The declination is 6°34'S, this added to 90° gives the polar distance 96°34'. To the sun's observed altitude 13°32', add 12 miles [minutes] and subtract the refraction 4', the remainder is the Sun's corrected altitude, 13°40'.]

Although the Longitude by Chronometer method was widely used, it had one fundamental flaw: the accuracy of the longitude calculation depended on the accuracy of the value for latitude used in the calculation. Ships were lost because of incorrect longitudes resulting from use of inaccurate values for latitude. Captain Sumner was acutely aware of this problem and, as we shall see, the discovery of his Line of Position method resulted from his exploration of the effect of errors in latitude on his calculation of longitude.

Of course, longitude by chronometer was no more accurate than the ship's chronometer. The best practice for determining time at sea and thence chronometer error and longitude was by "lunars". This method, more formally called Lunar Distances, was developed in the mid 1700's as a way of determining time from celestial observations in contrast to the mechanical method using clocks. Ultimately, John Harrison's clocks became the common method of telling the time at the prime meridian but lunars were used until the early 1900's to determine time and chronometer error at sea and ashore.

Think of the moon as the hands of a clock moving across the sky. The angular distance between the moon, the sun or the fixed stars at a given time could be predicted with sufficient accuracy and recorded in the Nautical Almanacs. The basic concept was to measure the angular distance between the moon and one of the tabulated celestial bodies and thus derive the time at the prime meridian at which that distance was predicted to have occurred.

Good practice in the early 1800's was to determine time and chronometer error once every day or two, the more frequently the better. The sun was a commonly used reference since atmospheric visibility was best during the daytime. Four observers were used for most accurate results: one to use the sextant to measure the angle between one of the moon's limbs and one of the sun's limbs; one to measure the altitude of the moon; one to measure the altitude of the sun; and one to record the times and sextant readings. A multitude of corrections were required. The almanac data were based on observations made from the center of the earth so that parallax corrections were required. Almanac predications used the center of the sun and moon for the tabulated values but observations were made at the limbs so that semidiameter corrections had to be made. Altitude observations had to be corrected as usual for sextant index error, dip, and refraction. Altitudes also needed to be corrected to the time of the distance measurement if the observations were not taken simultaneously. In addition, times as kept by "sea account" had to be corrected for astronomers' time as recorded in the almanacs. Fortunately, much of the required corrections and the arithmetic had been produced in tabular form in publications like the almanacs, Bowditch,[1] Mackay,[2] and Moore,[3] thus importantly expediting calculations. Even with this, Bowditch divided the calculations into two steps; "Preparation" and "To find the correct distance and the longitude."

Example[1, p186] Suppose the following observations were made May 18, 1804, sea account at 7h 15m 25s P.M., the distance of the nearest limbs of the sun and moon 106°3'58", altitude of the moon's upper limb 23°30', altitude of the sun's lower limb 11°54', the longitude by account being 24°W. Required the true longitude?

Preparation			h m s
May 18 by sea account is May 17 by Nautical almanac			7 15 25
Longitude 24°W, in time			1 36
Reduced time May 17d			8 51 25

☽'s S.D at noon	15' 11"	☽'s Horizontal Parallax noon	55' 45"	☽'s Observ. Altitude	23°30'		
at midnight	15' 6"	midnight	55' 26"	Subtract	20'		
difference	5"	difference	19"	☽'s Apparent. Alt	23°10'		
Table XII[a]	4"	Table XII[a]	14"	☽'s Zenith Dist	66°50'		
	15' 7"	☽'s Horizontal Parallax	55' 31"	☉'s Observed Alt	11° 54'		
Table XVI[b]	6"	Correction for Parallax[c]		add	12'		
		55'31";and ZD 66°	48' 35"	Apparent Altitude	12°06'		
☽'s Semidiam.	15' 13"	**d** = 10',Parallax=1"	1"	☉'s Zenith Distance	77°54'		
		D = 17", Z.D. = 50'	14"				
		Correction to ☽'s Altitude	48' 50"				
		Observed distance 106°	3' 58"				
☉'s refraction	4' 21"	☽'s Semidiameter	15' 13"				
☉'s Parallax	9"	☉'s Semidiameter	15' 51"				
☉'s Corrected Altitude	4' 12"	Apparent Distance 106° 35'					

To find the correct distance and longitude

Apparent Distance	106°35'	Constant Logarithm	9.6990		
☽'s Zenith Distance	66°50'	Half-sum 125°39' logcosec	10.0901		
☉'s Zenith Distance	77°54'	Distance 106° 35 logsine	9.9815		
Sum	251°19'	Reserved logarithm	9.7706	Reserved Log	9.7706
Half Sum	125°39'	☉'s Z.D. 77°54' logsine	9.9902	☽'s Z.D. 66°50' logsine	9.9635
☽'s Zenith Distance	66°50'	1ˢᵗ Rem 58°49' logcosec	10.0678	2ⁿᵈ Rem. 47°45' logcosec	10.1306
1ˢᵗ Remainder	58°48'	Corr. ☉'s Alt. 4'12" P.L	1.6320	Corr.to ☽'s Alt. 48'50" P.L.	.5666
Half Sum	125°39'	1ˢᵗ Correction 6'14' P.L	1.4606	2ⁿᵈ Correction 1°6'41 P.L.	.4323
☉'s Zenith Distance	77°54'				
2ⁿᵈ Remainder	47°45'				

			Distance at 9ʰʳ	106°12' 9"		
			Distance at 12ʰ	107°37' 3"		
Apparent Distance	106° 35' 2"			1°24'54"	P.L.	.3264
+First correction	6'14"		Distance at 9ʰʳ	106°12' 9"		
+Corr. ☽'s Altitude	48'50"		Corrected dist	106°19' 8"		
	107° 30' 6"			6' 59"	P.L.	1.4112
-Second correction	1° 6'41"	Time	0ʰʳ14ᵐ48ˢ		P.L.	1.0848
-Corr. ☉'s Altitude	4'12"	Add	9ʰ			
	106° 19'13"	Time at Greenwich	9ʰʳ14ᵐ48ˢ			
Table XIXᵈ(6-1)	5"	Time at ship	7ʰʳ15ᵐ25ˢ			
Corrected Distance	106° 19' 8"	Longitude in time	1ʰʳ59ᵐ23ˢ = 29°51'W			

ᵃ Table XII relates time to values such as parallax, proportional logarithms or Semidiameter.

ᵇ Table XVI provides the "Augmentation" i.e., the increase in the moon's Semidiameter as a function of the moon's altitudeᶜ

ᵈ Table XIX gives the effect of parallax on the moon's distance from the sun or a star.

P.L. Proportional Logarithm

The examples cited above show that it was entirely possible for an early 1800's navigator to find time and get a reasonably precise fix of latitude and longitude. As with most navigation techniques, regular practice with the sextant, frequent checks of chronometer error and rigorous attention to the calculations were required for best results. Failure of the ship's captain to perform the required observations frequently enough, whether due to bad weather, boredom, or simple inattention to duty, was a common reason for putting the ship in peril. The Lunar Distance method for determining time and thence longitude was particularly laborious and error prone and navigators were not always diligent in doing the work required to find their position accurately. But navigators of the early nineteenth century were no different from navigators of all other times. They continually searched for faster, easier and more accurate methods of fixing their position on a chart.

Chapter 2

Captain Thomas H. Sumner
and His Line of Position Method

ON THE MORNING of December 17, 1837, Captain Sumner was 22 days out of Charleston, South Carolina bound for Greenock, Scotland.[7] The weather was foul with heavy gales and thick overcast. As he approached St. George's Channel between Ireland and Wales, he desperately needed a fix to ensure that the strong winds out of the South-South East had not set him onto the rocks and shoals of the southeast coast of Ireland. A critical checkpoint was Small's Light off the western coast of Wales that he expected to sight late in the morning. At about 10:15 the clouds parted just enough for Sumner to take the sun's altitude and to note chronometer time. He used these data to calculate Longitude by Chronometer using his DR latitude. The calculation gave him a position comfortably south of the hazardous Irish coast and only 9 miles east of his DR position. Acutely aware of the effect on an error in DR Latitude on Longitude by Chronometer, Sumner then asked himself the pivotal question: What if I have been set further to the North by these strong winds out of the SSE and my DR latitude is in error resulting in an erroneous longitude? Sumner redid the calculation using a latitude 10' north of his DR. This placed the ship 27 miles ENE of the DR position. He then did the calculation once more, this time using a latitude 20' north of his DR. This new calculation placed the ship an additional 27 miles ENE of his DR. His plot of these positions on a Mercator chart is shown in Figure 2.

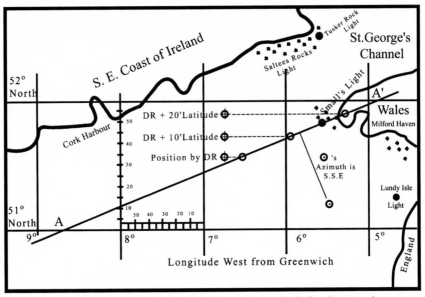

Figure 2. Captain Sumner's plot of his DR position and calculated Longitudes by Chronometer while looking for Small's Light on the morning of December 17, 1837. Redrawn from Sumner's Plate III.[7] See Appendix A.

Captain Sumner then brought his stroke of brilliant insight to derive two far-reaching conclusions:

First: "It then at once appeared that the observed altitude must have happened at *all the three* points, and at *Small's light*, and at the ship, at *all the same instant of time*;…"

Second: "…these three positions were then seen to *lie in the direction of Small's light* …and it followed that Small's light must bear E.N.E. if the Chronometer was right."

Sumner's recognition of the fact that the sun's altitude at that moment would be the same at the three calculated positions led him directly to formulate the concept of "parallels [circles] of equal altitude." This was not a new concept since even ancient planispheric astrolabes provided *almucanters* that were circles of equal altitude. In modern terms, the idea is that the altitude of a celestial body will be the same anywhere on a circle on the earth, the point on the earth's surface directly below the celestial body (GP, the Geographic Position) being the center. Furthermore, the azimuth of the celestial body will be perpendicular to the tangent of the circle at the point of observation. These concepts, further refined by Marcq Saint-Hilaire 40 years later in his "Intercept" method, are the foundation of today's celestial navigation procedures.

It was an incredible stroke of luck that the clouds parted at 10 AM when the sun's azimuth was SSE. This gave Sumner a line perpendicular to the sun's azimuth running ENE that just happened to pass through Small's light. He steered down this line and came upon Small's light close aboard in less than an hour. If he had made the sun sight an hour later, the azimuth of the sun would have been further to the south and the Line of Position would have run more to the east, crossing land well south of Small's light.

Sumner's second conclusion, that a line of equal altitudes gives the true bearing of land was an important improvement in navigation techniques of that time. Navigators depended on making a landfall at an identifiable point and then sailing up or down the coast as necessary to find the next way station or their final destination. Previously, it was necessary for the celestial object to bear precisely east or west or be on the meridian in order to derive a bearing to land. Sumner made it possible to find the bearing any time the celestial body could be observed.

Before long, navigators realized that Sumner's concept of a "line of position" could be used to fix the ships position precisely, either by plotting on a chart or by calculation of the latitude and longitude. As we shall see, forty years later Marcq Saint-Hilaire used the Line of Position concept as the fundamental starting point in has "Intercept" method. Establishing a fix by the crossing of lines of position from the simultaneous observations of two or three celestial bodies is still the basic concept of today's celestial navigation methods.

Captain Sumner formally published his methods in 1843,[7] almost six years after his original observations off the coast of Ireland. The title page reads: *A New and Accurate Method for Finding A Ship's Position at Sea, by projection on a Mercator's chart when the Latitude, Longitude and Apparent Time at the ship are uncertain; one altitude of the Sun, with the true Greenwich Time, determines, First, The True Bearing of the Land; Secondly, The errors of Longitude by Chronometer consequent to any errors in Latitude; Thirdly, The Sun's true Azimuth.* Appendix A is a reprint of the entire First Edition of this historic book where Sumner explains his "parallels of equal altitude" method.

By the time of publication of his book, Sumner had refined his "Method of Projection" i.e. a plot on a chart. His first rule was to choose two latitudes in round degrees, no minutes, for the calculation of Longitude by Chronometer. One latitude was less than the DR latitude and the other greater than the DR latitude (See Points A and A' in Figure 2, above), thus avoiding the complexity of interpolation between degrees in the tables. He extended the concept of "Double Altitudes" to produce two parallels of equal altitude that would gave a fix of the ship's position at the point where the two parallels of equal altitude cross. He also emphasized the point that a line perpendicular to a tangent to the parallel of equal altitude gives the azimuth of the celestial body from the point where the tangent touches the arc of the circle of equal altitude. As we shall see in the following chapter, this fact is a critical concept in Marcq Saint-Hilaire's intercept method.

The first example Sumner gives in his book reproduces the situation as he urgently looked for Small's Light in St. George's Channel:

Example I.[7, p14] On 17th December, 1837, sea account, a ship having run between 600 and 700 miles without an observation, and being near the land, the latitude by D.R. was 51°37' N., but supposed liable to an error of 10 miles on either side, N. or S. The altitude of the sun's lower limb, was 12°02' at about 10 ½ A.M., the eye of the observer being 17 feet above the sea; the mean time at Greenwich, by Chronometer, was 10^{h}47^{m}13^s A.M.

Required: The true bearing of land; what error of longitude the ship is subject to, by Chronometer, for the uncertainty of the Latitude; the true sun's azimuth.

Dip	4' 3"	SemiDiameter	16' 8"
Refraction	4' 23"	Parallax	+ 8"
	-8' 26"		+16' 16"
			-8' 26"
	Correction to Observed Altitude		+8'
Observed Altitude ☉'s Lower Limb	12°		02'
	Correction		+ 8'
	True Altitude ☉'s Center	12°	10'

1st. The Latitude by D.R. was 51°37' N. The Latitude of the next degree *less*, without odd minutes is 51° N. and that, the next degree *greater*, is 52° N.

2nd and 3rd. Find the Longitude of these two points, as follows:

⊙'s Altitude 12°10'				
For the point A in Latitude 51°N.				
Latitude	51° N		sec.	0.20113
Declination	23° 23' S		sec.	0.03722
Sum	74° 23'	Natural cos 26920		
⊙'s Altitude	12° 10'	Natural sin 21076		
H M S		Difference 5844	Log	3.76671
1 43 59	from noon = log rising =			4.00506
12 hours				
10 16 01	Apparent time at ship			
- 3 37	Equation of time			
10 12 24	Mean time at ship			
10 47 13	Mean time by chronometer			
34 49	= 8°42¼' West of Greenwich			

⊙'s Altitude 12°10'				
For the point A' in Latitude 52°N.				
Latitude	52° N		sec.	0.21066
Declination	23° 23' S		sec.	0.03722
Sum	75° 23'	Natural cos 25235		
⊙'s Altitude	12° 10'	Natural sin 21076		
H M S		Difference 5159	Log	3.61899
1 28 28½	from noon = log rising =			3.86687
12 hours				
10 31 31½	Apparent time at ship			
- 3 37	Equation of time			
10 27 54½	Mean time at ship			
10 47 13	Mean time by chronometer			
19 18½	= 4°49½' West of Greenwich			

4th. On Mercator's Chart, Plate III [see Figure 2, above], project the point A in Latitude 51°N, Longitude 8°42¼' W; and project the point A' in Latitude 52° N, Longitude 4°49½' W.

5th. Join the points A and A' by a straight line; and the ships position is *upon* this line; which referred to the compass, is found to tend E.N.E. true; and shows that *Small's Light* bears E.N.E. true from the ship.

6th. The error in Longitude for which the ship was subject for 10 miles error of Latitude is 39 minutes, as projected.

7th. The sun's true azimuth is 2 points from South or S.S.E. as projected.

Several important conclusions can be drawn from this example. Sumner's method produces a great deal of useful information from a single observation. First, the ship's position is on a line that is an arc of a circle of equal altitude. Second, the calculations avoid any error that might arise from an error in the D.R. latitude as it was commonly used to derive Longitude by Chronometer. Third, a line perpendicular to a tangent to the circle of equal altitude gives the true azimuth of the sun, or said conversely, the ship is on a line that is perpendicular to the azimuth of the sun. He emphasized the critical advantage of his method that observations can be taken at any convenient time whereas conventional techniques required that observations of altitude be made precisely as the sun passes through the meridian or when the sun bears precisely east or west.

Sumner went on to describe in his book how to produce a fix of position from observations of the sun at two different times by advancing the earlier circle of equal altitude to the time of the second observation according to the ship's movement during the interval. He also provided instructions and examples of how to use the sun, a fixed star, a planet or the moon alone or in combination to obtain a fix, thus importantly extending the usefulness of his method.

Prior to the publication of his book, Sumner revealed his method broadly and it received positive assessment from many quarters. A key endorsement came from a special committee convened by the Naval Library and Institute at the Boston Navy Yard in 1843. Their report stated: "…your committee is of the opinion, that in practice Capt. Sumner's discovery (for we can call it nothing less,) will prove a useful auxiliary to the present knowledge of Navigators, and, as such, would recommend it to the attention of all persons interested in the promulgation and improvement of Nautical Science."[7] Sumner's method was adopted almost immediately thereafter throughout the U.S. Navy.

Sumner's method was so intuitive and simple that it was rapidly put to use by American navigators. It quickly became common practice to "plot a Sumner line" or simply "do a Sumner". Sumner wrote of "…a ship's position on a line…" but he did not use the specific term "Line of Position" or "LOP" by which the method is now known. American textbooks of navigation of the 1850's had not yet adopted the term. The English Navy navigation manual by Lt. Henry Raper, RN of 1866[8] uses the name "Position on a Line of Bearing" for Sumner's method. By that time, the U.S. Naval Academy was using the term "Line of Position" to describe Sumner's "Circles of Equal Altitude Method".[9]

It was the same Lt. Henry Raper who first described the Sumner method in print in England in 1844 in an article in the *Nautical Magazine*.[10] Practicing English navigators appear to have accepted the method readily and it became common practice throughout the Royal Navy and particularly with the navigators of the Pacific and Orient Company. Recognition and acceptance in France seems to have been slower. Biographical notes on Marcq Saint-Hilaire in the files of the Marine Nationale, Vincennes, report that Sumner's method "…was not known in France until 1847 and expanded very slowly. In 1868 and 1870, the method was presented by Caillet, examiner in the marine and hydrographic schools, and by Fasci, Professor of Hydrographics. About the same time, the Naval officers Mottez and Fleuriais were teaching the method of lines of altitude on the school-ship Jean-Bart."[11]

While the Americans preferred graphic techniques to plot lines of position on a chart, French navigators calculated the actual latitude and longitude of their positions. One of the steps in establishing a line of position, whether graphically or by calculation, is determination of the azimuth of the celestial body **Z**, the angle **PZX** in the spherical triangle. Azimuth could be determined by calculation or simply by sighting with the magnetic compass.

Captain Sumner was well prepared to deal creatively with the mathematical techniques of navigation.[12,13] He was born on March 20, 1807, the son of a Boston architect. He entered Harvard at the age of fifteen. In his freshman year he studied plane geometry; solid geometry in his sophomore year; and "Analytic Geometry including Trigonometry", differential calculus and astronomy in his junior and senior years. He graduated in 1826. A hasty marriage ended in divorce in 1829. He promptly "ran away to sea", signing on as a common seaman in the China trade. His talents and training quickly progressed him through the ranks and by 1837 he held the rank of captain and was Master of his own ship. It was late that year, while sailing through the St. George Channel off the coast of Wales, that he conceived his "Line of Position" method that would quickly establish the name Sumner in the vocabulary and practice of navigators the world over.

Despite these successes, Thomas Hubbard Sumner's life was destined to end tragically. Shortly after his book was published in 1843, his mind began to fail. By 1850, at age 43, he was admitted to the McLean Insane Asylum, Boston. On his birthday in 1865 he was admitted to the Lunatic Hospital at Taunton, Massachusetts where he died in 1876 at age 69.

Chapter 3

Marcq Saint-Hilaire
and His "Intercept" Method

DESPITE THE POLITICAL TURMOIL of the 1860's and 70's in France, the French Navy continued to protect and expand the nation's foreign territories and colonies. Advancement of the art and science of navigation was a timely subject among French scientists and Naval officers. Officers on active duty published frequently in the *Revue Maritime et Coloniale* and sometimes were coauthors with astronomers from the Paris Observatory and with members of *l'Académie des Sciences* of the *Institut de France*. It was in this climate that Marcq Saint-Hilaire, *Capitaine de frégate*, developed and published his simplified method for finding a line of position that would become the world-wide standard.

Adolph Laurent Anatole Marcq de Blond de Saint-Hilaire had a brilliant and diversified career in the French Navy.[11,14] He entered the Naval service at age 15 in 1847. He attained the rank of Ensign of Vessels in 1854 and progressed regularly up the ranks to Rear Admiral in 1883. He published the critical elements of his *méthode du point rapproché* while Captain of the school ship *Renommée* from 1873 through 1875. He advanced to Commander in the Legion of Honor in 1881. He had a reputation for unusual competence and insight in mathematics and trigonometry. The record shows that Saint-Hilaire served extensively on ships on remote stations where he developed and sharpened his skills in navigation. He died of an infection at age 57 while Commandant of Marines in Algiers in 1889.

Saint-Hilaire published his instructions and critical assessment of the techniques of navigation in two papers in the *Revue Maritime et Coloniale*: the first, *Note sur la Détermination du Point*[15] in 1873 and the second, *Calcul du Point Observé*[16] in two parts in 1875. The Musée de la Marine, Paris, graciously provided copies of the original papers.

Appendix B is a translation of those sections of these historic articles that deal with the invention of the Intercept method.

In the first paper,[15] Saint-Hilaire provides detailed instructions on the methods of establishing a position on a chart that were in use in the French Navy in the early 1870's. He had not yet crystallized the elements of his new method but he clearly recognized the critical basic concept:

> Therefore, if one notices after the calculation and the construction of an altitude, that a certain small error [such as H_o - H_e] was committed in this altitude, one corrects the resultant altitude by taking a parallel to the line already drawn [Line of Position] at a distance in miles equal to the expressed error in minutes in the direction of the celestial body [azimuth, Z] or to the opposite, according to whether the employed altitude was too small or too large.[15]

The idea that errors in altitude from whatever source could be corrected by moving the line of position towards or away from the geographic position of the celestial body along the azimuth by a distance in miles equal to the minutes of error was not new. Most textbooks of navigation of the era expressed the concept when discussing the Sumner Line of Position method. Saint-Hilaire's contribution was to recognize that the same concept could be applied to the difference between the *observed* altitude of a celestial body and the altitude *calculated from an assumed position* to determine the true line of position.

In his second paper,[16] Saint-Hilaire begins with a concise description of his method of "estimated altitudes." He describes his method for calculating the results of a single observation based on the difference between the observed altitude of a celestial body and the altitude and azimuth that would have been observed at an estimated position at the time of the observation. He summarizes the technique as follows:

> …to calculate an observation, make the calculation of the altitude, [H_e] and the azimuth, [Z] of the celestial body for the estimated position, [e] and the time of observation. Subtract the estimated altitude from the observed altitude, [H_o - H_e]. Consider this difference as a displacement of the ship. The course is given by the azimuth and the distance is given by the difference in altitude. Correct the position [e'] along this track.

Figure 3 illustrates the simplicity of the concept. Using Saint-Hilaire's notations, **A** is the Geographic Position (GP) of the celestial body; **P** is the pole; **Z** is the azimuth of the celestial body; **e** is the estimated position, for example, the DR position; H_o is the observed altitude of the celestial body; H_e is the altitude of the celestial body calculated for the estimated position; $H_o - H_e$ is the difference in altitudes, in this case, the observed altitude is greater than the estimated altitude and the observed position, e', is *toward* the GP along the line of the azimuth; cc is a Line of Position drawn through e' perpendicular to the azimuth. QQ is the equator.

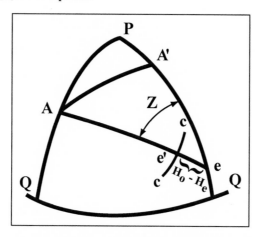

Figure 3. A plot of an observation by Saint-Hilaire's method.

Saint-Hilaire gives the following example to illustrate the method. In this example he calculates the difference between the latitude and longitude of the estimated position and the observed position, as was the practice in the French Navy at that time, but he goes on to give the method for plotting the positions on a chart with a Line of Position, as has become common practice.

Numerical example.[16, p347] On 24 October 1874, at 8 o'clock in the evening, at the estimated position $L_e = 35°30'$ N and $G_e = 9°30'$ W, one obtains the corrected altitude of Vega, $H_o = 48°51'00''$. The terrestrial coordinates of Vega, determined by the chronometer, will be L_a or D = 38°40'13'' N, and $G_a = 62°16'00''$ W.

$$\left.\begin{array}{l}\tan D' = \dfrac{\tan D}{\cos P} \\[1.5em] \cos Z = \tan(D'-L_e)\tan H_e\end{array}\right\} \sin H_e = \dfrac{\sin D}{\sin D'}\cos(D-L_e)$$

Latitude	Longitude		
$D = 38° 40'13"N$	$G_a = 62° 16'00"W$	$\tan D = \overline{1}.90325$	$\sin D = \overline{1}.79577$
$L_e = 35° 30'00"N$	$G_e = 9° 30'00"W$		
	$P = 52° 46'00"W$	$C \cos P\ \underline{0.21820}$	
$D' = \underline{52° 54'30"N}$		$\tan D'\ \underline{0.12145}$	$C\sin D'\ 0.09818$
$D'-L_e = 17° 24'30"N$		$\tan(D'-L_e)\ \overline{1}.4963$	$\cos(D'-L_e)\ \overline{1}.\underline{97964}$
		$\tan H_e\ \underline{0.0512}$	$\sin H_e\ \overline{1}.87359$
		$\cos Z\ \overline{1}.5475$	$H_e = 48°22'15"$
			$H_o = 48°51'00"$
	$\varepsilon\quad 26.9^{miles}$		
$\lambda = \quad 10'10"N$	$g\quad 33'06"W$	$Z = N69°20'\ W$	
$L_{e'} = 35° 40'10"N$	$G_{e'} = 10° 03'06"W$		$H_o-H_e = \quad 28'45"$

L$_a$ or **D** = declination or latitude of the GP; **G**$_a$ = longitude of the GP; **L**$_e$ = estimated latitude; **L**$_{e'}$ = observed latitude; **G**$_e$ = estimated longitude; **G**$_{e'}$ = observed longitude; **H**$_e$ = estimated altitude; **H**$_o$ = observed altitude; λ = dLatitude; **g** = dLongitude; ε = Departure, miles east or west; **Z** = azimuth.

The basic equations are (see Technical Note V, Appendix C):

(1) $\tan D' = \dfrac{\tan D}{\cos P}$; **(2)** $\sin H_e = \dfrac{\sin D}{\sin D'}\cos(D' - L_e)$;

(3) $\cos Z = \tan(D' - L_e)\tan H_e.$

Saint-Hilaire clearly recognized the advantages of his new method. He observes that the usual methods derive the latitude and longitude of the position when what is desired is the position itself. He emphasizes the generality of his method, regardless of whether the observation is made near the zenith, away from the prime meridian or near the observer's meridian.

Saint-Hilaire's *méthode du point rapproché* roughly translates as "the method of finding that position which is closest to the true position." It was quickly picked up by the French navigation community of officers on active duty in the Navy, scientists at the Paris Observatory and at the *Académie des Sciences*. Improvement in the techniques for establishing the accuracy of sea-going chronometers also was a subject of active investigation and publication in this community in the 1870's. Together, these two concepts, chronometer accuracy and Saint-Hilaire's method of finding position, were promptly incorporated into *la nouvelle navigation*, the new navigation.

The first published use of the term *nouvelle navigation* was in a paper presented to the *Institut de France, Académie des Sciences*[17] by M. Yvon Villarceau, Astronomer at the Paris Observatory and member of l'*Institut et du Bureau des Longitudes*. The paper, entitled *Transformation de l'Astronomie nautique, à la suite des progrès de la Chronométrie*, was published less than one year after the appearance in print of Saint-Hilaire's method. The term was further ingrained with the publication of *Nouvelle Navigation Astronomique*[18] in two parts: *Théorie* by Villarceau and *Pratique* by M. Aved de Magnac, a Naval Lieutenant and recognized expert in chronometer management. The term was translated and used in English language publications well into the twentieth century.

The other, more modern term used to describe Saint-Hilaire's method is the "intercept method". This is an English mathematical term, not found in French. Its definition is "to include or bound between two points or lines along a line or a curve." In this context, the term applies to the distance along the azimuth bounded at one end by the estimated position and at the other end by the observed position, specifically, H_o-H_e expressed in miles. Many publications refer simply to the "Marcq Saint-Hilaire method."

Saint-Hilaire's contribution to the *nouvelle navigation* was not an immediate, universal success as was Sumner's work. Publications in France by Villarceau and de Magnac[18] and others[19] provided an enthusiastic endorsement of the advancements in the management of chronometers and the new techniques of position finding. Adoption of the *nouvelle navigation* in England came more slowly despite timely publications in English by Bolt[20] and du Boisy.[21] It was introduced to the Royal Navy in 1886.[22] Students preparing for a career in the English Merchant Navy were not exposed to the preferred haversine tables and formulae until about 1908 and therefore did not use the intercept method.[23]

Use of the Saint-Hilaire method seems to have expanded in the United States at about the same pace as in England. The twentieth edition, 1888, of the popular Thoms textbook of navigation[24] makes no mention of Saint-Hilaire nor does MacArthur in his 1906 pocket-sized handbook.[25] As with the British Navy, the United States Navy adopted the method and put it to practical use before the method became common practice in the Merchant Marine. Commander W. C. P. Muir, Head of the Department of Navigation, U. S. Naval Academy, published

A Treatise on Navigation and Nautical Astronomy, the Second Edition of 1908, for use as a textbook at the Academy.[26] In the preface, Cdr. Muir reports that he has given much space to Sumner but also to the later work of Saint-Hilaire and others. He goes on to observe that:

> All of these methods are worthy of close examination …however, if the student is pressed for time, he is advised to confine his attention to what will be described as the "chord method" [of establishing a Sumner Line of Position] which embodies the present practice of the United States Naval Service.

As we shall see in the following chapter, it was the needs of the aviators for a rapid method of position finding that drove the further evolution of the Saint-Hilaire method.

Chapter 4

SUMNER'S AND SAINT-HILAIRE'S METHODS
IN THE TWENTIETH CENTURY

THE BASIC CONCEPTS of Sumner's Line of Position and Saint-Hilaire's Intercept method were well established and broadly used by the end of the nineteenth century. The innovative work in the early decades of the twentieth century was directed toward sight reduction techniques that would speed the task of plotting a fix using these methods. As airplanes flew further and faster, more rapid methods became imperative. The aviator's needs for quicker methods, even with the sacrifice of accuracy, drove the effort.

The preferred way to simplify the arithmetic of sight reduction is to precompute the values of azimuth and calculated altitude and present the results in tabular form. Tabulation of values shortens the time required to obtain a fix and eliminates the opportunity for error that is inherent in the calculation approach. A detailed table of azimuths was given in early U.S. Hydrographic Office publications, H.O. 120[27] based on tables prepared in 1902 and H.O. 171 of 1917.[28] A particularly popular graphic construction yielding azimuth, given declination, hour angle and altitude, was published by Captain Armistead Rust, USN, in 1918.[29]

Of course, azimuth is only one of the two factors needed to find a line of position by the Saint-Hilaire method. The other required value is the computed altitude. The first half of the twentieth century saw the publication of an international flood of innovative tabular methods know as Sight Reduction Tables, for finding both altitude and azimuth.

A major benefit of the Saint-Hilaire method is that it calculates an altitude and azimuth from an *assumed* position. The technique is to assume a position near the DR that has an integral number of degrees for latitude, L, and a longitude that, when applied to the Greenwich Hour Angle (GHA) of the celestial body, yields a Local Hour Angle (LHA), t, with an integral number of degrees. This approach markedly reduces the number of entries in the table and leaves only declination, **d**, to be extrapolated.

The Reverend Frederick Ball, a navigation instructor in the Royal Navy, is credited with being the first to capitalize on these principles with the publication of his *Altitude or Position-Line Tables* in 1907.[30] Even with these simplifications; the work ran to three volumes of 800 pages and cost an almost prohibitive 15 shillings per volume.

The modern approach to solving the celestial triangle for azimuth and altitude is to divide the celestial triangle into two spherical right triangles. This method was used by a number of navigators, mathematicians and astronomers to produce tables to quickly find azimuth and calculated altitude to establish a Sumner line of position by the Saint-Hilaire method.

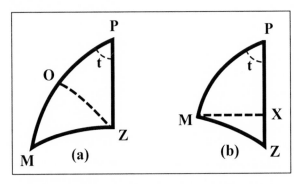

Figure 4. The celestial triangle divided into two right triangles.

There are two different ways to construct the two right triangles in the celestial triangle while preserving the known angle **t**, as illustrated in Figure 4. In Figure 4(a), arc **OZ** is perpendicular to arc **PM**. In Figure 4(b), arc **XM** is perpendicular to arc **PZ**. The option to divide the triangle two different ways plus the option to use a variety of formulae, led to the proliferation of tables specifically designed to simplify and speed the determination of Saint-Hilaire's azimuth and computed altitude in order to calculate the intercept.

The common arguments for entering the tables are latitude, **L**, declination, **d**, and local hour angle, **t**. The problem with tabular values is deciding how much data to include in the table. The more data points included in the tables, the less the error in interpolation between values but with too much data, the size of the tables becomes unwieldy. To tabulate values for latitude, declination and hour angle for each minute of the three values would lead to a table with over three billion data points. The most common simplification of the early tables was to limit the range of latitudes and/or declinations covered in the tables. Although these tables commonly required two or three openings to derive the required values, a principal advantage of this approach was the compactness of the tables. For example, Dreisonstok in H.O. 208[31] was able to produce two tables in whole degrees of latitude from 0° to 90°; whole degrees of local hour angle from 1° to 360°; and declination in whole minutes from 0° to 90° in 85 pages.

The series of the Hydrographic Office's precalculated tables began with H.O. 201, *Simultaneous Altitudes and Azimuths of Celestial Bodies*, published in 1919.[32] Hour angle is entered in time from noon in hours and increments of ten minutes; latitude is from 0° to 60° with facing pages for each latitude depending on whether declination is the same or the contrary name to latitude for each whole degree of declination. The publication is hard bound and runs to over 600 pages. H.O. 204, *The Sumner Line of Position*,[33] published in 1923, is arranged slightly differently, provides more detailed data, consists of 870 pages and weighs almost five pounds.

Through the 1920's and 30's the needs of the sailor and the aviator continued to diverge. The seagoing navigator refused to sacrifice accuracy for reduced weight and volume of his almanac and sight reduction tables. On the other hand, the aviators were content with accuracy within up to ten miles provided the methods were quick and easy and the tables compact.

The military buildup in preparation for World War II was a major stimulus to the development of improved sight reduction tables. H. O. 214, *Tables of Computed Altitude and Azimuth*, first published in 1936, appeared in an improved version in 1940[34]. See Figure 5. American surface and air navigators used H.O. 214 throughout the war. The series existed in six volumes, each spanning ten degrees of latitude with each degree of latitude comprising a section of 24 pages. Columns for each half-degree of declination up to 75° and hour angles in increments of whole degrees were provided. Extrapolation values for one minute of declination, Δd, and one minute of hour angle, Δt, were listed conveniently as an integral part of the tables. H. O. 214 was an immensely useful publication and is still used by many surface navigators.

Lat. 40°   2   DECLINATION SAME NAME AS LATITUDE

H.A.	0° 00' Alt.	Δd Δt	Az.	0° 30' Alt.	Δd Δt	Az.	1° 00' Alt.	Δd Δt	Az.	1° 30' Alt.	Δd Δt	Az.	2° 00' Alt.	Δd Δt	Az.
00	50 00.0	1.0 01	180.0	50 30.0	1.0 01	180.0	51 00.0	1.0 01	180.0	51 30.0	1.0 01	180.0	52 00.0	1.0 01	180.0
1	49 59.4	1.0 03	178.4	50 29.4	1.0 03	178.4	50 59.4	1.0 03	178.4	51 29.4	1.0 03	178.4	51 59.3	1.0 03	178.4
2	49 57.5	1.0 05	176.9	50 27.5	1.0 05	176.9	50 57.5	1.0 05	176.8	51 27.4	1.0 05	176.8	51 57.4	1.0 05	176.8
3	49 54.4	1.0 07	175.3	50 24.3	1.0 07	175.3	50 54.3	1.0 07	175.2	51 24.2	1.0 08	175.2	51 54.1	1.0 08	175.1
4	49 50.0	1.0 09	173.8	50 19.9	1.0 09	173.7	50 49.8	1.0 10	173.7	51 19.7	1.0 10	173.6	51 49.6	1.0 10	173.5
05	49 44.5	99 11	172.2	50 14.3	99 11	172.2	50 44.1	99 12	172.1	51 14.0	99 12	172.0	51 43.8	99 12	171.9
6	49 37.6	99 13	170.7	50 07.4	99 14	170.6	50 37.2	99 14	170.5	51 06.9	99 14	170.4	51 36.7	99 14	170.3
7	49 29.6	99 15	169.2	49 59.3	99 16	169.1	50 29.0	99 16	169.0	50 58.7	99 16	168.8	51 28.3	99 16	168.7
8	49 20.4	99 17	167.7	49 50.0	99 18	167.5	50 19.6	99 18	167.4	50 49.1	99 18	167.3	51 18.7	99 18	167.1
9	49 10.0	98 19	166.2	49 39.5	98 20	166.0	50 09.0	98 20	165.9	50 38.4	98 20	165.7	51 07.9	98 20	165.6
10	48 58.4	98 21	164.7	49 27.8	98 21	164.5	49 57.1	98 22	164.3	50 26.5	98 22	164.2	50 55.8	98 22	164.0
1	48 45.7	98 23	163.2	49 14.9	97 23	163.0	49 44.2	97 24	162.8	50 13.4	97 24	162.7	50 42.6	97 24	162.5
2	48 31.8	98 25	161.7	49 00.9	97 25	161.5	49 30.0	97 25	161.3	49 59.1	97 26	161.1	50 28.1	97 26	160.9
3	48 16.8	97 27	160.2	48 45.8	97 27	160.0	49 14.7	96 27	159.8	49 43.7	96 28	159.6	50 12.6	96 28	159.4

Figure 5. H.O. 214. Vol. V. Reproduction of a portion of the first page of the altitude/azimuth tables.[34]

The special needs for sight reduction tables for "avigation" became increasingly critical as the threat of war loomed in the late 1930's. The British Air Commission produced their *Astronomical Navigation Tables* in 1940.[35] This work was photocopied by the U.S. Hydrographic Office and released to U.S. Naval Aviation and the U.S. Army Air Corps as H.O. 218 with the same name.[36] These publications ran to twelve volumes, each covering four degrees of latitude. A unique feature was tables of altitude and azimuth for twenty-two stars in addition to tables yielding altitude and azimuth for use with the sun, moon, and planets using declination and hour angle from the *Air Almanac*.

A closely related development during the pre-war period was the simplification of the almanacs used for air navigation. The *Lunar Ephemeris for Aviators*, published as a supplement to the *American Nautical Almanac* of 1930, was the first of what would become an annual series of especially constructed almanacs for aviators. The original idea was to make the moon accessible for daytime sights rather than having to wait two or three hours for the sun's azimuth to change enough to make a second sight for a fix practical. The first *Air Almanac*, published by the U.S. Naval Observatory and the Hydrographic Office, appeared in 1933 but was discontinued. The French first published their version, the *Éphémérides aéronautiques*, in 1937 and the British version appeared later that year. The principal innovation in these almanacs was the first use of Greenwich Hour Angle rather than the astronomer's Right Ascension and an entering argument of Greenwich Civil Time.

This approach saved a number of steps in the calculations and is now the standard for all navigational ephemerides.

A preliminary version of the ultimate sight reduction tables for air navigation appeared in 1947 in the form of *Star Tables for Air Navigation*, H.O. 249.[37] In its final form, H.O. 249, and its British counterpart, A.P. 3270,[38] are a three volume series modeled after H.O. 218, described above. Volume I gives the required Saint-Hilaire parameters, calculated altitude, H_c, and the true azimuth, Z_n, for all but one of the first magnitude stars and for nineteen of the second magnitude stars. The data are tabulated as a function of latitude and the Local Hour Angle of Aries, γ, derived from the *Air Almanac* knowing Greenwich Civil Time and the right ascension of the star. Volumes II and III give H_c and Z for all latitudes with declinations from $0°$ to $39°$, given the Local Hour Angle of the celestial body from the *Air Almanac*. As before, the trick to getting the easiest, most accurate results is to choose the assumed latitude, $a\alpha$, and assumed longitude, aL, that yield values in whole degrees for entering the tables without the need for extrapolation except for declination, and this correction is obtained in one opening of a simple auxiliary table. An example from Volume II of H. O. 249 illustrates the simplicity of the method.

Example: On January 18, 1964, the GMT 0330 dead reckoning position of an aircraft is lat. $6°15'$ S, long. $137°21'$ E. The aircraft is on course $150°$, ground speed 340 knots. The sun is observed with an artificial horizon sextant as follows: GMT $3^{hr}30^m35^s$, height 30,000feet, IC [index correction] 0', hs [sextant altitude] $73°53'$. *Required:* Determine **a** [intercept] and **Zn** [azimuth measured from North] for plotting the line of position. *Solution:* For Jan. 18, 1964

GMT	3^h	30^m	35^s	From the Chronometer
$3^h30^m =$	$229°$	58'		From Table 3. Conversion arc to time
0^n30^s	$0°$	09'		
GHA	$230°$	07'		
	Aλ	$136°$	53' E	Assumed longitude to derive **LHA** in whole degrees.
LHA	$7°$	00'		
dec.	$20°$	45'	S	From the *Air Almanac* for date.
	AL	$6°$	00' S	Assumed latitude in whole degrees.
Tabulated **Hc**	$74°$	26'	Tab **Z** = $25°$	Saint-Hilaire's azimuth
Correction	(-)	40'		Interpolation for 45' of declination
Hc	$73°$	46'		Saint-Hilaire's calculated altitude
Ho	$73°$	53'		
a'		7'	Towards	Saint-Hilaire's intercept. Toward the GP as **Hc**<**Ho**.
				Zn = $205°$

Compare this calculation with the examples cited above from Bowditch's first edition of 1805. The plot of the fix on a Mercator chart is equally simple and direct. See Figure 6.

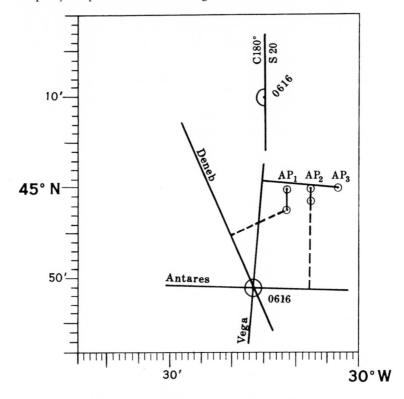

Figure 6. The plot of a three-star fix using Saint-Hilaire's intercept method. The assumed positions along Latitude 45°N are advanced for the run on course 180°, speed 20 knots during the intervals between observations.[39]

We owe Captain Sumner, Admiral Saint-Hilaire and the aviators of the first half of the twentieth century who gave us this quick, error free, accurate method of finding our position on a chart.

During the last half of the twentieth century the Saint-Hilaire intercept method was increasingly computerized. The almanacs became available on compact discs and computer programs were developed to handle the sight reduction calculations. Universal time, based on the average of a number of atomic clocks scattered around the globe, became instantly available.

The time-honored process of finding position by observing the celestial bodies has been replaced by increasingly more rapid, more exact methods. Radio Direction Finding, RDF, began to be used for aircraft navigation before World War II and for many years was the standard for aviation. A similar system, Long Range Radio Aid to Navigation, LORAN, was developed for marine navigation. Radar made position finding near the coastline much more dependable, particularly in foggy weather. Inertial guidance systems, developed in the 1960's, quickly became the universal, worldwide method for aircraft and were still in use at the end of the century.

The next revolution in navigation techniques, the Global Positioning System, (GPS), swept rapidly into universal use at the end of the twentieth century. Constellations of man-made satellites now blanket the globe. Receivers measure the time required for a signal to arrive from the several satellites within view, thus measuring distance from the satellite rather than its altitude. Virtually all ocean-going vessels now use GPS which, when coupled with computerized maps, gives a continuously updated visual presentation of position. Hand-held GPS receivers costing less than a decent sextant giving Latitude and Longitude to one-tenth of a degree have become requisite equipment for small-craft sailors, hikers and explorers. GPS has revolutionized surveying and map-making with accuracy beyond that achievable by mechanical techniques. Conversely, GPS has not been adopted broadly by commercial aviators out of concern that the United States system could be turned off instantaneously, without prior notice, by the President under eminent threat of attack. This constraint, along with the restriction of a degraded signal for civilian use, has been removed and thus GPS should find increasing application for aviation navigation.

Despite the advent of GPS, many navigators still insist on maintaining the skill required to find their position using a sextant, the chronometer, an almanac, sight reduction tables and the sun, the moon, the planets and the stars overhead. Let us not forget that we owe Captain Sumner, Admiral Saint-Hilaire and the creative astronomers, mathematicians and navigators who produced the almanacs and sight reduction tables for giving us the tools that make our job so quick, easy and precise and so intellectually satisfying.

Bibliography

1. Bowditch, Nathaniel. *The New American Practical Navigator*. First edition. Boston: John West, 1802.
2. Mackay, Andrew. *The Complete Navigator, or An Easy and Familiar Guide to the Theory and Practice of Navigation*. Philadelphia: B. B. Hopkins and Co., 1807.
3. Moore, J. H. *The New Practical Navigator*. 12th edition. London: 1788.
4. Nunes, Pedro. *Tratado da Sphera*. Lisboa, 1537.
5. Hues, *Tractatus de globis et eorum usu (Treatise on the Globes and Their Use)*. London, 1594.
6. Douwes, M. Cornelius, *Actes e3 l'Academie de Haarlem*. 1754.
7. Sumner, Capt. Thomas H. *A New Method of Finding a Ship's Position at Sea*. Boston: Thomas Groom & Co, 1843.
8. Raper, Henry, Lieut. R.N. *The Practice of Navigation and Nautical Astronomy*. Ninth Edition. London: J. D. Potter, 1866.
9. Coffin, J. H. C. *Navigation and Nautical Astronomy*. New York: D. van Nostrand, 1865.
10. Raper, Henry, Lieut. R.N. *On Captain Sumner's Method for Determining Position of a Ship*. *Nautical Magazine*. 1844.
11. Anonymous. *Contre-Admiral Adolphe, Laurent, Anatole MARCQ de BLOND de SAINT-HILAIRE*. Summary of service, 3 p; Notes biographique, 3p. cote CC⁷2ème Moderne M 3/3. Service Historique, Marine Nationale, Château de Vincennes, France.
12. Richardson, Robert S. *Captain Thomas Hubbard Sumner, 1807-1876*. *Navigation*, Journal of the Institute of Navigation, Vol. 1, No. 2, pp 35-40, June, 1946, Reprinted from *Publications of the Astronomical Society of the Pacific*. Vol. 55, pp 136-144. June, 1943.
13. Sumner, William Appleton. *Sumner Genealogy*. Boston. 1879. p 50 and p 96. Harvard College Library, Cambridge, Massachusetts.
14. Davis, T. D. *Navigation Personalities, Marcq Saint-Hilaire*, Volume 14, p 6-7.*The Navigator's Newsletter*. Foundation for the Art of Navigation. Fall, 1986.
15. Saint-Hilaire, Marcq. *Note sur la Détermination du Point, Revue Maritime et Coloniale*, pp41- 58. October, 1873.
16. Saint-Hilaire, Marcq. *Calcul du Point Observé, Revue Maritime et Coloniale*, Part 1 pp341- 376. August 1875; Part 2 pp714-742 September, 1875.
17. Villarceau, M. Yvon. *Transformation de l'Astronomie nautique, à la suite des progress de la Chronométrie*. Institut de France, Académie des Sciences. Extract from *Comptes rendus des séances de l'Académie de Sciences, t. LXXXII, séances des 6 et 13 mars 1876*. pp 14. Paris: Gauthier-Villars, 1876.
18. Villarceau, M. Yvon and de Magnac, M. Aved. *Nouvelle Navigation Astronomique*. XIII, pp 19, pp191. Paris: Gauthier-Villars, 1877.
19. du Bury, G. Tirant. *Etude sur la Nouvelle Navigation Astronomique, Revue Maritime et Coloniale*, pp 102- 122. March - October, 1878.
20. Bolt, W. H. *The New Navigation*. *Nautical Magazine*. London, 1880.

21. Boisy, M. le Comte du. *The New Astronomical Navigation, Nautical Magazine*. London, 1881.
22. Brent, Charles. *A Shorter and Accurate Method of Obtaining the Longitude at Sea… to Which Is Added a Brief Explanation of the New Navigation*. A. F. Walter & George Williams, 1886.
23. May, Commander W. E. *A History of Marine Navigation*. Henly-on-Thames, Oxfordshire.G. T. Foulis & Co. LTD, 1973
24. Thoms, Captain William. *Practice of Navigation at Sea*. Twenteeth Edition. New York: Published by the Author, 1888.
25. MacArthur, C. E., *Navigation Simplified*. New York: The Rudder Publishing Company, 1906.
26. Muir, Commander W. C. P. *A Treatise on Navigation and Nautical Astronomy*. Annapolis, Maryland: The United States Naval Institute, 1908.
27. Anonymous. *Azimuths of Celestial Bodies H. O. No. 120*. Washington: The Hydrographic Office.
28. Anonymous. *Line of Position Tables, H. O. 171*. Washington: The Hydrographic Office. 1916. Reprinted Fort Pierce, FL: Donald L. Pegg., 1978.
29. Rust, Capt. Armistead, U. S. Navy. *Practical Tables for Navigators and Aviators*. Philadelphia: Published by the author, 1918.
30. Ball, Rev. Frederick. *Altitude Tables Computed for Intervals of Four Minutes between the Parallels of Latitude 31° and 60° and Parallels of Declination 0° and 24° Designed for the Determination of the Position Line at All Hour Angles without Logarithmic Computation*. London: J. D. Potter, 1907.
31. Dreisonstock, J.Y.,Lieutenant Commander, Unites States Navy. *H. O. 208*, Sixth Edition, Washington:Hydrographic Office, Bureau of Navigation, United States Navy Department. United States Government Printing Office, 1942
32. Anonymous. *Simultaneous Altitudes and Azimuths of Celestial Bodies. H. O. 201*. Washington: Hydrographic Office, Bureau of Navigation, United States Navy Department, 1919.
33. Anonymous. *The Sumner Line of Position of Celestial Bodies H. O. No. 204*. Washington: United States Navy Department, Oceanographic Office, 1923.
34 Anonymous. *Tables of Computed Altitude and Azimuth H. O. 214*. Washington: Hydrographic Office, United States Navy Department, 1940.
35. Anonymous. *Astronomical Navigation Tables*. British Air Publication 1618. London: British Air Commission, British Air Ministry, 1940.
36. Anonymous. *Astronomical Navigation Tables, H.O. 218*. Washington: Hydrographic Office, United States Navy Department, 1941.
37. Anonymous. *Sight Reduction Tables for Air Navigation H. O. Pub. No. 249*. Washington:United States Naval Oceanographic Office,. Preliminary Edition of Vol. I, 1947; Later Editions: Vol. I, 1967; II, 1970; and III, 1965.
38. Anonymous. *Sight Reduction Tables for Air Navigation*. A. P. 3270. Volumes I, II and III. London: Her Majesty's Stationary Office, 1959-1961.
39. Anonymous. *Sight Reduction Tables for Marine Navigation*, Pub. No. 229. Washington: Defense Mapping Agency, Hydrographic/Topographic Center, 1981.

Appendix A

A NEW METHOD OF FINDING A SHIP'S POSITION AT SEA

BY CAPT. THOMAS H. SUMNER.

INTRODUCTION

CAPTAIN SUMNER published his Line of Position method in 1843, almost six years after his critical observations off the coast of Ireland. By this time his method was becoming known and gaining acceptance through informal channels. The formal publication of his work and the enthusiastic endorsement of a U.S. Navy Commission stimulated widespread acceptance both domestically and abroad.

Captain Sumner used the observations he made on December 17, 1837 as the first Example in the application of his method (Appendix A, pages [A-15]-[A-17]). He describes how to calculate the true bearing to land, the error in longitude from Longitude by Chronometer and the sun's true azimuth. Sumner's key observation is that "…the ship's position is upon…a line perpendicular to the sun's azimuth at the assumed latitude." This is the basic element of Sumner's Line of Position that later formed the fundamental basis for Saint-Hilaire's intercept method. Here we have the first pillar of modern celestial navigation.

Sumner went on to provide other examples of how his approach could be used to address a variety of navigation problems. He had a strong personal concern with the potentially disastrous consequences of using erroneous latitudes in the popular Longitude by Chronometer method. This clearly influenced his selection of examples for his book. He put great emphasis throughout on using his method to find the true bearing to land. This was a critical factor for navigators of that time because their method was to make landfall at some identifiable point on the coast and then sail up or down the coast to arrive at their destination.

Chapter III of Sumner's book gives a lucid explanation of his concept of "circles of equal illumination". He used this term in the sense that the altitude of the celestial body is the same at any point on the circle. He also used the term "pole of illumination" for what we now call the Geographic Position (GP) of a celestial body.

Interestingly, Sumner described how the altitude of a celestial body changes with distance from the ***pole of illumination***. "It is plain, then, that for ***every mile*** a ship sails on the great circle **MZ** [i.e., the azimuth of the sun] towards **Z** [the *pole of illumination*], that is, at right angles to the parallels [of equal illumination], she *increases* the sun's altitude *one* minute; and every mile sailed from **Z**, *decreases his altitude* one *minute*." This is the basic principle that Saint-Hilaire will use thirty years later for his intercept method. Saint-Hilaire would turn it around and say that the *circle of equal illumination,* the Line of Position, moves *away* from the Assumed Position *one* mile along the line of the azimuth of the sun for every *one* minute that the observed altitude is less than the altitude calculated for the Assumed Position.

A

NEW AND ACCURATE METHOD

OF

FINDING A SHIP'S POSITION AT SEA,

BY PROJECTION ON MERCATOR'S CHART.

———————

WHEN THE LATITUDE, LONGITUDE, AND APPARENT TIME AT THE SHIP ARE
UNCERTAIN; ONE ALTITUDE OF THE SUN, WITH THE TRUE
GREENWICH TIME, DETERMINES,

FIRST,

THE TRUE BEARING OF THE LAND;

SECONDLY,

THE ERRORS OF LONGITUDE BY CHRONOMETER,
CONSEQUENT TO ANY ERROR IN THE LATITUDE;

THIRDLY,

THE SUN'S TRUE AZIMUTH.

———————

WHEN TWO ALTITUDES ARE OBSERVED, AND THE ELAPSED TIME NOTED, THE
TRUE LATITUDE IS PROJECTED; AND IF THE TIMES BE NOTED BY
CHRONOMETER, THE TRUE LONGITUDE IS ALSO
PROJECTED AT THE SAME OPERATION.

———————

The Principles of the Method being fully explained and illustrated
by Problems, Examples, and Plates,

WITH RULES FOR PRACTICE, AND EXAMPLES FROM ACTUAL OBSERVATION.

———————

BY CAPT. THOMAS H. SUMNER.

———————

.

BOSTON:
PUBLISHED BY THOMAS GROOM & CO., 82 STATE STREET.
1843.

[A-I]

SAMUEL N. DICKINSON, PRINTER,
WASHINGTON STREET,
BOSTON.

RECOMMENDATIONS.

The following letter from Professor PEIRCE, of Harvard College, Cambridge, to J. INGERSOLL BOWDITCH, Esq., President of the American Insurance Company, is published by permission.

CAMBRIDGE, 16th March, 1843.

My dear Bowditch,

I have examined Capt. Sumner's processes, and they are founded on perfectly correct principles.

I think his methods are especially valuable, because they require but one formula; and the Geometry is so simple and obvious, that it can easily be made intelligible to any man of good sense.

Yours, truly,

(Signed)   BENJAMIN PEIRCE.

In obedience to a resolution adopted at the last stated meeting of the "Naval Library and Institute," in the following words, to wit: " Resolved, That a Committee of three members be appointed to investigate the ' New method of finding a Ship's Position at Sea,' by Capt. Sumner, and report at the next meeting,"

The Committee respectfully submit the following REPORT :

We have carefully examined the subject referred to, and find that Capt. Sumner's method of ascertaining " The Bearing of the Land; of finding a Ship's Position by projecting two of those Bearings, and of projecting the Sun's true Azimuth, &c.," are all founded on spherical principles, as applied to Nautical Astronomy.

And your committee is of opinion, that in practice, Capt. Sumner's discovery (for we can call it nothing less,) will prove a useful auxiliary to the present knowledge of Navigators, and, as such, would recommend it to the attention of all persons interested in the promulgation and improvement of Nautical Science.

(Signed)   JAMES ALDEN, Lt. U. S. Navy,
                SAM'L R. KNOX, Lt. U. S. Navy,   } Committee.
                GEO. H. PREBLE, Passed Mid. U. S. N. }

"Naval Library and Institute,"

Navy Yard, Boston, April 30th, 1843.

I certify the above to be a true Copy of the Report.

(Copy.)   (Signed)   W. WHELAN, Recording Secretary.

Navy Yard, Boston, 9th May, 1843.

ERRATA.

THE following errors the reader is requested to correct; the first six are all of more or less importance to the geometrical sense; the others are of minor consequence.

Page 23, line 2, instead of " P. M. The " read " P. M., when the."

Page 23, line 3, instead of " P. M., when the " read " P. M.; the."

Page 29, line 6, after " sun's " read " true."

Page 49, line 15, instead of " places " read " place."

Page 75, line 25, instead of " (or in-" read " (or de-"

Page 75, line 27, erase the comma after " Xa."

Page 30, line 27, instead of "their " read " the."

Page 30, line 27, instead of " chronometers " read " chronometer."

Page 38, line 24, instead of " placed " read " place."

Page 43, line 18, after " with " read " the."

Page 43, line 24, after " of " read " the."

Page 43, line 28, after " and " read " the."

Page 76, line 9, instead of a period after " 6 " read a comma.

[Letter from Captain Sturgis.]

BOSTON, JULY 8th, 1843.

Captain THOMAS H. SUMNER,

SIR,

I have examined with much care and attention your " New method for finding a Ship's position at Sea," which I consider a valuable discovery. I have no knowledge of any Nautical work that directs otherwise than that observations be taken when the Sun bears East or West, therefore I think your method, when published, will be universally adopted by Navigators. I therefore recommend it to all who feel an interest in the promotion of Nautical Science, as well as practical Navigators. Wishing you every success in your undertaking,

I am, very respectfully,

Your obedient servant,

JOSIAH STURGIS,

Captain U. S. Revenue Cutter Hamilton.

CONTENTS.

		Page
To the Reader, ...		7

I. The Practice of this Method, ... 10

To find the bearing of the land, &c., by one altitude at
any hour, ... 12
To find the latitude and longitude by chronometer, by
two altitudes at one operation, ... 19
To find the latitude by two altitudes; times noted by
"watch," 25
To find the latitude and longitude by chronometer with-
out projecting, ... 29
How to allow for possible errors of altitude, ... 30
Table and Rules, showing errors of longitude, &c., . . 31

II. The Advantages, ... 35

III. The Principles, ... 41

Explanation of them, ... 41
To project a parallel of equal altitude in latitude, . . . 45
To project two parallels, in latitude, showing their inter-
sections, ... 49
To project a parallel, in latitude and longitude by chro-
nometer, showing the bearing of the land, ... 51
To project two parallels, in latitude and longitude by
chronometer, showing the true latitude and longitude, 53
To project two parallels on a terrestrial globe showing
the latitude, ... 54
To project the change of station between two observations, 55
To project the sun's azimuth, ... 56
To project errors of longitude, &c., ... 57
To project any arc of a parallel of equal altitude, . . . 58
To project two arcs, change of station, &c., and the lat-
itude, &c., ... 59

IV. Application to Moon, Planets, and Fixed Stars, . . . 68

The most simple method to do this, in most cases, . . 69
Another process, ... 69

V. Currents in the Gulf and Stream of Florida, . . . 78

TO THE READER.

It is not so much the object of this work to present the navigator with a new method of " Double Altitudes," as to afford him an accurate method of finding, by *one Altitude of the Sun* taken at any hour of the day, with the Chronometer time, the *True Bearing of the Land*, the Latitude, &c., being, from any cause, uncertain; and to place him on his guard, when near a dangerous coast, (and all coasts are dangerous when the *Latitude* is not accurately known,) against those *errors of Longitude by Chronometer*, which arise from an *erroneous Latitude* used in finding the apparent time at the ship; directing, particularly, his attention *to the fact*, as shown in these pages, that when the Latitude is uncertain, a single altitude of the sun, at any time of day, when not less than say 7° high, is, with a good Chronometer, as *useful as a* Meridian Observation for the Latitude; and the errors above alluded to are rendered apparent.

When a single altitude is thus calculated, one half of the calculation of a double altitude is finished; and a second altitude furnishes all that can be desired, both Latitude and Longitude.

Hence, it seemed proper to explain "Double Altitudes" by this method of projection; and it is believed, that it has the advantage over any other method, in the *simplicity* of the calculation, and in *the fact*, that ship-masters universally understand, and daily practice the *numerical* calculation, namely, that of finding the apparent time at the ship, which is the only one used.

Many navigators, having taken morning sights for the Chronometer, supposing the observation useless without "the Latitude," wait for the meridian observation, in order to deduce the Longitude by Chronometer; or, if the sun be obscured till afternoon, think a single altitude under such circumstances is of small value; and, by the common methods, with good reason; for then the Latitude by dead reckoning from the preceding noon, must, in general, be used to find the apparent time at the ship; and here is the source of error; because, 26 to 30 hours having probably elapsed, in such time the ship may have sailed from 250 to 300 miles; if two days have passed without a meridian observation or double altitudes, then from 400 to 500 miles, in frequent cases; and while sailing so far, a small current, with a small error in the log, (if one is used, but they are much out of fashion in these days,) will easily make an error in the distance of half a mile an hour, and half a point in the course, and cause an error in the Latitude by dead reckoning, and consequently in the Longitude by Chronometer.

Suppose the course and distance sailed by Log to be East 300 miles, from a place in Lat. 50° N., when the sun's declination is 23.28 S.; but from accidental causes the true course and distance sailed is 315 miles E. $\frac{1}{2}$ N.; the difference of Latitude is, in this case, 30.9 miles; but the dead reckoning gives 50° N. for the Latitude to be used in finding the apparent time at the ship, if an observation should be now taken.

Now, with the *most favorable* altitude, (which is the one that is nearest to the East or West points, when observed,) the *least* error of Longitude by Chronometer is, in this instance, 1° 2′; and with other, *greater* altitudes, it may be *three or four times as much*, even when the Chronometer is strictly accurate.

None of the works on Navigation, within the writer's knowledge, exemplify, or even hint at this important source of error, but merely direct the observations to be taken when the sun bears as nearly "*East or West as possible*;" but it is *impossible*, for nearly 7 months in the year, to observe the sun in the East or West points.

It is hoped, that the "Method by Projection," which explains these errors, and renders a single altitude, taken at any bearing of the sun, available, in a similar *manner as a Meridian Observation*, will supply a want which every practical navigator must have frequently experienced.

The latter pages of this treatise are intended to show the Principles upon which this method depends; and the problems there solved, and the examples given, merely as illustrations of those principles, in the order in which they are explained.

It has been endeavored, to explain them in such a manner, that practical persons may be led, step by step, to the entire understanding of the Theory.

Notwithstanding they might prove amply sufficient to enable many readers to put the principles in practice, yet, since there may be persons who might not be inclined to give them the attention necessary for this purpose, the more Practical Rules are introduced, so that all such persons may proceed at once to the adoption of this method.

The present seemed a fit opportunity to offer the chart relating to the currents in the Gulf of Mexico, at the end of the book; if it serve no better purpose, it will put the mariner on his guard, in those parts so fatal to the commercial interests.

2

I.

THE PRACTICE OF THE METHOD BY PROJECTION,

WITH EXAMPLES FROM ACTUAL OBSERVATION.

IT is a direct inference from the Principles herein stated, that there is, by the common rules, but *one* proper instant of time in one day, namely, when the sun bears north or south, at which a single observation to find the Latitude can be taken with a correct result, unless *the apparent time* at the ship is accurately known.

And, when *the Latitude* is uncertain, that there are only *two* proper instants in *one* day; namely, when the sun bears *East* or *West;* at which his altitude can be taken to find the Longitude by Chronometer with accuracy.

All deviations from these bearings of the sun, at the time of observation, (in such circumstances,) are attended with errors of Latitude, or of Longitude, proportional to the angular distance of the sun from these points; and these errors are frequently very great.

To remedy this difficulty, and render a *single altitude* of the sun, taken at any angle from the meridian, or from the East and West points, available, when the Latitude and apparent time at the ship are, from accidental causes, uncertain, (the time of observation by Chronometer being given,) the method of projection affords a *substitute* for a *parallel of Latitude*, or a *meridian of Longitude;* namely, a line *diagonal* to either of these, and which is called a PARALLEL OF EQUAL ALTITUDE; which, when projected on Mercator's Chart, according to the Rules given, shows a ship to be *on such projected line*, corresponding to the observed altitude; in a similar manner as a ship is found to be on a certain *parallel of Latitude* by a *meridian observation;* consequently, the *projected line* shows the BEARING OF THE LAND, in a similar way as a parallel of Latitude.

And likewise if two altitudes be observed, the times being noted by Chronometer, and the *two lines*, corresponding to the two altitudes, be projected as before, then both the true Latitude and true Longitude is found at the *intersection* of the two projected lines.

The following remarks are offered upon the corrections to be made at sea to any observed altitude of the sun, or other body.

These corrections are commonly four; namely, for Parallax, Semi-diameter, Dip, and Refraction.

. The first two are found for the given time in the Nautical Almanac, and we have only to take them upon trust, as they are there laid down.

But with regard to the last two, accuracy depends, in a great degree, upon the observer himself.

With regard to Dip, it should be remembered, that in the large ships built at the present day, the eye is so elevated (especially from the poop-deck) that the dip is fully 1' more than has been usual.

With some persons it has become a habit always to add 12' to an observed *meridian* altitude of the sun's lower limb, and from inattention they neglect to subtract the *proper* Refraction, when the altitude is observed for the purpose of finding the apparent time for the Longitude by Chronometer: important errors will often occur, if the proper corrections be not strictly applied for different altitudes observed.

In all observations for the Latitude by two altitudes, by whatever method, all these four corrections should be applied with particular care.

Both Dip and Refraction being *subtractive*, if the proper corrections be not attended to, the error will be so much the greater.

The following THREE PRACTICAL PROBLEMS are deduced from the principles of the method.

PROBLEM I.

The Latitude, Longitude, and apparent time being uncertain, and one altitude of the sun being observed, at any hour, when sufficiently high above the horizon, the Chronometer time being noted, and declination given; it is required to project, on Mercator's Chart, a line, diagonal to the parallels of Latitude, and meridians of Longitude, called a *parallel of equal altitude*, which shall pass through the position of the ship, and show by inspection,

1st. The Bearing of the Land.

2d. The errors of Longitude by Chronometer, to which the ship is subject for any in the Latitude by dead reckoning.

3d. The sun's true azimuth.

RULE I.

1st. Select two Latitudes, one of which is the next *degree* (without any odd minutes) *less*, and the other, the next *degree greater* than the Latitude by dead reckoning.

2d. Find, in the usual way, the ship's Longitude by Chronometer, upon the supposition that she is in the *least* Latitude assumed; and project this position on your Chart in a point, which call A.

3d. Find, in the same way, the ship's position, supposing she is in the *greatest* assumed Latitude; and project this position also on your Chart in a point, which call A'.

4th. Join these two points by a straight line, which produce as far as necessary; this line is an arc of a "*parallel of equal altitude*"; and it passes through the *true* position of the ship; and whatever *land* it passes through, bears from the ship in the same direction as the line lays on the Chart.

5th. The error of Longitude by Chronometer, at the time of observation, to which the ship is subject for an error of Latitude by D. R. (when this Latitude is used to find the apparent time,) amounting to *one* degree, is the difference of Longitude between the points A and A′; for half a degree, half that difference of Longitude, &c.

6th. Erect a perpendicular upon the projected straight line A A′, on that side next towards the sun, and it will be in the direction of the sun's true bearing; and the angle it makes with the meridian is the true azimuth.

NOTE.

It will thus appear, that the ship is *always* situated *on a line, perpendicular* to the sun's true bearing or azimuth. It follows, that the nearer an observation is taken *to noon*, the more accurately the Bearing of the Land is ascertained, by this method, if the CHRONOMETER ITSELF BE ERRONEOUS.

If the observation be taken *near to Noon*, (at other times of day a mistake would not be likely to happen,) and the declination and Latitude in are both of the *same* name; the sun bearing South in North Latitude, or North in South Latitude, neither of the two *assumed* Latitudes must be *greater* than the *sum* of the *declination* and the *complement* of the sun's true central altitude; but if the Sun bears North in North Latitude, or South in South Latitude, then neither of the assumed Latitudes must be *less* than the *difference* between the *declination* and the *complement* of the sun's altitude; but when the declination and Latitude in are of *different* names, neither assumed Latitude must be *greater* than the *difference* between the *declination* and the *complement of the sun's altitude*.

It may happen, when the altitude is near noon, that the difference of Longitude of the two points, A and A′, to be projected, may be greater than the extent in Longitude of the '*particular*' chart in use; in such case, the points may be projected on a '*general*' chart; or what would be better, assume two Latitudes, which are less than one degree distant; namely, one on each side of the Latitude by D. R.; the one being only ten miles *greater*, and the other only ten miles *less* than the Latitude by account; or if it be very near noon, five miles *greater* and *less*: taking care not to assume a Latitude *too* great, or otherwise, as mentioned above.

With this restriction, it is immaterial what two neighboring Latitudes are chosen, they may be either *both greater* or *both less*, or *one greater* and the *other less* than the Latitude by D. R.; but, in general, when the sun is *not* very near the meridian, it will be more convenient to assume Latitudes, one less, the other greater, and which have no odd minutes; because their logarithms are more readily taken from the Tables, as they are always at the top or bottom of the page.

It is recommended to use Bowditch's third method, for finding the apparent time; because it is something shorter, and there is a convenience in placing the logarithms, which neither of the first two methods admit. The result, however, will be nearly the same, by either method. It is proper to mention, however, that method 1, (Bowditch,) has its own advantages, as explained in the Navigator.

Several of the logarithms used in finding *the apparent time* are the same for all the operations; which contributes to shorten the method, in particular when two altitudes are observed.

EXAMPLE I.

On 17th December, 1837, sea account, a ship having run between 600 and 700 miles without any observation, and being near the land, the Latitude by D. R. was 51° 37′ N., but supposed liable to error of 10 miles on either side, N. or S. The altitude of the sun's lower limb, was 12° 02′ at about 10 1-2 A. M., the eye of the observer being 17 feet above the sea; the mean time at Greenwich, by Chronometer, was $10^h 47^m 13^s$ A. M.

Required, { The True Bearing of the Land: what error of Longitude the ship was subject to, by Chronometer, for the uncertainty of the Latitude: The sun's true azimuth.

dip	4′ 3″	S. D.	16′ 8″
refra.	4′ 23″	Px.	+ 8″
—	8′ 26″		+ 16′ 16″
			8′ 26″
correction of alt. obs'd	+ 8′		

Obs'd Alt. ☉ L. L.   12° 02′
correction   + 8′

True Alt. ☉'s centre,   12° 10′

1st. The Latitude by D. R. was 51° 37′ N. The Latitude the next degree *less*, without odd minutes, is 51° N.; and that, the next degree *greater*, is 52° N.

2d and 3d. Find the Longitude of these two points, as follows:

☉'s. ALTITUDE 12° 10′

For the point A in Latitude 51° N.

Lat. 51°   N.   -   -   -   sec. 0.20113
Dec. 23 23   S.   -   -   -   sec. 0.03722
Sum 74 23   Nat. cos. 26920
☉ Alt. 12 10   Nat. sin. 21076
H. M. S.   Diff. - 5844   log, 3.76671
1 43 59   from Noon = log rising = 4.00506
12 hours.
10 16 01   App. Time at Ship.
— 3 37   Equa. Time.
10 12 24   Mean Time at Ship.
10 47 13   do.   by Chro.
    34 49   =   8° 42¼′ *West* of Greenwich.

For the point A′ in Latitude 52° N.

Lat. 52°   N.   -   -   -   sec. 0.21066
Dec. 23 23   S.   -   -   -   sec. 0.03722
Sum 75 23   Nat. cos. 25235
☉ Alt. 12 10   Nat. sin. 21076
H. M. S.   Diff. - 4159   log, 3.61899
1 28 28½ from Noon = log rising = 3.86687
12 hours.
10 31 31½ App. Time at ship.
— 3 37   Equa. Time.
10 27 54½ Mean time at ship.
10 47 13   do.   at Greenwich, by Chro.
    19 18½   =   4° 49½′ West Long.

4th. On Mercator's Chart, Plate III, project the point
A in Latitude 51° N., Longitude, 8° 42¼' W.; and project
the point A' in Latitude 52° N., Longitude 4° 49½' W.

5th. Join the points A and A' by a straight line; and
the ship's position is *upon* this line: which, referred to the
compass, is found to tend E. N. E. true; and shows, that
Small's Light bears E. N. E. true from the ship.

6th. The error of Longitude to which the ship was subject for 10 miles error of Latitude, is 39 minutes, as projected.

7th. The sun's true azimuth is 2 points from South, or
S. S. E., as projected.

NOTE.

The ship's true position, in Latitude and Longitude, at
the time of this observation, is shown on the plate, as was
actually proved by making Small's Light. (see page 38.)

Had it been required to make Tusker Light, a northerly course might have been shaped, and such a "departure" made from the straight line A A', (30 miles in this
case,) as would have brought Tusker to bear E. N. E., and
then the course again altered to E. N. E., and Tusker
would have been made as shown on the plate. But, as
the wind was S. E., when this observation was taken, it
was preferable to make Small's Light.

Thus, if the projected line does not pass through your
port, a proper course may be shaped, by which you will
ultimately make the land as desired, in the same manner
as by a meridian observation; which may place you on
a parallel of Latitude, which passes some miles to the
north or south of your port, or the head-land you wish to
make.

The accuracy of your work may be very readily *veri-
fied*, by assuming a *third* or intermediate Latitude; (for instance, the Latitude by D. R.,) and finding a *third* point,
which project *as before*; then, if the three points be not
very nearly *in the same straight line*, you have made a
mistake in your work. It should be observed, however,
that the middle point should in truth be a little out of the
straight line, and in a direction *from the sun;* agreeably
to the curves laid down in Plate I; but with altitudes

which are not great it would be a very trifling difference from a straight line, indeed, scarcely perceptible.

When the line is projected, your Latitude by D. R. gives your *approximate position in the line;* that is, your approximate *distance* from the head-land through which the line passes.

If the line runs parallel to a coast, it gives your *true* distance from such coast. In the above example, the true *distance* from the *Irish coast* is found to be 30 *miles;* and the true *bearing of Small's* E. N. E.

Example II.

On 4th April, (sea account,) 1840, at about 1, P. M., the correct central altitude of the sun was 60° 32′ the mean time at Greenwich, by Chronometer, $6^h\ 13^m\ 56^s$ P. M.; the Latitude by dead reckoning was 32° 20′ N., but supposed liable to an error of 10 miles on either side.

Required, the true bearing of the land; the error of Longitude by Chronometer consequent to 10′ error of Latitude; and the sun's true azimuth.

1st. The two Latitudes to be used in the calculation, are 32° N., and 33° N.; one on each side of the Latitude by D. R.

2d and 3d. Find the Longitudes of the points A and A′, having those two Latitudes, as follows:

For the point A in Latitude 32° *N.*

Lat.	32°	N. - - -		sec.	0.07158
Dec.	5 35	N. - - - -		sec.	0.00207
Diff.	26 25	Nat. cos. 89558			
☉ Alt.	60 32	Nat. sin. 87064			
	H. M. S.	Diff. -	2494	log,	3.39690
P. M.	0 55 51	= log rising,	=		3.47055
	+ 3 21	Equa. Time.			
	0 59 12	Mean Time P. M. at Ship.			
	6 13 56	do. by Chronometer.			
Diff.	5 14 44	= 78° 41′ West Longitude.			

3

For the point A' in Latitude 33° *N.*

Lat. 33°   N.   -   -   -   sec. 0.07641
Dec. 5 35   N.   -   -   -   sec. 0.00207
Diff. 27 25   Nat. cos. 88768
⊙ Alt. 60 32   Nat. sin. 87064
     H. M. S. Diff. -   1704   log, 3.23147
P. M. 0 46 23   =   log rising, =   3.30995
   + 3 21 Equa. Time.
   0 49 44 Mean Time P. M. at Ship.
   6 13 56   do.   Chronometer.
Diff. 5 24 12   =   81° 03' West Longitude.

4th. On Mercator's Chart, Plate IV, project the point A, in Latitude 32° N., Longitude 78° 41' W., and project the point A', in Latitude 33° N., Longitude 81° 03' W.

5th. Join the points A and A', by a straight line; this line passes through the position of the ship; it is found to tend N. W. by W. ½ W., showing that the land, situated about 10 miles S. Westerly, from Charleston light, bears N. W. by W. ½ W.

6th. The error of Longitude by Chronometer, to which the ship was subject from 10' error of the Latitude, is seen to be 24', as set off on the Plate.

7th. The sun's true azimuth is also projected; his bearing being nearly S. S. W. ½ W.

NOTE.

If it be required to make Charleston light, then sail northerly from the line AA', until a departure from AA' is made equal to about 10 miles, then haul up N. W. by W. ½ W. until the light is seen.

PROBLEM II.

Two correct altitudes of the sun's centre being observed; and the times of observation noted by Chronometer;
the declinations at both times, and the Latitude by D. R.
being given, and A. M. and P. M. times of observation
noticed;

Required to project the two corresponding "*straight
lines*" on Mercator's chart, showing their mutual intersection; the true Latitude and Longitude, and likewise the
results of Problem I.

RULE.

1st. Proceed as in Problem I, to project the first
straight line AA', which will correspond to the first observed altitude.

2d. Proceed in exactly the same manner, to project
the second straight line, (using the very same *assumed
Latitudes*, as before,) and it will correspond to the second
observation; name the two points in it, which have the
assumed Latitudes, B and B'; taking care to correct the
declination, if any change has taken place in it between
the observations, and likewise the equation of time.

3d. These two straight lines will be found *to intersect*
each other, for the most part, between the two assumed
Latitudes; if they do not intersect, then produce them to
an intersection; and the intersected point will be in the
Latitude and Longitude of the ship, if she has not changed
her station between the observations.

4th. If the ship has changed her station; then, set off
the distance sailed between the observations, in the direction of the course made good, from *any* point in the
straight line AA'; through this point draw a straight line,
parallel to AA', and produce it until it intersects the
straight line BB'; this new intersection with BB' is the
position of the ship in Latitude and Longitude at the
time of the second observation corrected for change of
station.

5th. The other requisitions of the Problem are explained in Problem I.

NOTE.

It follows from the principles hereafter explained, that all observations for the Latitude by double altitudes, by whatever method, are to be preferred, when the observations are taken at right angles to each other, by compass.

If it is preferred, you may correct the *first* altitude for change of station, *before finding the apparent times;* and then the intersection of the two straight lines, AA′ and BB′ will be the ship's position in Latitude and Longitude at the time of *the second observation.*

EXAMPLE I.

January 1st, 1839. The sun's correct central altitude, A. M., was 14° 23′; the mean time at Greenwich, by Chronometer, being 11ʰ 8ᵐ 18ˢ A. M.; and when the time by Chronometer was 12ʰ 6ᵐ 44ˢ P. M., his correct central altitude was 19° 33′ A. M.; the Latitude, by account, being 43° 45′ N. Between the observations the ship sailed only one mile N. E. by E.

Required the true Latitude, and the true Longitude, at the time of the second observation, &c.

1st. The two Latitudes to be used are 43° N. and 44° N.

FOR THE FIRST ALTITUDE 14° 23′ A. M.

To find the point A. in Latitude 43° N.

Lat. 43° N. - - - -		sec.	0.13587
Dec. 23 03 S. - - -		sec.	0.03613
Sum. 66 03	Nat. cos. 40594		
☉ Alt. 14 23	Nat. sin. 24841		
H. M. S.	Diff. - 15753	log,	4.19736
2 40 3 =	log rising,	=	4.36936
12 hours.			
9 19 57	App. time A. M. ship.		
+ 3 42	Equa. time.		
9 23 39	mean time at ship.		
11 8 18	mean time Chronometer.		
1 44 39 =	26° 9′ 45″ West Longitude of A.		

To find the point A', in Latitude 44° N.

Lat. 44°   N.   -   -   -   sec. 0.14307
Dec. 23 03 S. -   -   -   -   sec. 0.03613

Sum. 67 03   Nat. cos. 38993
⊙ Alt. 14 23   Nat. sin. 24841

H. M. S.   Diff. - 14152   log, 4.15082
2 32 40   =   log rising,   =   4.33002
12 hours.

9 27 20 App. time, A. M. at ship.
+ 3 42 Equa. time.

9 31 02 mean time at ship.
11 08 18   do   Chronometer.

1 37 16 = 24° 19' West Longitude of A'.

For the Second Altitude 19° 33' A. M.

To find the point B, in Latitude 43° N.

Lat. 43 00 N.   -   -   -   sec. 0.13587
Dec. 23 03 S. -   -   -   -   sec. 0.03613

Sum. 66 03   Nat. cos. 40594
⊙ Alt. 19 33   Nat. sin. 33463

H. M. S.   Diff. - 7131   log, 3.85315
1 46 28   =   log rising   =   4.02515
12 hours

10 13 32 App. time at ship, A. M.
+ 3 43 Equa. time.

10 17 15 mean time at ship, A. M.
12 06 44   do   Chronometer.

1 49 29 = 27° 22' 15" West Longitude of B.

To find the point B', in Latitude 44 *N.*

Lat. 44 00 N. - - - sec. 0.14307
Dec. 23 03 S. - - - - sec. 0.03613

Sum. 67 03   Nat. cos. 38993
☉ Alt. 19 33   Nat. sin. 33463

H. M. S.   Diff. - 5530 log. 3.74273
1 34 21 = log rising, = 3.92193
12 hours.

10 25 39 App. time at ship, A. M.
+ 3 43 Equa. time.

10 29 22 mean time at ship.
12 06 44   do.   Chronometer.

1 37 22 = 24° 20' 30" West Longitude of B'.

2d.   On   Mercator's
Chart, Plate V, project
{ the point A, in Latitude 43° N.
   Longitude 26° 9' 45" West.
   the point A' in Latitude 44° N.
   Longitude 24° 19' West.

Join A and A', and this line will pass through the position of the ship at the time of the first observation.

Project
{ also the point B, in Latitude 43° N. and in
   Longitude 27° 22' 15" West,
   and the point B' in Latitude 44° N., and in
   Longitude 24° 20' 30" West.

Join B and B', and this line will pass through the position of the ship at the time of the second observation.

3d.   It is seen that these two lines intersect each other in Latitude 44° 1' N., which is the true Latitude, and the true Longitude is 24° 18' W.

4th.   No correction is required for change of station, since the course sailed was *on the first* projected straight line AA' tending N. E. by E., the same as the course sailed.

5th.   The other requisitions of the Example are projected as in Problem I.

Example II.

On December 21st, 1838, the sun's correct central altitude was 20° 23' A. M., when the Chronometer time was 1ʰ

34ᵐ P. M.; and his correct central altitude was 25° 10′
P. M. ⋆ The mean Greenwich time was 5ʰ 55ᵐ 34ˢ
P. M., when the Latitude by account being 36° 08′ N., and
between the observations the ship sailed E. N. E. ¾ E., 25
miles. Required to project, on Mercator's Chart, the true
Latitude and Longitude by Chronometer, &c.

1st. The two Latitudes to be assumed, less and greater, than 36° 8′ N. are 36° N. and 37° N. The declination is 23° 27′ S. and Equation of time as under.

For the First Altitude, 20° 23′ A. M.

For the point A, in Latitude 36° N.

Lat. 36 00 N.   -   -   -   sec. 0.09204
Dec. 23 27 S. -   -   -   -   sec. 0.03744
Sum. 59 27   Nat. cos. 50829
☉ Alt. 20 23   Nat. sin. 34830
H. M. S.   Diff. - 15999   log, 4.20409
2 33 20   =   log rising,   =   4.33357
12 hours.
9 26 40 App. time at ship, A. M.
— 1 40 Equa. time.
9 25 00 mean time at ship.
13 34 00   do.   Chronometer.
4 09 00   =   62° 15′ West Longitude of A.

For the point A′, in Latitude 37° N.

Lat. 37 00 N.   -   -   -   sec. 0.09765
Dec. 23 27 S. -   -   -   -   sec. 0.03744
Sum. 60 27   Nat. cos. 49318
☉ Alt. 20 23   Nat. sin. 34830
H. M. S.   Diff. - 14488   log, 4.16101
2 26 37   =   log rising,   =   4.29610
12 hours.
9 33 23 App. time at ship, A. M.
— 1 40 Equation.
9 31 43 mean time at ship.
13 34 00   do.   by Chronometer.
4 02 17   =   60° 34⅛′ West Longitude of A′.

For the Second Altitude, 25° 10′ P. M.

For the point B, in Latitude 36° N.

Lat. 36 00 N. - - - sec. 0.09204
Dec. 23 27 S. - - - - sec. 0.03744
Sum. 59 27   Nat. cos. 50829
☉ Alt. 25 10   Nat. sin. 42525
H. M. S.   Diff. - 8304 log, 3.91929
1 49 27 P. M. = log rising, = 4.04877
— 1 30 Equation time.
1 47 57 mean time at ship, P. M.
5 55 34   do.   Chronometer.
4 07 37 = 61° 54¼′ West Longitude of B.

For the point B′ in Latitude 37° N.

Lat. 37 00 N. - - - sec. 0.09765
Dec. 23 27 S. - - - - sec. 0.03744
Sum. 60 27   Nat. cos. 49318
☉ Alt. 25 10   Nat. sin. 42525
H. M. S.   Diff. - 6793 log, 3.83206
1 39 28 = log rising, = 3.96715
— 1 30 Equation time.
1 37 58 mean time at ship. P. M.
5 55 34   do.   Chronometer.
4 17 36 = 64° 24′ West Longitude of B′.

Project on Mercator's Chart, Plate VI, the four points A, A′, B, B′; in their respective Latitudes and Longitudes; and join A and A′; B and B′. If the ship had not changed her station, her true place would be at their intersection.

3d. But since this is not the case, from any point, as P, in the line AA′, set off the point D, 25 miles E. N. E. ¾ E., the course and distance made good between the observations; through D, parallel to AA′, draw an indefinite straight line DB; the intersection of DB with BB′, is the ship's place at the second observation.

4th. The correction in miles of the *first altitude*, for change of station, is the perpendicular upon AA' from B to C, equal to 10' additive.

The true Latitude is 36° N.; and the Longitude by Chronometer is 61° 54¼' West of Greenwich.

NOTE.

This observation was found to be accurate by meridian observation of the sun, as follows:

⊙'s observed altitude was 30° 24' bearing S.

$$11 \text{ correction.}$$
$$\overline{30° 35'}$$
$$59 \ 25 \text{ Zenith distance N.}$$
$$23 \ 27 \text{ Declination S.}$$

The ship's intermediate ⎫
position between the obser- ⎬ 35 58 Latitude N.
vations was at noon. ⎭

PROBLEM III.

When two altitudes of the sun are observed, and the times are noted by a " well-regulated watch," for the elapsed time, the course and distance being given; and it is required to find the Latitude only; we may consider, in such case, that the " *watch* " shows mean time at *any meridian*, which we may please to *assume;* in the same way as the " *Chronometer* " shows mean time at the *known* meridian of Greenwich.

We may, then, assume, as a first meridian, that of Greenwich; and set the hands of the watch, previously to any observation, to the Greenwich mean time, *as nearly as we may be able to estimate it*, according to the supposed Longitude of the ship by account. And then we may regard the " *watch* " as a " *Chronometer*."

Having done this, proceed *exactly as in the last two Examples*, to find the Longitudes of A, A', B, B'; and project them *by that rule*, and the *true Latitude* will be found as before; but the Longitude from Greenwich *will not* be found; since the watch shows only the *approximate* time at Greenwich.

4

But it is not absolutely necessary to set the hands of the watch to the Greenwich time, but merely see how much the watch is *fast*, or *slow*, of such estimated time, and allow for the error, accordingly. Thus it is quite immaterial what hour and minute the watch shows; it is only required, that the going of the watch between the observations is known to be accurate.

By assuming that the watch shows Greenwich time, the resulting Longitudes will be such as correspond in degrees to the chart in use; otherwise, any other meridian might be assumed with equal success.

The above method will be found the most simple, and is to be always used when the sun is the object observed; but to familiarize the learner with the principles of this method, so that he can apply the method in all cases to the fixed stars and planets, the following example is given, in which the *four* points are projected by a different process; for the rule to do this, the reader will refer to Problem VI. and Example (page 59.)

EXAMPLE.

On the 4th of January, 1839, sea account, between 2 and 3 o'clock, P. M., the sun's true central altitudes were 15° 10′; and 10° 30′; and the elapsed time was 46^m 5^s. The course and distance made good between the observations, being E. N. E., 6 miles; the Latitude by account 46° 25′ N. Required the true Latitude, at the time of the second observation; the correction of the first altitude for change of station; the sun's azimuth at each observation.

1st. The elapsed time is 46 m. 5 s. = 11° 31′ 15″, or the difference of Longitude of Z′, West of Z.

2d. The two Latitudes to be assumed, will be 46° N. and 47° N.

3d. Find the apparent times *"from noon,"* as follows:

For the First Altitude, 15° 10′ P. M.

For the point A, in Latitude 46° N.

Lat. 46 00 N. - - - sec. 0.15823
Dec. 22 51½ S. - - - - sec. 0.03552
Sum. 68 51½ Nat. cos. 36068
☉ Alt. 15 10 Nat. sin. 26163

H. M. S. Diff. - 9905 log, 3.99585
2 9 12 = log rising, = 4.18960
2 9 12 = 32° 18′ diff. Longitude East of Z, be- ⎱
cause P. M., of a point A, in Latitude 46° N. ⎰

For the point A′ in Latitude 47° N.

Lat. 47 00 N. - - - sec. 0.16622
Dec. 22 51½ S. - - - - sec. 0.03552
Sum. 69 51½ Nat. cos. 34435
☉ Alt. 15 10 Nat. sin. 26163

H. M. S. Diff. - 8272 log, 3.91761
1 58 55 = log rising, = 4.11935
1 58 55 = 29° 43¾′ diff. Longitude East of Z, ⎱
because PM, of a point A′ in Latitude 47° N. ⎰

For the Second Altitude, 10° 30′ P. M.

For the point B, in Latitude 46° N.

Lat. 46 00 N. - - - sec. 0.15823
Dec. 22 51½ S. - - - - sec. 0.03552
Sum. 68 51½ Nat. cos. 36068
☉ Alt. 10 30 Nat. sin. 18224

H. M. S. Diff. - 17844 log, 4.25149
2 55 22 = log rising, = 4.44524
2 55 22 = 43° 50½′ diff. Longitude East of Z′, ⎱
because P. M. of a point B in Latitude 46° N. ⎰

For the point B', in Latitude 47° N.

Lat. 47 00 N. - - - sec. 0.16622
Dec. 22 51½ S. - - - - sec. 0.03552
Sum. 69 51½   Nat. cos. 34435
☉ Alt. 10 30   Nat. sin. 18224

H. M. S.   Diff. - 16211   log, 4.20981
2 48 23   =   log rising,   =   4.41155
2 48 23 = 42° 5¾' diff. Longitude East of Z', ⎫
because P. M. of a point B', in Latitude 47° N. ⎰

A in Lat. 46 N., is East of Z,   32° 18'
Z is East of Z', - - -   11 31¼
A is, also, East of Z',   - =   43° 49¼'
Project A, on the chart, Plate VII., in Latitude 46° N.,
and in any Longitude; and mark it, *East of Z*, 32° 18';
and *East of Z*, 43° 49¼'.

A', in Lat. 47° N., is East of Z   29° 43¾'
A   46° N., is East of Z   32 18
A' is West of A - - =   2 34¼
Project A', in Lat. 47° N.; and 2° 34¼' West of A, mark
it 29° 43¾' *East of Z*.

A is East of Z' - - =   43° 49¼'
B in Lat. 46° N. is East of Z'   43 50½
B is East of A - - =   1¼
Project B', in Lat. 46° N., 1¼', East of A, and mark it
43° 50½ *East of Z'*.

A is East of Z' - - -   43° 49¼'
B', in Lat. 47° N., is East of Z'   42 5¾
B' is West of A - - =   1 43¼
Project B', in Lat. 47° N., 1° 43¼' West of A. and mark it
42° 5¾' *East of Z'*.

5th. Join by straight lines A, A', and B, B', from any
point, as P, in AA', set off the point D, with the course
and distance, E. N. E., 6 miles; through D, draw a line
parallel to AA', and its intersection with BB', is the true

Latitude at the time of the second observation, namely, 46° 15¼' N.

6th. The correction of the first altitude is 5 miles subtractive, as projected by the rule; the bearings of the sun are also projected. _____

If the sun's azimuth could be always *exactly observed*, it would be necessary to find the Longitude of *only one* point in each straight line; and that might be found by using the Latitude by dead reckoning to get the apparent time; for then, if a line be drawn on the chart, through this point in the *exact* direction of the sun; and a second line be drawn through the same point, and perpendicular to the first line; it would show the bearing of the land &c. as before; and if two altitudes were taken, and the lines thus projected, the Latitude and Longitude would be very easily found — but unless under very favorable circumstances this cannot be done with sufficient accuracy; and the only *safe* way is to find the position of two points in each line as directed.

It is evident, that, having found the position in Latitude and Longitude of the two points in either straight line, the bearing of one from the other is easily found *by case I. Mercator's sailing;* and thence the bearing of the land; but still it is preferable to project them.

The Latitude may be found by this method of calculation from two altitudes, *without projecting the straight lines,* as follows. Note the elapsed time by watch or Chronometer, (in example, Problem III, this was 46^m 5^s;) with both altitudes, find the apparent times from noon, using either *one* of the two assumed Latitudes; take the difference of these times; (in example, Problem III, the times for ☉'s Altitude, 15° 10' and 10° 30', in assumed Latitude 46°, were 2^h 9^m 12^s and 2^h 55^m 22^s; their difference is 46^m 10^s;) which difference of times (46^m 10^s) *would have been* the *elapsed time*, if the true Latitude had been 46°; but 46^m 10^s is 5^s *greater* than the elapsed time *noted* by watch; do likewise with both altitudes, using the other assumed Latitude; (we have, example Problem III, for Latitude 47°, the times 1^h 58^m 55^s, and 2^h 48^m 23^s; their difference is 49^m 28^s,) which difference would have been the elapsed time if the true Latitude had been 47°; but

49^m 28^s is 3^m 25^s *greater* than the elapsed time noted, (46^m 5^s;) therefore, in this example, the further north we assume a Latitude the greater we make the error in the elapsed time; and we may already see that the true Latitude is not so much as 46° N. Now take again the difference between 46^m 10^s, (the elapsed time if the Latitude be 46°,) and 49^m 28^s, (the elapsed time if the Latitude be 47°;) this difference is 3^m 18^s; then make this proportion; if 3^m 18^s is the error of elapsed time, caused by an error of Latitude of 1°, what is the error of Latitude (to be subtracted from 46° N.) caused by an error of 5^s of elapsed time? by proportional logarithms (Table XXII, Bowditch,) we have

$$3^m\ 18^s \text{ Arith. Comp. log } 8.2632$$
$$1° \qquad\qquad\qquad .4771$$
$$0^m\ 5^s \qquad\qquad 3.3345$$

$$\text{Ans.} = 1'\ 31'' \qquad\qquad \log 2.0748$$
$$46°\ 0'\ 00''$$

45° 58' 29'' Latitude of the intersection of
AA' and BB'.

By reference to Plate VII, we see that the straight lines, AA' BB', intersect each other a little to the *south* of Latitude 46°; *no change of station* being allowed; to find the *true* Latitude, according to the example, we should have *first* corrected the first altitude for change of station; and then proceeded as above. The Longitude also may be found when their times are noted by Chronometers, by a similar process.

What are the errors to which observations calculated by the method of projection are subject?

The only calculation used, is that for finding the apparent time; for this purpose, three things are necessary; the latitude, the declination, and the altitude; if all these be accurate, we have the true apparent time; and if the chronometer is right, we have *no error;* excluding such as may arise from inaccuracy of noting the times, of adjustment, reading off, &c., which ordinary care will prevent.

Now, by assuming the latitudes used, no error exists in

this element; the declination also may be considered accurate; and the only remaining source of error is in the altitude observed.

This is usually less than two miles; but we may find, that by the common rules this will make a large error in the ship's *position* by Chronometer, as the sun approaches the meridian; because the resulting time is applied *directly* to finding the Longitude. When the sun bears east or west, the error would be exactly equal to the error of altitude turned into time; but as the sun approaches the meridian, the error of time may be regarded as the hypotheneuse of a right-angled triangle, one of whose angles is very acute; and the short leg opposite to this as the error of altitude; and while the short leg always remains the same, the hypotheneuse continually increases, thus causing continually increasing errors in the *position* by Chronometer.

But by this method, the same things existing in the triangle, the error in *the bearing of the land* is always *equal* to the error of altitude; as when a meridian observation is observed one mile too great, the bearing of the land in the parallel of Latitude resulting, is one mile erroneous. There is no reason, then, why we may not observe the sun at *any* bearing.

We may then readily find by *inspection* of any projected observation, the small limit of error to which it is liable; or by drawing a parallel line on each side of each projected "parallel of equal altitude," at the *greatest* distance from it that it is possible for the altitude to be erroneous, we shall have the *extreme* limit of error; and thus know what degree of confidence can be placed in every altitude observed; and hence in the bearing of the land, by one altitude; and in the Latitude, and Longitude by Chronometer, when two altitudes are observed.

———

That the navigator may see, at a glance, the errors of Longitude by *a strictly accurate Chronometer*, to which he is subject, for an error of the Latitude used in finding the apparent time of the ship, when he cannot get sights of the sun at the time he bears E. or W., the following Table is calculated upon the principles of this method.

This will serve as a guide to know the *greatest* error of Longitude consequent to *any* observed altitude; but then the *greatest possible* error of Latitude must be allowed for this purpose.

But since the *real error* of Latitude *cannot* be known by *one* altitude, (except it be a meridian observation,) it will still be necessary "to project" the observation as directed, finding thereby the *Bearing of the Land*, in a similar way as by meridian observation.

TABLE,

Showing the errors of Longitude by Chronometer, in Nautical miles, (60 to a degree of Latitude,) for *one mile* error of the Latitude used in finding the apparent time at the ship; when the sun *does not* bear true E. or W., at the time of observation.

⊙'s TRUE AMPLITUDE IN POINTS.	ERROR IN NAUTICAL MILES.	⊙'s TRUE AMPLITUDE IN POINTS.	ERROR IN NAUTICAL MILES.
$\frac{1}{4}$	0.049	$4\frac{1}{4}$	1.103
$\frac{1}{2}$	0.098	$4\frac{1}{2}$	1.219
$\frac{3}{4}$	0.148	$4\frac{3}{4}$	1.348
1	0.199	5	1.497
$1\frac{1}{4}$	0.250	$5\frac{1}{4}$	1.669
$1\frac{1}{2}$	0.303	$5\frac{1}{2}$	1.871
$1\frac{3}{4}$	0.358	$5\frac{3}{4}$	2.115
2	0.414	6	2.414
$2\frac{1}{4}$	0.473	$6\frac{1}{4}$	2.795
$2\frac{1}{2}$	0.535	$6\frac{1}{2}$	3.297
$2\frac{3}{4}$	0.599	$6\frac{3}{4}$	3.992
3	0.668	7	5.027
$3\frac{1}{4}$	0.742	$7\frac{1}{4}$	6.741
$3\frac{1}{2}$	0.821	$7\frac{1}{2}$	10.153
$3\frac{3}{4}$	0.907	$7\frac{3}{4}$	20.356
4	1.000	8	Infinite.

To know if this error of Longitude be to the E. or W. of the *true* Longitude, the following Rules are given, and will be found to include every case.

I.

If the ☉ bears $\begin{Bmatrix} \text{Southerly when in N. Latitude,} \\ \text{Northerly when in S. Latitude,} \end{Bmatrix}$

And the time of observation is A. M., then, if the *Latitude*, used in finding the apparent time, be $\begin{Bmatrix} greater \\ less \end{Bmatrix}$ than the *true* Latitude, the Longitude will be too far $\begin{Bmatrix} East. \\ West. \end{Bmatrix}$

But if the time of observation be P. M., then, if the *Latitude* used in finding the apparent time be $\begin{Bmatrix} greater \\ less \end{Bmatrix}$ than the *true* Latitude, the Longitude will be too far $\begin{Bmatrix} West. \\ East. \end{Bmatrix}$

II.

And when the ☉ bears $\begin{Bmatrix} \text{Northerly in North Latitude,} \\ \text{Southerly in South Latitude,} \end{Bmatrix}$

And the time of observation is A. M., then, if the *Latitude* used in finding the apparent time be $\begin{Bmatrix} greater \\ less \end{Bmatrix}$ than the *true* Latitude, the Longitude will be too far $\begin{Bmatrix} West \\ East \end{Bmatrix}$

But if the time of observation be P. M., then, if the Latitude used in finding the apparent time be $\begin{Bmatrix} greater \\ less \end{Bmatrix}$ than the *true* Latitude, the Longitude will be too far $\begin{Bmatrix} East \\ West \end{Bmatrix}$

Note. After the vernal equinox, when in north Latitude, observations may be often taken when the sun bears to the northward of the E. and W. points; and in south Latitude, after the autumnal equinox, when he bears to the southward of them; also when the Latitude and declination are of the *same* name, and the declination is *greater* than the Latitude in.

The method of using this Table will be best shown by

Example.

If the sun bore S. W. by S., *true*, at the time of observation, in Latitude 50° N. by D. R., what will be the error of Longitude by Chronometer, if the Latitude used in finding the apparent time at the ship is erroneous 10 miles?
Ans. 23.3 minutes of Longitude.

S. W. by S. is five points from W. In the Table opposite five points Amplitude is the error for *one* mile, in

Nautical miles -   -   - = 1.497
Multiply by -   -   -   -   10
gives the error for ten miles = 14.97 in Nautical miles.

Enter Table II, (Bowditch,) with the Latitude in, 50°, as a course, at the bottom of the page; and over it, in the Latitude column, find 14.97; opposite to it, in the Distance column, is 23.3, the error of Longitude in minutes of Longitude.

In the foregoing example, if the Latitude was erroneous 10 miles to the *north* of the *true* Latitude; we have "the ⊙ bearing *southerly* in *north Latitude;*" and "the time of observation P. M.;" and the "*Latitude* used in finding the apparent time, "*greater*" than the *true* Latitude;" and the rule gives the Longitude too far *west;* the error by the Table was 23' 3 minutes of Longitude; which must be *subtracted* if in *west* Longitude, from the Longitude by Chronometer, but *added* if in *east* Longitude. When such observations, however, are projected, these errors are evident by *inspection*, and the *bearing of the land* found.

II.

SOME REMARKS UPON THE ADVANTAGES OF THIS METHOD.

There is no difficulty, by the common methods, in determining the position of places on the earth's surface, when these places are situated on the land; for then sufficient time may be taken to select the moment of observation; and every circumstance can be taken advantage of, which will conspire to produce a correct result. But when at sea on board a ship, which is constantly changing her position, and frequently approaching with rapidity a dangerous coast, numerous circumstances often render the case one of considerable difficulty at an important moment.

The common methods of finding the ship's place are these: a meridian observation of the sun for the Latitude; an altitude of the sun, bearing as nearly as possible E. or W. for the Longitude by Chronometer; lunar observations; double altitudes; dead reckoning; and occasional meridian altitudes of the fixed stars, planets, or moon. Of all these methods, the first two are those which are chiefly relied on, by a great majority of navigators in all cases; and if these observations could be had daily at the *proper* moment, the ship's position would always be easily known, and no danger need ensue.

But the proper moment cannot at all times be chosen to take these observations; for the first must be taken when the sun is *on the meridian*, unless the apparent time is exactly known; and the second when he bears *E.* or *W.*, except the Latitude be previously accurately known; and the observations will be partially or entirely prevented, when thick weather prevails, or be liable to error, if the sun does not bear E. or W. at any time during the day.

For after the sun crosses the equator, throughout the whole hemisphere from which he is receding in declination, he daily rises and sets, at points further removed from E. or W.; and since an altitude cannot be relied on, which is not greater than 6° or 7° at least, this cause increases the angle from the E. and W. points at which he is observable. So throughout a whole hemisphere, for nearly 7 months in the year, *the sun is not observable* in the proper E. or W. points; and it may be found, that, when the sun is 23° 28' S. of the equator, he will rise and set in Latitude 50° N., at an angle from E. and W. of 38° 17'; or by compass SE. ⅜ E. and SW. ⅜ W, *true;* and when only 7° above the horizon, he will bear SE. ¼ S. nearly; and thus the least error of Longitude by Chronometer, to which a ship is liable for an error of Latitude of 30 miles, is 1° 2'; whenever, then, the *Latitude by account* is used to find the apparent time at the ship; and the sun does *not bear exactly E.* or *W.*, the Longitude, by a good Chronometer, will be always *wrong*, unless the Latitude by account is strictly accurate. The necessity of some method of finding the ship's place, when the Latitude is uncertain, is then apparent.

A meridian altitude shows the ship to be in some point of a small circle of the sphere, called a *parallel of Latitude*; (or else on the equator, which is a great circle;) and that the *land*, through which this small circle passes, bears *E.* or *W.*

The observation for the Chronometer shows in a similar manner, (the Latitude being previously correctly obtained,) that the ship is *likewise* situated on *another* circle of the sphere, called a meridian of Longitude; and that the *Land*, through which *this* circle passes, bears *N.* or *S.*

And at the intersection of these *two circles*, (allowing for change of station between the observations,) is the ship's position on the earth's surface.

But since the accuracy of the position depends upon the accuracy of the *Latitude* and apparent time, how, when these are uncertain, or even unknown, can the ship's position be fixed upon either of these *two circles*, by either of these two methods, as they are usually directed to be used, when only *one altitude* of the sun can be observed, and that when he bore *neither E. nor W., nor on the meridian?*

No practical rules are laid down which include so important a case; the only resource is, to use the Latitude by dead reckoning. How very erroneous this may prove, is herein shown.

But *these are the cases* to which the Method of Projection is *peculiarly adapted.* For if it be possible, at *any* time of day when the sun is sufficiently high above the horizon, to observe at all, *one altitude* of the sun; by noting the Chronometer time, and observing roughly his bearing, we shall find the ship to be, not on a *parallel of Latitude*, it is true, running E. and W.; nor on a *meridian of Longitude,* running N. and S.; but on as actual and as simple a circle as either of these, namely, a *parallel of equal altitude;* running diagonally to those circles, at an angle which depends on the bearing of the sun; which parallel, when projected on the chart, by the rules, will pass through the position of the ship, and show the bearing of the land, in its course as it lies projected on the chart, as truly as by a Meridian Observation, which can be observed but *once* in a day; and if two altitudes be projected, both the true Latitude, and Longitude by Chronometer, are evident by inspection.

When approaching the land, (and this is the time when it is of the most importance to know the true position of the ship,) it unfortunately happens, that thick weather frequently prevails at considerable distances seaward, so that the sun is visible only for a few moments during a run of several days, and it is certainly important that a single observation at such times should be rendered available.

There is no part of the seas, that is liable in a greater degree to fogs and thick weather, than the English Channels, North Seas, &c.; and there is no part more crowded by the fleets of all nations; the coast, too, is dangerous; and the Westerly gales are severe, and of long duration; and ships are often placed in situations there, from uncertainty of their position, which render it dangerous "to run," and often more dangerous to "lay by," or to "stand off and on."

Having sailed from Charleston, S. C., 25th November, 1837, bound to Greenock, a series of heavy gales from the Westward promised a quick passage; after passing the

Azores, the wind prevailed from the Southward, with thick weather; after passing Longitude 21° W., no observation was had until near the land; but soundings were had not far, as was supposed, from the edge of the Bank. The weather was now more boisterous, and very thick; and the wind still Southerly; arriving about midnight, 17th December, within 40 miles, by dead reckoning, of Tusker light; the wind hauled S. E., true, making the Irish coast a lee shore; the ship was then kept close to the wind, and several tacks made to preserve her position as nearly as possible until daylight; when nothing being in sight, she was kept on E. N. E. under short sail, with heavy gales; at about 10 A. M. an altitude of the sun was observed, and the Chronometer time noted; but, having run so far without any observation, it was plain the Latitude by dead reckoning was liable to error, and could not be entirely relied on.

Using, however, this Latitude, in finding the Longitude by Chronometer, it was found to put the ship 15′ of Longitude, E. from her position by dead reckoning; which in Latitude 52° N. is 9 nautical miles; this seemed to agree tolerably well with the dead reckoning; but feeling doubtful of the Latitude, the observation was tried with a Latitude 10′ further N., finding this place the ship E. N. E. 27 *nautical* miles, of the former position, it was tried again with a Latitude 20′ N. of the dead reckoning; this also placed the ship still further E. N. E., and still 27 *nautical miles* further; these three positions were then seen to lie in the direction of *Small's light*. It then at once appeared, that the observed altitude must have happened at *all the three* points, and at *Small's light*, and at the ship, at the *same instant of time;* and it followed, that Small's light must bear E. N. E., if the Chronometer was right. Having been convinced of this truth, the ship was kept on her course, E. N. E., the wind being still S. E., and in less than an hour, Small's light was made bearing E. N. E. ½ E., and close aboard.

The Latitude by dead reckoning, was erroneous 8 miles; and if the Longitude by Chronometer had been found by this Latitude, the ship's position would have been erroneous 31½ *minutes of Longitude*, too far *W.*, and 8 *miles* too far *S.* The ship had, from current, tide, or error of log, overrun her reckoning, 1 mile in 20. (See Plate III.)

Thus it is seen, that an observation taken at *any* hour of the day, and at any angle between the meridian and *E.* or *W.* points, is rendered *practically* useful, inasmuch as the Chronometer can be depended on.

A great proportion of the Chronometers now in use, are sufficiently accurate to determine the ship's position; and particularly when they have been out of port only a month or two; the government of Great Britain have spent thousands to perfect them; but it should be recollected that the Greenwich time is only *one* of the quantities which must be correct, to find the Longitude; we must be *sure* that the *time at the ship* is correct also; and it can scarcely be doubted, that *errors of Latitude* have caused the loss of as many ships, as errors of Chronometers; while Chronometers have borne the blame not only of their own occasional imperfections, but also of these *errors of Latitude,* to which the navigator is subjected, from the prevalence of thick weather, gales of wind, and when a ship is under short sail, wearing, and tacking, and in tide-ways near the land; making leeway, and changing the rate of sailing with different cargoes on board.

The proverb, that "a seaman always knows his Latitude," had its origin in those days, when *the Longitude* was the great point to be determined; for before lunar observations were used, or Chronometers invented, the only observations which could be relied on, were those for finding the Latitude; and thus the Latitude was *comparatively* certain; but the Longitude was estimated by the log, and great errors were common.

But, at present, the case is almost completely reversed; for with a good Chronometer, used with care, it is *the Latitude* which is the great desideratum; if the Latitude is *accurately* known, a single altitude is sufficient to find the ship's place; and if it be *uncertain,* the Method of Projection affords the *most complete substitute* for a meridian observation, the altitude being observed at *any* hour.

By this method, if the Chronometer is *wrong,* and the Latitude *uncertain,* the *bearing of the land* would be erroneous, by a quantity equal to the whole error of Chronometer, when the sun is observed bearing *E.* or *W.;* but as the angle *increases*, from the E. and W. points, at which an observation *is* taken, the error in the bearing of the land, caused by the error of the Chronometer, constantly *diminishes ;* and when the sun is on the meridian, *vanishes ;* when the observation becomes a real *meridian altitude*, whence the true Latitude may be found as usual. But by the usual method no approximation to correctness can be made.

The case when a second altitude is observed, is deduced from the manner in which the first is projected ; and in an analogous manner, as a meridian observation, and one taken when the sun bears East or West, by the usual method, place the ship at the intersection of a circle of Longitude with a parallel of Latitude, allowing for change of station, so the intersection of the first projected parallel of equal altitude with the second, is the ship's place.

The extra work to project the second parallel is trifling, for it will be noticed that many of the logarithms are the same as in the first.

The Advantages of the Method by Projection may be summed up as follows :

1. When the Latitude, &c., are uncertain, one altitude of the sun, at *any* hour, with the Chronometer time, is available in a similar manner as a meridian observation, which can be taken only *once* in a day.

2. The errors of Longitude by Chronometer, consequent to any error in the Latitude, are shown by inspection.

3. The sun's azimuth is found at the same operation.

4. In addition to these results, found by one altitude, two similar altitudes give the true Latitude, and also the Longitude by Chronometer. By the common methods of double altitudes, the Longitude must be found by a subsequent calculation ; which circumstance renders this method much the *shortest*.

5. The usual simple calculation for finding the apparent time at the ship, is known and daily practiced by every shipmaster who uses a Chronometer. No other formula is used.

6. Double altitudes of the sun are therefore within the reach of all persons who use Chronometers, and who are unacquainted with the various formulas laid down in the books.

41

III.

EXPLANATION OF THE PRINCIPLES UPON WHICH THIS METHOD DEPENDS.

To facilitate the understanding of the theory of this method, a reference to the following common definitions relative to spherical bodies may be necessary.

A *sphere* is a uniformly round body, every point on the surface of which is equally distant from a certain point within the body, called the centre.

If any plane or flat surface pass through the sphere, the intersection of the surface of the sphere by the plane is the circumference of *a circle*.

A *great* circle of a sphere is one whose plane passes through the centre of the sphere, and so divides the sphere into two *equal* parts, called hemispheres.

A *small* circle of a sphere is one whose plane does not pass through the centre of the sphere, and consequently divides the sphere into two *unequal* parts.

The *pole* of *any* circle of a sphere is a *point* on the surface of the sphere from which every point in the circumference of the circle is equally distant; thus every circle of the sphere has two poles, and the straight line joining them is the diameter of the sphere.

One half* of the spherical surface of the earth being illuminated by the sun at a given instant, while at the same time the opposite portion is in the shade, that line, which is the boundary between the illuminated and dark hemispheres, is called by geographers "THE CIRCLE OF ILLUMINATION."

---

* The corrections being made by the usual tables, for Parallax, Semidiameter, Refraction, and the Spheroidal Figure of the Earth — and if the eye be elevated, for Dip also.

It is a *great circle*, and its plane passes through the centre of the earth, dividing it into two equal parts; in the same manner as the equator is a great circle of the earth, and divides it into the Northern and Southern hemispheres.

But these are also divided by *small circles* of the sphere, parallel to the equator, which are called "parallels of Latitude;" and by their means the Latitude is reckoned, all places situated on the equator having their Latitude equal to 0°; and proceeding towards the poles, the Latitude of places on these small circles increases regularly, until, arriving at them, it becomes equal to 90°.

In like manner, all those places which are situated on the *circle of illumination*, since they have the sun's centre in the horizon, have his *altitude* equal to 0°, and that point on the surface of the earth, next towards the sun, and which is *the pole* of the circle of illumination, has the sun in the zenith; consequently, at that point his altitude is equal to 90°. The *intermediate* altitudes of the sun may likewise be reckoned on *small circles*, parallel to the circle of illumination; and which may be called PARALLELS OF EQUAL ALTITUDE; since they serve the purpose of showing all those places on the earth's surface, which have an *equal* altitude of the sun, at *the same instant* of time; the pole, at which the sun is in the zenith, may be called the POLE OF ILLUMINATION, and the whole system of circles, THE SYSTEM OF CIRCLES OF ILLUMINATION.

Thus it appears, that, as all those places on a given *small circle* of the earth, called a parallel of Latitude, have the *same Latitude*, and that degree and minute which is the name of that parallel; so, all those places, on a given *small circle*, called a parallel of equal altitude, have the SAME ALTITUDE of the sun, and the same degree and minute which is the name of this parallel.

Since the poles of the equator, and of the parallels of Latitude, coincide with the extremities of the earth's *axis*, the system of circles of Latitude is not affected by the daily rotation of the earth; but always remains constant; indeed, it has been constructed with particular reference to this object.

Such, however, is not the case with the system of circles of illumination; because, the *poles* of this system do *not* coincide with the extremities of the earth's *axis;* for the sun being always vertical to one of its poles, this follows the sun (at the rate of 15° per hour) in his apparent daily course from East to West, and also in the ecliptic, through all the degrees of the sun's declination.

But if at any instant, we can project upon the earth's surface the position of this moving system, or any parallel of equal altitude belonging to it, which may correspond to an observed altitude of the sun, we shall have as sure a method of determining the position of places on the earth's surface, as by means of the system of parallels of Latitude.

But it may be well to consider in what manner the system of circles of illumination intersects the different parallels of Latitude, and the meridians of Longitude.

Because the sun is always vertical to the pole of illumination, and the parallels of Latitude on the earth's surface are concentric with parallels of declination on the celestial sphere, the *Latitude of this pole is always equal to the Sun's declination.*

If, then, about a point (as Z, Plate I,) in any Longitude, but in that parallel of Latitude which is equal to the sun's declination as a centre, we describe small circles of a sphere at every 10° distant, after the manner of parallels of Latitude, and this may be seen to advantage on a terrestrial globe, we shall observe, that the parallels of equal altitude, which we are describing, cut the parallels of Latitude and meridians of Longitude at all possible angles; in the N. W., N. E., S. W., and S. E., directions from the pole of illumination, Z, they will cut them diagonally; in the North, South, East, and West points from this pole, they will touch them as tangents; and at intermediate bearings will make intermediate angles with them.

Each parallel of equal altitude, it will be observed, is described round the pole of illumination, as a centre, at a distance, measured on the arc of a *great* circle passing through this pole, which is equal to the *complement* of the *sun's altitude* corresponding to each parallel respectively.

Hence, with a given altitude of the sun, the corresponding parallel of equal altitude cuts only certain parallels of Latitude, not North of a particular Latitude in the Northern, nor South of a particular Latitude in the Southern hemisphere. The distance, then, of the North and South points, in any parallel of equal altitude from the pole of illumination, is equal in degrees and minutes to the complement of the sun's altitude; but these points being on the same meridian as the pole of illumination, this distance is also equal to the *difference of Latitude* between the pole and either point; and because they are on the same meridian as this pole, the apparent time at these points will be *noon*, for it is always noon at the meridian of the point which has the sun in the zenith.

Now the difference of Longitude, between any two places on the earth's surface, is expressed by the difference of the apparent times at those places, turned into degrees, 15° to the hour.

The difference of Longitude of *any point* in a parallel of equal altitude, corresponding to any observed altitude of the sun, from the meridian of its pole of illumination, will then be expressed by the difference of the apparent times at those places; that is, by the difference between 0^h 0^m 0^s, and the *apparent time from noon* at the point, in the parallel of equal altitude, which may be given. And the difference of Longitude between *any two points given* will be expressed in a similar manner.

But if the altitude, and declination of the sun be given, the apparent time will vary only with the different *Latitudes* which may be used in the calculation.

If, then, we *assume* any Latitude, not North of the North point, nor South of the South point of the parallel of equal altitude corresponding to an observed altitude of the sun, the declination being known also; and thence find the apparent time from noon, (by Method 3, Bowditch,) the *difference* between such time, and 0°, 0^m, 0^s, turned into Longitude, (15° per hour,) will be the *difference of Longitude* of the point in the parallel, from the meridian of the pole of illumination, and *its Latitude is had by the assumption:* thus the position of such point is found *relatively* to the pole of illumination, which is situated in a certain given Latitude.

In the same way, by assuming *two* Latitudes, with the same restrictions, the difference of their apparent times will express the difference of Longitude of the two points having the *two* assumed Latitudes; and their positions *relatively to the pole* will be expressed by their times from noon, turned into difference of Longitude.

———

Each point, thus found, has two positions in its parallel of equal altitude, in the assumed Latitude of each respectively; namely, one on each side of the meridian of the pole, and at equal differences of Longitude from it; and they correspond to A. M. and P. M. times of observation; and to distinguish on which side of the meridian of the pole of illumination the point lies with which we have to do, we should notice in practice the bearing of the sun. The required point being Westward from the pole, if an observation be A. M.; and Eastward, if P. M.

By assuming as many Latitudes as we please, we may thus project as many points as are necessary; and by joining all the points determined by a curve line, the whole parallel of equal altitude corresponding to any observed altitude of the sun, will be projected, in Latitude, *relatively* to the pole of illumination.

From the foregoing considerations the rule for solving the following Problem is deduced.

PROBLEM I.

The correct altitude of the sun's centre being observed, and his declination being given, it is required to project, on Mercator's chart, the corresponding parallel of equal altitude relatively to its pole of illumination, showing what parallels of Latitude it cuts, and in what manner it cuts both them and the meridians of Longitude.

Note. — Owing to the distorted shape of the earth's surface by Mercator's chart, the curves will not appear as circles, as they would be if projected on the earth, or on a terrestrial globe.

RULE.

1st. Find the complement of the sun's altitude; which gives the difference of Latitude between the pole of illumination and the North and South points of the parallel of equal altitude.

2d. Project then on the chart (Plate I,) in a Latitude equal to the sun's declination, the pole of illumination, the point Z, in any assumed Longitude, as 0°; and on the meridian of Z, in their respective Latitudes just found, project the North and South points N. and S.; at which the apparent time is noon, or 0^h 0^m 0^s.

3d. *Assume* a Latitude, as that of any point, A, B, or C, &c., not North of N., nor South of S.; and with the given altitude and declination, find the apparent time from noon (Method 3, B.) which, turned into Longitude, 15° per hour, will be the difference of Longitude between Z, and A, B, or C, &c., and its Latitude is had by assumption.

4th. In the Latitude assumed, (if that of A,) on each side of the meridian of Z, project the points A, A', with the difference of Longitude found above; then A and A' will be *two points* in the parallel required; in the same manner find as many points as are necessary.

5th. By joining all the adjacent points with a curve line, the whole parallel, and the Latitudes it cuts, &c., are evident by inspection.

Note.—In this problem the difference of Longitude of the points have been reckoned from the meridian of Z; but the curve could be also projected, by taking the meridian of any point, as A, for a starting-point, and thence might be reckoned the points B, C, &c., and finally the meridian of Z, and then Z be projected.

Example I.

The sun's central altitude is 60°; the declination 10° N., it is required to project the parallel of equal altitude, &c.

1st. To find the complement of the sun's altitude, and the Latitude of the N. and S. points.

From   90°
sub.   60
remains $\overline{30°}$ = complement of the sun's Altitude.

To   30   comp. ☉ Alt.
add   10° Dec.

sum   40°= Lat. of N.
diff.   20° = Lat. of S.

2d. Project (Plate I) the points Z, N, and S, in their

proper Latitudes, and in any one assumed Longitude, as 0°.

3d. To find and project any point; as one in Latitude 30° N., which call A.

Lat. 30 00 N. -   -   -   -   sec. 0.06247
Dec. 10 00 S.   -   -   -   sec. 0.00665

Diff. 20 00   Nat. cos.   93969
⊙ Alt. 60 00   Nat. sin.   86603

H. M. S.   Diff.   7366   log. 3.86723
1 35 57.05   =   log rising   =   3.93635

1 35 57.05 = 23° 59' 15".75, or the difference of Longitude of A in Latitude 30 N., from the meridian of Z, where it is noon.

4th. On each side of NZS with this difference of Longitude project two points, A and A', in Latitude 30° North; which will be two points in the curve required; the altitude is observed at A, when the time is P. M., and at A', when A. M.

Find other points B, B', C, C', &c.

5th. Join all the points, and the requisitions of the Problem are evident by inspection.

In the same manner are projected the parallels of equal altitude, corresponding to sun's altitude, 0°, 10°, 20°, 30°, &c., when the sun's declination is 10° N.

———

After any lapse of time, the sun, and, consequently, the pole of illumination, to which the sun is always vertical, will have passed, at the rate of 15° per hour, due West; (no change of declination having taken place;) and will have arrived after such time at some point, as Z', (Plate I,) whose difference of Longitude from Z will be equal to the elapsed time turned into Longitude, 15° for an hour; because the angular space passed over is equal to the product of the time by the angular velocity.

But if, at the expiration of such time, a second altitude be *observed*, and its corresponding parallel of equal altitude be projected as before, it will have for its pole Z'; and it must intersect the first projected parallel in two points, one to the Northward and one to the Southward of the poles Z and Z'; and one of these two intersected points must be the position of the observer; because both altitudes are observed at one station; and if a point is situated at the same time in two circles, it can only be at one of the *two* intersected points; which one of the intersections is the observer's place, obviously depends on the bearing of the sun at the times of observation; and the two curves being projected on the chart, the intersection will be situated in a *Latitude* which is evident by inspection.

———

The difference of Latitude between the two poles of illumination, Z and Z', is equal to the difference in the sun's declination, which may have taken place during the elapsed time. This change of declination must not be neglected, but each pole projected in that Latitude which is equal to the sun's declination at each observation respectively.

Two altitudes of the sun may be observed, either both A. M., or both P. M.; or one A. M., and the other P. M.; for as the system of circles of illumination passes westward, the *western* arcs of the parallels of equal altitude, which are *interior* to the *first* projected parallel, cut its *western* arc in two points, and poles being to the *eastward* of the intersections, the time at which the altitudes are observed at either intersected point, will be A. M.

So also, the *eastern* arcs of the *exterior* parallels, cut the *eastern* arc of the *first* projected parallel, in two points; but the poles now being to the *westward* of the intersections, the time will be P. M.

And after a greater time has elapsed, *eastern* arcs of both *exterior* and *interior* parallels will cut the *western* arc of the first projected parallel, and the intersected points lie *between* the Longitudes of the two poles, and show that the time at which the first altitude was observed, is A. M., since its pole is *eastward;* and the time of the other is P. M., since its pole is *westward* of the two intersected points.

We shall now be able, using the rules of Problem I, to project the parallels of equal altitude, corresponding to *two* observed altitudes of the sun; the elapsed time giving the distance between their respective poles of illumination; and intersection which takes place, and which is designated by the bearing of the sun, giving the *true Latitude* of the place of observation.

From these considerations are deduced this Problem and Rule.

PROBLEM II.

Having noted the elapsed time between two observed altitudes of the sun's centre, the declination at each time, and the sun's bearing being given, required to project on Mercator's chart the two corresponding parallels, showing how they cut the parallels of Latitude and meridians of Longitude, within their respective limits of Latitude, how they intersect each other, and the *true Latitude* of the places of observation.

RULE.

1st. By Problem I, project the parallel corresponding to the first altitude.

2d. Turn the elapsed time into difference of Longitude, 15° for an hour.

3d. With which difference of Longitude, project, *westward* always from Z, the point Z', in a Latitude equal to the sun's declination at the time of the second observation; and Z' will be the pole of illumination of the parallel corresponding to the second observed altitude.

4th. Proceed, as in Problem I, to project the parallel corresponding to the second altitude relatively to Z'.

5th. Upon inspection, the curves will be seen to intersect, as at A and *a*. (Plate I.)

6th. The true Latitude is at one of the intersected points; which it is depending on the bearing of the sun.

The other requisitions are evident by inspection.

EXAMPLE II.

The two altitudes are 60° and 40°; the declination 10° N.; supposed invariable between the observations;

7

the elapsed time is 1ʰ 41ᵐ 18ˢ 89; the sun bearing between S. and W., it is required to project, &c.

1st. The first altitude is the same as in Example I, and is already projected.

2d. The elapsed time, 1ʰ 41ᵐ 18ˢ 89, is equal to 25° 19′ 43″.4, (15° for an hour.)

3d. In Latitude 10° N. project Z′, 25° 19′ 43″.4 west from Z. (Plate I.)

4th. Project N′ and S′ as in Prob. I; and to find any point, as one in Lat. 30° N., which call X, proceed as under.

Lat. 30°	N.	-	-	-	sec. 0.06247
Dec. 10	N.	-	-	-	sec. 0.00665
Diff. 20		Nat. cos. 93969			
☉ Alt. 40		Nat. sin. 64279			

H. M. S.   Diff. - 29690   log, 4.47261

3 17 15.94   =   log rising, =   4.54173

3 17 15.94   =   49° 18′ 59″.1 or Difference

Longitude of X in Latitude 30° N. from the meridian N′ Z S′, where it was noon at time of 2d observation.

On each side of N′ Z S′ with this difference of Longitude, project two points, X and X′, in Latitude 30 N.; which are two points in the curve required.

Find the other points Y, Y′, &c., in the same way. Join all the points, and the whole curve will be projected.

5th. It is now evident, how the curves intersect each other, as at A and a.

6th. The sun having been west of the place of observation for both altitudes, shows that both were taken P. M.; and having borne southerly, also, the northern intersection, A, is at the *true Latitude* of the place; and it will be found to be on the chart in 30° N.

————

Thus far we have determined the positions of the projected parallels, *relatively* to their poles, and the distance of these from each other; and the whole only in relation to the Latitude of the place of observation; consequently, it is only the bearing of the land in that Latitude which has become known.

To determine their actual position, in Longitude, also, on the earth's surface, and project them at any instant, we must have means to arrest, in their passage, both systems of circles of illumination, while moving from east to west.

If the Longitude of the place of observation be known, or if the time be noted by Chronometer which shows true mean time at a known meridian; and the altitudes calculated by assumed Latitudes as before, to find the apparent time, the difference between the apparent times and the Chronometer time, will give the Longitude of each point, and the actual position of each curve is fixed in both Latitude and Longitude.

By such means, having a single altitude of the sun and Chronometer time, we may find a ship at sea to be on some point of a *small circle,* which has for its pole, the pole of illumination, in like manner, as a meridian altitude of the sun fixes the position of the ship in some point of a *small circle,* called a parallel of Latitude, and which has for its pole, the pole of the equator.

Hence, the bearing of any land, through which the curve passes, is seen by inspection, as we may observe the bearing of the land, through which the parallel of Latitude passes.

Hence, we can solve the following problem.

PROBLEM III.

The true altitude of the sun being observed at any place, his declination and bearing, and the true mean time at Greenwich, by Chronometer, being given; it is required to project the corresponding parallel of equal altitude, showing *what* meridians of Longitude it cuts, east or west of Greenwich, and what parallels of Latitude; and in what directions; consequently, what land it passes through, and how such land bears from any point in the curve.

RULE.

Proceed, as in Problem I, to project the curve; only taking notice, that when "*the apparent time*" is found for any point, the difference between it and the Chronometer time, (corrected for equation of time and rate,) gives the Longitude of such point, *East or West of Greenwich*— (while its difference of Longitude, from the meridian of *its pole* of Illumination will still be expressed by the *"apparent time from noon,"* as in Problem I.) Thus, are all the points projected in *Latitude* and *Longitude*, and the requisitions of the Problem are obvious on inspection.

EXAMPLE III.

Sun's altitude 60°; declination 10° N.; corrected time at Greenwich, by Chronometer, 0^h 0^m 0^s, sun bearing southwesterly. It is required to project the curve passing through the position of the observer, showing how the land bears from any point in the curve.

1st. This example is the same as Example I, except the Chronometer time. It will be necessary, then, only to see how this time affects the position of the curve; (by Example I, the curve was projected in *any* assumed Longitude.)

We have Greenwich time corrected, for rate and equation, - - -

The apparent time, Example I, in assumed Latitude 30°, at a point A, (Plate I,) sun bearing South westerly, was - - - -

	H.	M.	S.	
	0	0	0	M.
	1	35	57 05	P.M.
Difference, - - -	1	35	57	

The apparent time is greater than the Greenwich time, showing that the point A, in Latitude 30° N., is 1^h 35^m 57^s, or 23° 59' 15".75 East of Greenwich. Project A, then, in such Longitude and Latitude, and its *actual* position is determined.

In the same manner are all the other points projected, and the curve drawn.

The other requisitions of the example will appear if we refer all the points A A', B B', &c., to a Chart, on which the land is designated; thus A is situated on the North coast of Africa, in the same meridian as part of Greece; B, near the South of Sicily; and the curve passes likewise near the South of Sardinia; over Majorca, through

Spain, near Madrid; through Portugal, near Lisbon; not far from Maderia; thence to within 6° West of Cape Verde Islands; thence 10° East of Cape St. Roque, S. A.; thence 3½°South of St. Helena; and thence reaches the continent of Africa again, in Latitude 18° S., near Cape Negro; thence over the interior of Africa, towards Egypt to the point A again; all these places having the same altitude of the sun at the same instant; the place of the observer, being of course in the curve, having OBSERVED the *same* Altitude at the *same* time.

Thus, the land, through which the curve passes is evident, by inspection; and also its bearing from any point in the curve; and thus, by projecting the curve for any observed altitude, we have as sure a method of determining the position of places, as by means of parallels of Latitude and a meridian observation.

From the foregoing three Problems, the following one is directly deduced.

PROBLEM IV.

Having two altitudes of the sun, the declinations at both observations, and his bearings, and the Greenwich times by Chronometer; to project the corresponding parallels of equal altitude, showing *what* meridians of Longitude and parallels of Latitude it cuts, and in what manner; what land they pass through; how it bears from any point in either curve; and the true Latitude and Longitude of the place of observation.

RULE.

1st. Project both parallels as in Example II, applying the Greenwich time, as in Example III.

2d. The requisitions of the Problem will be evident by inspection.

NOTE.

The "*Elapsed Time*" does not appear, as such, in this Problem; for it enters into the Longitudes of the points of the second parallel, *placing them* always so much *further West*, as *greater* time elapses between the observations.

Example IV.

Sun's central altitude was 60°; when Chronometer time corrected for equation was 0ʰ 0ᵐ 0ˢ; and 40° when Chronometer time corrected, was 1ʰ 41ᵐ 18ˢ.89; declination 10° N.; invariable between the observations; sun's bearings Southwesterly, required to project, &c.

This example is the same as Example II, except Chronometer time; project the curves as directed, (Plate I,) applying the Chronometer time, as in Example III.

This being done, the requisitions are manifest; the Latitude sought, being 30° N., and the Longitude 23° 59′ 15″.75 East; since if, from the apparent time at A, or X, (which two points coincide, at the time of the second observation,) namely:

H. M. S.

3 17 15.94 P. M. (sun bearing Southwesterly.)

Subtract, 1 41 18.89 P. M. the corrected Chro. time.

The diff. is 1 35 57.05 = 23° 59′ 15″.75 East Longitude, since the Chronometer time is least.

The Problem of Double Altitudes, admits, on these principles, another simple solution, as follows.

PROBLEM V.

Two correct central altitudes of the sun, his declinations, and bearings, at each observation, and the elapsed time being given; required, to project, on a terrestrial globe, the Latitude of the place of observation.

RULE.

1st. Turn the elapsed time into degrees, 15° to an hour.

2d. In the Latitude equal to the sun's declination, at each observation, project the two poles of illumination in two points, distant a difference of Longitude found above.

3d. On the Eastern pole, (or that corresponding to the *first* altitude,) as a centre, and with a distance measured on a great circle, equal in degrees and minutes to the *complement* of the *first* altitude, describe, with a pair of dividers, an arc in that direction from the pole indicated by the bearing of the sun, at first observation.

4th. On the Western pole, as a centre, with a distance equal to complement of the second altitude, describe an arc cutting the former arc.

5th. The intersection will be in the Latitude of the place of observation, if both altitudes be observed *at one station.*

1.

In the foregoing Problems, it has been supposed, that both altitudes were taken at one station; but it is necessary to show how to allow for any change of station between the observations.

The curve Z M, Plate I, is an arc of a great circle, passing through Z, the *pole of illumination,* where the sun's altitude is 90°; and through M, a point in the *circle of illumination,* where the sun's altitude is 0°; it is of course perpendicular to all the parallels of equal altitude.

It is plain, then, that for *every mile* a ship sails on the great circle M Z towards Z, that is, at right angles to the parallels, she *increases* the sun's altitude *one minute;* and every mile sailed from Z, *decreases* his altitude *one* minute.

And if she sails at right angles to M Z, that, is *on* a parallel of equal altitude, she would *neither increase nor diminish* it for short intervals of time.

So, in sailing at greater or less angle than 8 points from a parallel of equal altitude, we should increase or diminish the *altitude* in a proportional manner; and in so sailing should make a "difference" of *altitude,* in a similar manner as, in sailing from a parallel of *Latitude,* we make a "difference" of *Latitude,* proportional to the course and distance sailed.

In sailing from the point, then, which was the ship's place in the parallel of equal altitude corresponding to the first altitude, we shall arrive at a point in another parallel which belongs to the same *system of circles of illumination,* with the first projected parallel, on a certain course and distance; and this new parallel will corres-

56

pond to an altitude which would have been observed at the instant of the first observation, had the ship been at this new point at the same time; but this new point *is that* at which the *second* altitude is taken, after the time elapsed as noted by the watch.

The "difference" of *altitude* made good, then, proportional to the course and distance sailed from the first projected parallel, will be the correction of the first altitude for change of station, additive or subtractive, as explained before. This "difference" of *altitude* will be measured on the arc of a great circle, passing through Z, (perpendicular to the parallels of equal altitude,) and this new point to which the ship may have sailed; and the arc, which is intercepted between this point and the first projected parallel, will be the correction in miles. We have, then, the following rule.

Set off, from the first projected parallel, the distance sailed in the direction of the course made good between the observations. Through this point project a curve line parallel to the first projected parallel, and the intersection of this curve line with the *second* projected parallel, will be the true Latitude corrected for change of station.

II.

Since M Z, is an arc of a great circle passing through Z and M, perpendicular to all the parallels; and the sun's centre, and Z and M, are all in one plane, and the sun is perpendicular to Z, therefore the arc Z M, lies wholly in this plane, and the direction of the sun, from any point in Z M, is projected in the direction M Z, on the chart; but the angle at any point on the earth's surface, which the bearing of the sun projected, makes with the meridian projected at that point, is the sun's true azimuth. Thus, at M, the sun bears in the direction M n, or about E b N$\frac{1}{2}$ N.; and the angle which M n makes with the Meridian passing through M, is the sun's true azimuth at M; now Mn is perpendicular to the circle of illumination, and n o is perpendicular to the parallel of equal altitude for 10°, and so of the other portions of M Z; so, in order to project the sun's azimuth, at the time of observation of his altitude, at any point in the corresponding parallel of equal altitude, we have this rule;

Draw a tangent, or chord parallel to the tangent, to the given point, erect a perpendicular to the tangent or chord at the point given; and the perpendicular will be in the direction of the sun at that point, and the angle it makes with the meridian, passing through this point, is the sun's true azimuth.

III.

From the manner in which the parallels of equal altitude cut the meridians of Longitude and parallels of Latitude, may be seen how, with a given altitude of the sun, and the Chronometer time, different Latitudes, used in finding the apparent time, give different Longitudes by Chronometer.

For if the sun be observed A. M., in North Latitude, when he bears Southerly, then Latitudes at *greater* distances from Z, (Plate I,) give *smaller* differences of apparent time from noon, and, therefore, a *less* difference of Longitude, if in *West* Longitude, and a *greater* difference of Longitude, if in *East* Longitude, and analogous differences under other circumstances.

It may be seen, too, that, when the sun bears *East or West*, a considerable difference in the Latitudes used in finding the apparent time at the ship, will occasion but a trifling error in the Longitude by Chronometer.

Hence, it is *not only* because the sun is "*rising or falling faster*," when bearing East or West, that this is the best time to take Chronometer sights for the Longitude; but because, also, at such times, an *erroneous Latitude* will not much affect the result.

So, also, when the sun bears North or South, it is easy to find the *Latitude* by *meridian observation;* but the Longitude by Chronometer is subject to great errors, owing to the difficulty of finding the apparent time at the ship, and not only because the sun is "rising or falling" *slower*, but also because a slight error of Latitude gives a very great error of Longitude by Chronometer.

The errors of Longitude by Chronometer, then, consequent to an erroneous Latitude used in finding the apparent time at the ship, *increase* regularly, from the time the sun bears *East*, until he reaches the meridian, when the error is a *maximum*; and thence diminish until he bears *West*, when they *vanish*.

8

58

By reference to Plate I, and from these remarks, it will be found, that the *error of Longitude* any *error of Latitude* produces, at the instant of observing an altitude of the sun, is equal to *the difference of Longitude between any two points in the projected parallel, whose difference of Latitude is the error of Latitude.*

Thus, in the winter season, when the sun *does not rise or set either East or West,* and is not observable, frequently, until he bears S. E., or more Southerly, it is of the utmost importance to estimate such errors.

IV.

In practice it is not necessary to project the whole curves, but only such *arcs* as will include the intersected points required. Two points in each arc are sufficient, that part of the curve which is required being indicated by the bearing of the sun.

It will be found convenient, in finding the apparent times, for these two points, to assume two Latitudes to be used in the calculation, one on each side of the Latitude by D. R.; one being the next degree less and the other the next degree greater than such Latitude, and without any odd minutes; the position of the four points, and their arcs, being projected, will, in general, be found to *include* the intersected point, or be very near to it; for if we join the points by *straight* lines, they will either intersect each other, or converge towards a point beyond the limits of the assumed Latitudes; in this case we have only to produce the lines *to an intersection.*

These two *straight* lines, although they do not lie strictly in the curves, but may be regarded as chords of their respective arcs, will not sensibly differ from the arcs themselves, or even from their tangents, at points near the intersection; particularly as the parallels most frequently used, have a large Radius.

Should, however, the altitudes be *great,* in which case, the curves have a smaller Radius, we can choose such Latitudes as shall be nearer the intersected points, and thus reduce the error, on this account, as much as we please. Also, if the altitude be observed when near *noon,* the *assumed* Latitudes should not be chosen too great, or otherwise, as mentioned in the note to Rule 1, Practical Part; and they should be such as are much *nearer* to the supposed Latitude.

Hence, the following Practical Problem is deduced, when the times are noted by a common watch.

PROBLEM VI.

Two correct central altitudes of the sun being given, and also the elapsed time, the declinations and bearings of the sun at both observations, the course and distance made good *between* the observations, and the Latitude by dead reckoning; it is required to project on a "*particular*" Mercator's chart, those ARCS of the corresponding parallels of equal altitude, which are mutually intersected; showing, 1st. The true Latitude. 2d. The correction for change of station. 3d. The sun's true azimuth at each observation. 4th. The errors of Longitude consequent to any error of Latitude, when the times are noted by the Chronometer.

RULE.

1st. Turn the elapsed time into degrees, (15° to an hour,) which will be the difference of Longitude between the two poles of illumination, Z and Z'.; the *Eastern* pole, or that which corresponds to the *first* altitude, being called Z, and the *Western* pole, which corresponds to the *second* altitude, Z'.

2d. Assume *two* Latitudes, one of which is the next degree *less*, (without any odd minutes,) and the other the next degree *greater* than the Latitude by account.

3d. With the first altitude and declination find (method 3, B,) the apparent time *from noon* with *each* of the two assumed Latitudes; turn these resulting times into differences of Longitude, 15° to an hour; and, if the altitude was observed A. M., they will show the differences of Longitude of *two points* in the required arc, WEST of the meridian of Z.; but if the altitude was P. M., EAST of the meridian of Z.; these two points having the *assumed* Latitudes respectively; name that point which has the *least* assumed Latitude, A, and the other, A'.

Do the same with the second altitude; and name that point which has the *least* assumed Latitude, B; and the other B'. The difference of Longitude of B and B', will be reckoned from Z', and not from Z.

4th. Project on the Chart, Plate II, the four points A, A'; B, B', in their respective Latitudes; and distant their respective differences of Longitude, from the meridians of their respective poles Z and Z'; (which poles are distant from each other a difference of Longitude equal to the elapsed time turned into degrees;) and the points must be projected on that side of these meridians, designated by A. M. and P. M. times of observation.

Explanatory Note.

Project A in its respective Latitude, and in *any* assumed Longitude; if A. M., mark it "A, West of Z;" (*so many degrees* as have been found from the corresponding apparent time from noon;) but if P. M., mark it "A, East of Z," (*so many degrees.*)

Project A' in its respective Latitude, but with a difference of Longitude from A, (East or West,) equal to the difference between the Longitudes of A from Z, *and* A' from Z; and mark it "A' (East if P. M., or West if A. M.,) of Z," (so many degrees and minutes, as the case may be.)

Now to project B, B', with reference to A, A', we must first find the difference of Longitude of A from Z'; because their difference of Longitude are not reckoned from Z, but from Z'; this is done by means of the elapsed time, or the difference of Longitude between Z and Z', thus:

I. If both observations be A. M., then difference of Longitude of A, West of Z' = difference of Longitude of A, West of Z — difference of Longitude of Z', West of Z.

II. If both observations be P. M., then difference of Longitude of A, East of Z' = difference of Longitude of A, East of Z + difference of Longitude of Z, East of Z'.

III. If one observation be A. M., the other P. M., then difference of Longitude of A, East of Z' = difference of Longitude Z', West of Z — difference of Longitude of A, West of Z.

Project B in its respective Latitude, with a difference of Longitude from A, (East or West,) equal to the difference between the Longitude of *A from Z'*, (found by one of these three rules,) and B from Z', (found by method 3 B,) mark it "B (East or West) of Z', (so many degrees.")

Project B' in its respective Latitude, with a difference of Longitude from A, (East or West,) equal to the difference between the Longitudes of A from Z' and B' from Z'; and mark it "B' (East or West) of Z' (so many degrees.")

5th. Join by *straight* lines A and A', B and B'; and if they do not intersect each other, produce them to an intersection; and if the ship has not changed her station between the observation, this intersection will be in the *true Latitude.* But, if the station has been changed, then in the direction of the course made good, set off the distance from *any* point in the straight line A A'; through *this* point draw a *straight* line parallel to A A', and its intersection with B B' is the *true Latitude;* corrected for change of station.

6th. From this point let fall a perpendicular upon A A', and the length of this is the correction in miles to the first altitude; additive, if the course sailed was towards Z, subtractive, if from it.

7th. Produce this perpendicular towards the pole of illumination Z, and the angle it makes with the meridian is the sun's true azimuth.

8th. The *difference of Longitude* between any *two points* in either *one* of the two *straight* lines, is the error of Longitude consequent to an error of Latitude as great as the difference of Latitude between the same points at their respective times of observation.

Example V.

[From Bowditch.]

" In a ship running N. by E. ¾ E. per compass, 9 miles per hour, at 10ʰ A. M. per watch, the correct altitude of the sun's centre, was 13° 18', bearing S. ¾ E. per compass; at 1ʰ 40ᵐ P. M. per watch, the altitude of the centre was 14° 15'; the declination being 23° 28' S.; the Latitude by account, 48° 17' N. Required the true Latitude."

And also by this method are shown the true correction of the first altitude for change of station; the sun's true azimuth and errors of Longitude by Chronometer, consequent to any error in the Latitude, when the time is noted by Chronometer.

1st. The elapsed time, 3^h 40^m is equal to 55°, or the difference of Longitude of Z' West of Z. (Plate II.)

2d. The two Latitudes less and greater than the Latitude by account, are 48° N. and 49° N.

3d. Find the apparent times from noon (method 3. B) with these Latitudes, for each altitude.

For the First Altitude, 13° 18' A. M.

For a point A, in Latitude 48° N.

Lat.	48	N.	-	-	-	sec. 0.17449
Dec.	23 28	S.	-	-	-	sec. 0.03749

Sum.	71 28	Nat. cos.	31786
⊙ Alt.	13 18	Nat. sin.	23005

H. M. S.   Diff. -   8781   log,   3.94354

2   4   6   =   log rising,   =   4.15552

2 4 6 = 31° 1½' or diff. Longitude (West, because A. M.) from Z, of the point A in Latitude 48° N.

For a point A' in Latitude 49° N.

Lat.	49	N.	-	-	-	sec. 0.18306
Dec.	23 28	S.	-	-	-	sec. 0.03749

Sum.	72 28	Nat. cos.	30126
⊙ Alt.	13 18	Nat. sin.	23005

H. M. S.   Diff. -   7121   log,   3.85254

1   52   37   =   log rising,   =   4.07309

1 52 37 = 28° 9¼' or diff. Longitude (West, because A. M.) from Z, of the point A' in Latitude 49° N.

For the Second Altitude, 14° 15' P. M.

For a point B in Latitude 48° N.

Lat. 48   N.   -   -   -   sec. 0.17449
Dec. 23 28 S. -   -   -   - sec. 0.03749

Sum. 71 28   Nat. cos. 31786
☉ Alt. 14 15   Nat. sin. 24615

H. M. S.   Diff. -   7171   log, 3.85558
1 51 53 =   log rising, =   4.06756
1 51 53 = 27° 58¼' or diff. Longitude (East, because
P. M.) from Z' of the point B in Latitude 48° N.

For a point B' in Latitude 49° N.

Lat. 49   N.   -   -   -   sec. 0.18306
Dec. 23 28 S. -   -   -   - sec. 0.03749

Sum. 72 28   Nat. cos. 30126
☉ Alt. 14 15   Nat. sin. 24615

H. M. S.   Diff. -   5511   log, 3.74123
1 38 51 =   log rising, =   3.96178
1 38 51 = 24° 42¾' or diff. Longitude (East, because
P. M.) from Z', of a point B' in Latitude 49° N.

4th.   To project A, A', B, B', Plate II.

A. { In Latitude 48° N., and in any Longitude, project a
    point; mark it "*A 31° 1½' West of Z.*"

A'. {

From   31° 1½' = Long. of A, West of Z,
Subtract 28° 9¼' = Long. of A', West of Z,

Diff. is   2 52¼ = Long. of A', East of A.
    Project A', then, in Latitude 49° N., 2° 52¼' East
from A, and mark it "*A' 28° 9¼' West of Z.*"

Now find the difference of Longitude of A from Z';
one observation is A. M., the other P. M., (see rule.)

Z' is West of Z = 55° 00 by the elapsed time.
A is West of Z = 31 01½

A, then, is East of Z' = 23 58½
Mark A, then, also, "*A 23 58½ East of Z'.*"

$$
\text{B.} \begin{cases}
\text{From} \quad 27° \ 58\tfrac{1}{4} = \text{Long. of B, East of } Z', \\
\text{Subtract } 23 \ 58\tfrac{1}{2} = \text{Long. of A, East of } Z', \\[4pt]
\hline \\[-6pt]
\text{Diff. is} \quad 3 \ 59\tfrac{3}{4} = \text{Long. of B, East of A.} \\
\text{Project B, then, in Latitude } 48° \text{ N., and } 3° \ 59\tfrac{3}{4} \\
\text{East from A, and mark it } ``B \ 27° \ 58\tfrac{1}{4}' \textit{ East of } Z'.\text{''}
\end{cases}
$$

$$
\text{B'.} \begin{cases}
\text{From} \quad 24° \ 42\tfrac{3}{4}' = \text{Long. of B', East of } Z', \\
\text{Subtract } 23 \ 58\tfrac{1}{2} = \text{Long. of A, East of } Z', \\[4pt]
\hline \\[-6pt]
\text{Diff. is} \quad 0 \ 44\tfrac{1}{2} = \text{Long. of B', East of A.} \\
\text{Project B', then, in Latitude } 49° \text{ N., and } 0° \ 44\tfrac{1}{2}' \\
\text{East from A, and mark it, } ``B' \ 24° \ 42\tfrac{3}{4}' \textit{ East of } Z'.\text{''}
\end{cases}
$$

5th. Join A, A'; B, B', with straight lines; from any point in AA', as for instance A, set off a point D; 33 miles N. by E. ¾ E.; through D, parallel to AA', draw a straight line DL; its intersection with BB' at the point L, is in the *true Latitude* at the time of the second observation, namely, 48° 51½' N.

6th. From the point L, let fall a perpendicular LC on AA'; and LC is the correction in miles of the first altitude for change of station : namely, 22 miles subtractive by the scale.

7th. Produce LC, *towards* Z, and it will make an angle CxM, with the meridian; this angle, or its opposite, which is the same, is the sun's true azimuth, equal to S. 28° 16' E., or 2½ points from S. nearly; and at the first observation the sun bore S. S. E. ½ E. nearly: (see note this Ex.)

8th. If the Chronometer time had been noted at the first observation, in order to find the Longitude by Chronometer, and a second observation had not been observed, the true Latitude being, as we will suppose, 48° N.; then the ship would have really been at the point A, in the straight line AA'; but if the Latitude by account had been erroneous 20' *to the N.;* or 48° 20' had been used to find the "apparent time at the ship," instead of 48° N., then the error of Longitude by Chronomer would be equal to the difference of Longitude between A and the point P in the line AA', in Latitude, say 48° 20' N.; or 57' of Longitude; that is *one mile* error of Latitude gives nearly *three minutes* error of Longitude in this case.

NOTE.

The Latitude found above is 48° 51½′ N., the Latitude by Bowditch, old editions, is 48° 55′, by two operations; new editions, 48° 54′. The cause of this difference affords a good opportunity of testing the correctness of this method, without impeaching the accuracy of his rules.

The reason of this apparent difference is, that he has accidentally stated the sun's bearing to have been S. ¾ E., instead of S. S. E. ½ E., at the time of the first observation. It is an error of no consequence in itself, as it serves *to exemplify* his rules as well as the true bearing would.

This method gives 48° 55′ for the Latitude, supposing the sun to have borne S. ¾ E.; and Bowditch's method gives 48° 51½′ for the Latitude, if the sun bore S. S. E. ½ E. For the Latitude of the *place of the first observation* by this method, is 48° 19′; and by his, 48° 23′, the Dec. is 23° 28′ S., and the first altitude 13° 18′; we have, then;

```
☉ Alt.  13° 18′      -    -    -     sec.  0.01181
P. D.  113° 28′   -    -    -    -   sec.  0.17717
Lat.    48° 19′
Sum.  175° 05′    -    -    -        cos.  8.63238
½Sum. 87° 32½′
P. D.  113° 28′
Diff.   25° 55½′   -    -    -    -  cos.  9.95394
                                       2)18.77530
2  ×  75° 52′            cos.   =     9.38765
     151° 44′  ☉'s azimuth from N.
     180° 00′
      28° 16′  ☉'s azimuth from S.
```

If calculated with Latitude 48° 23′, the ☉'s azimuth will be 28° 06′, only 10′ difference.

Now S. S. E. ½ E. is S. 28° 07′ E. So it appears that the sun bore S. S. E. ½ E. nearly, and not S. ¾ E.

Let us see, that supposing the sun bore S. ¾ E., the two methods agree. From L, Plate II, *the true Latitude*, draw a line LP, parallel to AD, meeting AA′ in P; it will be 33

9

miles in length, on a course S. by W. ¾ W., or N. by E. ¾ E.; and P. will be the place of the first observation.

Upon P, erect a perpendicular Py, which will be the sun's *true* bearing (S. S. E. ½ E.) at first observation; the angle yPL is the angle of the course sailed with respect to Py, or the sun's bearing; make the angle yPs equal to 1¾ points, and Ps will be in the direction S. ¾ E.; make angle LPp, equal to yPs; then yPp will be the angle of the course sailed with respect to Py, if the sun bore *S.¾ E.*; from P set off the point, p, on Pp, at the distance of 33 miles; through p, draw a straight line pq, parallel to AA', and the intersection at q is the true Latitude 48° 55', if the sun bore S. ¾ E.; which is the same as Bowditch.

From q, let fall a perpendicular on AA', meeting it in c'; qc', should be the correction in miles to be subtracted from the first altitude if the sun bore S. ¾ E.; this distance, qc', measured on the Chart is 29 miles; now 29 miles is the correction in reality used by Bowditch.

Thus it appears the two methods agree, but that the *true* azimuth is apparent by this method on inspection; and we learn, that an error of 1¾ points in the sun's bearing, by his method, makes an error of about 4 miles in the Latitude, in this example.

The preceding Problem includes the whole theory of double altitudes by this method; and however useful it may prove, it becomes much more so, when the times are noted by Chronometer; for then the Longitudes of the points A, A', B, B', become known at once; and thus the "elapsed time," will not appear as such in the Problem; for it enters into the Longitudes of the points B, B', placing them so much *further West* as greater time elapses between the observations; thus we shall only have to find in the usual way, the Longitude of the points by Chronometer, and project them in their respective Longitudes from Greenwich, and assumed Latitudes.

And likewise, in accordance with Problem III, when the Latitude is uncertain, a *single* altitude of the sun becomes of great value to determine the ship's position, because it shows the bearing of the land at *any* hour ; in fact, as useful as two altitudes by any other method, when the times are noted by a common watch; and of equal value with a meridian observation ; because these *only* show the *bearing of the land*, in the parallel of Latitude ; this last only *once* in day ; and the first usually requires *two* observations.

IV.

APPLICATION OF THESE PRINCIPLES TO THE FIXED STARS, PLANETS, AND MOON.

Double Altitudes may be classified as follows:

CLASS I.

When the same body is observed at two different times.

Case 1. The sun.
2. A fixed star.
3. A planet.
4. The moon.

CLASS II.

When two different bodies are observed at the same time.

Case 5. Two fixed stars.
6. Two planets.
7. A planet and fixed star.
8. Moon and fixed star.
9. Moon and planet.
10. Moon and sun.

CLASS III.

When one body is observed at one time, and a different body at another time.

Case 11. Two fixed stars.
12. Two planets.
13. A planet and a fixed star.
14. The sun and a fixed star.
15. The sun and a planet.
16. The moon and a fixed star.
17. The moon and a planet.
18. The moon and the sun.

It is plain that the same results will follow, if any celestial body is used, from which the apparent time at the ship can be known. It will be only necessary to consult the epitome upon the manner of finding the apparent time by any object observed; and apply this time in the same manner as when it is found by the sun's altitude.

The apparent time for the assumed Latitudes can be found from any of the fixed stars, or planets, with accuracy, with a good horizon, and from the moon, when her right ascension and declination can be had. In all these cases, the *arcs* of the parallels of equal altitude corresponding to each altitude, are to be found in the same way as before. If the apparent time at the ship can be found from the altitude by any of *the rules in the epitome*, and the Chronometer time is noted, then the Latitude and Longitude of each point may be at once projected, as in the case of the sun; and if the times of observation be noted by a common watch, then it may be *assumed* that the "watch" shows approximate Greenwich time, by allowing its error, if fast or slow, as in Problem III, Practical Part. The above will in general be the most simple method.

———

But we may also proceed as follows, the times being noted by watch.

Assume two Latitudes, as before, with which, and the true declinations of the body at each observation, and the correct central altitudes, find the *hour angles*, or "apparent times from the meridian," to which the body is vertical, (Method 3, B,) turn these times into degrees for their respective differences of Longitude, (East or West, according to which side of the meridian of the place of observation the body was observed,) from their respective poles Z and Z'.

The points A and A' can be projected, as before; but to project B, B', with reference to AA', the value of the arc ZZ' must be found by one of the following Rules; because the elapsed time turned into degrees will not in all cases express the difference of Longitude between Z and Z'.

This being done, BB' can be also projected, and the intersection will show the *true Latitude* as before, allowing for change of station.

———

All cases in which the moon is one of the bodies will be liable to error, unless the ship's position in Longitude is nearly known beforehand, for her right ascension and declination must be known with accuracy at the time of observation, her motion being greater than any other body; in Case 4, however, it is only *hourly motion* in R. A. and the declinations that are required, and these can be ascertained nearly enough for common use. (See Appendix, Bowditch.)

The sun's and planets' proper motion is much slower, and their R. A. and Dec. can be had accurately.

The arc ZZ' is greater than 180° (or must be subtracted from 360°) when the great circle which passes through the positions in the heavens, in which the bodies were observed, passes also *below* the elevated pole, the bodies being also observed on different sides of the meridian. In all other cases ZZ' is less than 180°.

All bodies situated below a great circle passing through the East and West points of the horizon and the elevated pole are *below* the pole.

Care must be taken not to mistake *which pole*, Z or Z', belongs to *which object;* for this purpose it will be useful to remember, that the body which has the *greatest* altitude has its pole of illumination the *nearest* to the observer; and always name the Eastern pole Z, the Western one Z'.

The nearer the bodies are observed at right angles to each other, whatever method of calculation is used, the more likely is the result to be accurate.

———

Two of these bodies may be observed, either *both East-ward* from *the meridian,* or *both Westward;* or *one Eastward,* and *one Westward;* and in this respect, the times of observation are similar to the *two* altitudes of *the sun,* which are observed either *both A. M.,* both P. M., or *one A. M.* and *one P. M.;* in every case, for uniformity, it will be proper always to call the *Eastern* pole Z, and the *Western* pole Z′; and having found the value of the arc ZZ′, to project the points A, A′; B, B′, *Eastward* or *Westward* of Z and Z′, as is designated by the body's having been observed when *East or West of the meridian.*

With the exception of Class II, in all cases in which the sun is *not* one of the bodies, a correction is to be applied to the elapsed time, and is that quantity which is called XS in the following formulas.

The motion of the stars is *quicker* than that of the sun; it takes the sun 24 mean solar hours to make an apparent revolution round the earth; but .the stars do the same thing in about 23^h 56^m; in any given elapsed time, then, the stars will be a proportional distance *West* of the place where the sun would have been, had the sun been the body observed. The elapsed time being usually noted by watch, which shows *solar* time. The motion of the planets and moon is compounded of this motion, and their own proper motions in R. A. and Declination.

This correction is $9^s.85647$ for every hour of elapsed time. The following Table is calculated to make this allowance in those cases where it is required.

Table for finding the value of XS, *in the formulas, during* ET (*Elapsed Time.*)

ET	XS		ET	XS	
Hours.	min.	sec.	min.	sec.	
1	0	09.856	1	0.164	EXAMPLE.
2	0	19.713	2	0.329	
3	0	29.569	3	0.493	The Elapsed Time is
4	0	39.426	4	0.657	5^h 17^m, what is the value
5	0	49.282	5	0.821	of " ET+XS."
6	0	59.139	10	1.643	5^h = $49^s.282$
7	1	08.995	15	2.464	15^m = 2.464
8	1	18.852	20	3.285	2^m = 0 .329
9	1	28.708	25	4.107	52 .075 = XS
10	1	38.565	30	4.928	5 17 00 = ET
11	1	48.421	35	5.750	Ans. 5^h 17^m 52^s = ET+XS.
12	1	58.278	40	6.571	
			45	7.392	
			50	8.214	
			55	9.035	
			60	9.856	

FORMULAS OR RULES

To find the ·value of the Arc ZZ′ in hours, minutes, and seconds, which, being turned into degrees, 15° to an hour, gives the Diff. Long. between Z and Z′.

CLASS I.

When the same body is observed at two different times.

Case 1. The Sun
$$ZZ′ = ET, \text{ or the Elapsed Time.}$$
Case 2. A fixed Star
$$ZZ′ = ET + XS.$$
Case 3. A Planet
$$ZZ′ = ET + XS \begin{Bmatrix} - \\ + \end{Bmatrix} \text{ Planets } motion \text{ in R. A.}$$
during ET, if R. A. is $\begin{Bmatrix} \text{Increasing} \\ \text{Decreasing.} \end{Bmatrix}$
Case 4. The Moon
$$ZZ′ = ET + XS - ☽\text{'s motion in R. A.}$$
during ET.

In explanation of the rules. In Case 1st it has already been seen, that ZZ′ is equal to ET; but let P, (Plate VIII. fig. 1,) be the elevated pole, ESS′W be a parallel of declination on which the R. A. is reckoned, HH′ a part of the horizon, O the place of the observer on the earth's surface, and PO the meridian passing through P and O, the arrows show the direction of the apparent motion.
Let S be the sun at the first observation, it is vertical to Z, (below the horizon.) After an elapsed time, the sun is again observed at S′; S′ is vertical to Z′; the arc SS′ is described by the sun, at the rate of 15° per hour of ET; the 'arc ZZ′ is then described in the same time; for the earth is a sphere, concentric with the celestial sphere; and difference of Longitude between Z and Z′, or the arc ZZ′, is equal to the apparent difference of R. A. of S and S′ and is expressed by the elapsed time turned into degrees, 15° to an hour; therefore ZZ′ = ET.
Case 2d, (Lower portion figure 2.) Let * be the position of a star, after an elapsed time by watch showing *solar* time it will at *′; if it had been the sun the second

altitude would have been taken when he was at ⊙S, and the arc * S would be equal to ET = ZZ'; but since the star moves quicker than the sun, it will have reached the position *' at X, during the elapsed time by watch; being an excess = the arc XS; * is vertical to Z', and *' is vertical to Z; ZZ' then is equal to **' or = ET + XS; but since it is required to reckon the difference of Longitudes of Z and Z' from O, the place of the observer on the earth's surface, ZZ' must be taken greater than 180°; that is, ZZ' in degrees, must be subtracted from 360°; because the great circle GC, which passes through the positions where the body was observed, and also observed on different sides of the meridian, passes *below* P, the elevated pole.

This case is a simple one.

Case 3d, (upper portion, figure 2,) Let P be the position of a planet when first observed; it is vertical to Z; after an elapsed time by watch, it may be taken at P', vertical to Z'; therefore ZZ' = PP'. If it had been the sun it would have been observed at S⊙ the second time; but PS = ET; and being a star, the correction XS must be added as before; and ⁑ is the place in which it would have been observed, had it been a fixed star; but during ET, it has moved from ⁑ to P', by its own proper motion in R. A., *towards the East;* * P' then must be subtracted (the R. A. increasing): we have then (PX,) or (ET + XS)— (XP', or planet's motion East, in R. A., during ET) = PP' = ZZ' as in the formula. If the planet's proper motion be to the West, or (R. A. decreasing,) it must be *added* to ET + XS.

This is an easy case, by this method.

Case 4. The moon, figure 2. This is sufficiently explained by the last; the moon's motion in R. A. being *always* E., is always subtractive.

CLASS II.

When two different bodies are observed at the same time.

ZZ' = Difference of R. A. of the bodies at the instant of observation, in all the cases of this class.

In figure 3. The objects are observed on *different sides* of the meridian PO; and the great circle GC passes *above* the pole P ; ZZ' is therefore *less* than 180°. But in figure 4, the objects are observed on *different sides* of the meridian, and the great circle GC, passing through the position of the two objects, passes also *below* the pole P; therefore, ZZ' will be *greater* than 180° : then the *Difference R. A.* must be turned into degrees and subtracted from 360° to find ZZ'.

In the *two* cases in figure 5. Because the objects are both observed on the *same* side of the meridian PO, ZZ' is *less* than 180° in both cases, although in one case GC is *above*, and in the other *below* the elevated pole.

It is evident ZZ'= Difference of R. A. of the bodies, in all these cases.

Those cases of this Class, in which the moon is *not* one of the bodies, are important, as the observations can be frequently taken with great accuracy ; particularly in the twilight, and they are attended with but little more trouble than the observations of the sun, because it is not required to find the "*apparent time at the ship*," but only the *hour angle*, or that time which is found (Method 3, Bowditch,) in Table XXIII, in column, "*log rising*."

But, if the apparent time at the ship is found for *one* point in each arc, and the *Chronometer* time is noted for each altitude, then the Longitudes of the other points, A', B', may be found, and the position of the ship in Latitude and Longitude.

The RA of the fixed stars and planets, is, too, readily found, in the large edition of the Nautical Almanac.

CLASS III.

When one body is observed at one time, and a different body at another time.

This class comprehends a great variety of circumstances, under which the bodies may be observed. By a few examples, the manner of finding the value of ZZ', in any case, will be understood.

Let A. figure 6, be the *Eastern* body, and the *first* observed ; and B, the other body, Westward from it.

The arc AB, is the difference of R. A. of the bodies at the time of 1st observation. After A is observed, and a time has elapsed by watch, A will have advanced West to a point S; and B will have reached T; let B be now observed at T, and TS is the difference of R. A. of the bodies at 2d observation.

If A is the *sun*, the arc AS, will be equal to the elapsed time, ET; and ZZ' is equal to the sum of the arcs AS, and ST; that is,

ZZ' = ET + (difference of R. A. of the bodies at *time of 2d observation.*)

And ZZ' is less than 180°; because GC is *above* the elevated pole.

If A is a *fixed star*, it would have arrived at X, in the same elapsed time, instead of S; then, TX will be difference of R. A. of the bodies at *2d observation; and* AX + TX = ZZ', that is,

ZZ' = ET + XS + difference of R. A., 2d observation.

If A is a *planet*, and had no proper motion in R. A., it would be the same case as the last, and would arrive at X; but having arrived at X, if it have a proper *motion in R. A.*, increasing, (or going E.,) it will during ET, arrive at some point b; and Tb will be the difference of *R. A., 2d observation;* we have, then, ZZ' = AT = ET + XS — (Zb, or planet's motion in R. A., during ET,) + difference of R. A. at 2d observation.

But when the planet's motion in R. A. is West, (or increasing,) *then it would have* arrived at some point *a*, during ET, and *Xa*, must be *added.* T*a* would then be the difference of R. A. at 2d observation.

If A is the moon, her motion in R. A., during ET, being always East, (or increasing,) must be always subtracted, and we have

ZZ' = ET + XS—Xb + R. A., 2d observation.

Figure 7. If A be the *Eastern* body; and B, the *Western* body, is *first* observed, and A is not observed until it reaches S, having passed the position in the heavens where B was observed at B, then,

If A is the ☉; AS, is the elapsed time, *and AB*, the difference of R. A. at 1st observation; SB is equal to ZZ', and ZZ' = ET — difference of R. A., 1st observation.

But if B is the sun, TB is the elapsed time, and TS the difference of R. A., 2d observation, then

ZZ' = ET — difference of R. A., 2d observation.

Figure 8. If A is the Sun, the *Eastern* body, and *first* observed, after an elapsed time, it will reach S; and B, the other body, will reach T, which then observe; then, AS = ET; and TS = difference of R. A., 2d observation; and AT = ZZ'; then

ZZ' = difference of R. A., 2d observation — ET.

The bodies being observed on the same side of the meridian, ZZ' is less than 180°.

In figure 6. A, the sun, was also the *Eastern* body, and *first* observed, but the rule for finding ZZ', is different, because both objects were *above* the pole, and the apparent motion was from East to West; but in this case, both bodies being *below* the pole, the apparent motion is reversed, or from West to East, and in this case we might with propriety call A *West* of B, although it appears to be East of it, and will appear so, when both are *above* the pole.

In this manner, by attention to the *circumstances* of the observation, a rough diagram may be made, and the value of ZZ' may be readily found; and it will be necessary, for this purpose, for one of the cases of " Class III," to notice

1st. *What two* bodies are used.

2d. Which was *first* observed.

3d. Which was the *Eastern*.

4th. Which *side* of the meridian was *each* observed.

5th. Did the great circle passing through the positions in the heavens where observed, pass also *below* the elevated pole?

6th. Does the body *2d observed, after* it passed the position in the heavens, when the other body was *previously* observed?

These two last considerations will seldom be required, but to include all *possible* circumstances they are given.

By using discrimination in the bodies used, these observations will be found useful, and when familiar with the principles, they will be found quite simple.

The motion of the planets in R. A. is generally small during ET, and can for the most part be neglected; a glance at the Ephemeris of the planets in the Nautical Almanac, is sufficient to determine this. The planets, when in the most favorable situation for observation, are stationary; and they will be found exceedingly useful for these observations; or for their meridian observations for the Latitude; but the moon cannot be always relied on *for a meridian altitude*, because her *meridian altitude* is not always her *greatest* altitude; and unless the ship's position in Longitude, or the Greenwich time is well known beforehand, it will be impossible to be accurate in finding *her R. A. and Declination.*

V.

CURRENTS IN THE GULF OF MEXICO AND THE FLORIDA STREAM.

By Plate IX, are shown the currents experienced in the Gulf, in June, 1840.

The position of the ship was found by the method of projection; and the accuracy of the work was tested by the *usual meridian* observations, and Chronometer sights, the sun bearing E. or W.

The land was not seen, neither any light, after leaving the Mississippi. Soundings were had on the Tortugas Bank, on the evening of 21st June, but the ship was some 20 miles further E. than marked on the chart for the noon of that day; for only the distances, *made good* from *noon to noon*, are shown by the chart.

The full black line ————— shows the true course and distance daily, by Chronometer, &c.

The light black line ————— shows the course and distance by log, carefully attended to; and is carried out without correction for the observations, for the whole distance from the 10th to the 25th inclusive:

The dotted lines . . . . show the daily courses and distances by log, reckoned from the position of the ship at each preceding noon determined by observation; and the daily differences caused by currents.

The arrows point in the direction of the current, and the velocity is marked in miles and parts. To prevent confusion on the chart, they are placed at the ends of the dotted lines. They should be referred to the *full* black lines, in order to show the *place where* the currents existed; thus, between 18th and 19th, on the full black line, the current was S. by W. ⅔ W., 2¼ miles per hour.

The figure of the ship on the 10th, shows which way she headed, while the full black line shows which way she was going over the ground.

79

EXTRACT FROM THE JOURNAL.

IN THE GULF OF MEXICO.

Sea act. 1840.	Dist.	Course.	Winds.	Clear weather throughout.	Under what sail.	error in 24 hours.	Velocity. miles.	Direction.
June 10	105	SE ½ S	ENE ½ E	strong br'zs.	s. reefs	75	3 1-8	W ⅞ N
11	96	SE b S	ENE ¾ E	do.	do.	34	1 1-2	NE b N
12	95	SSE ½ E	E ¾ N	do.	do.	43	1 3-4	NE ½ N
13	83	SSE ½ E	E ½ N	fresh	reefs out	42	1 3-4	NNW ¾ W
14	35	SE b E	E ENE	light	all sail	53	2 1-5	W b N ½ N
15	84	SE b E ¼ E	NE	fresh	do.	86	3 1-12	W b N ¼ N
16	98	ENE	SE ¼ S	do.	do.	50	2 1-12	W ¾ N
17	82	NE b E ¼ E	SE ½ E	do.	do.	17	3-4	NW ⅞ N
18	70	NE b·E ¾ E	SE	moderate	do.	54	2 3-4	S b W ½ W
19	65	S b E ¼ E	E ½ S	do.	do.	20	5-6	WNW
20	71	E ½ N	SSE ¼ E	do.	do.	26	1 1-12	WNW ¾ W
21	95	S ½ W	SE b E ¾ E	fresh	do.	25	1	N b E ½ E

IN THE FLORIDA STREAM.

22	53	ESE two tacks	ESE	strong	do.	70	2 1-12	E ½ N
23	150	NNE	ESE	fresh	do.	70	2 11-12	NE ½ N
24	156	N ¼ W	ESE	moderate	do.	68	2 5-6	E ¼ N

Whole amount of current in every direction in 15 days = 735 miles.

It will be seen by the Plate, that if no observation had been taken, that the "Dead Reckoning" placed the ship in the Fair Way of the Stream, on *the* 19*th of June*. But if a course had then been shaped to the Northward, a run of 40 hours would have put the ship ashore, in about Longitude 84° Latitude 30°.

The various directions and velocities of the currents, and the uncertainty of their duration, show how little dependence is to be placed in any "Reckoning" when thick weather prevents observations, and that a good *lookout* is essentially necessary.

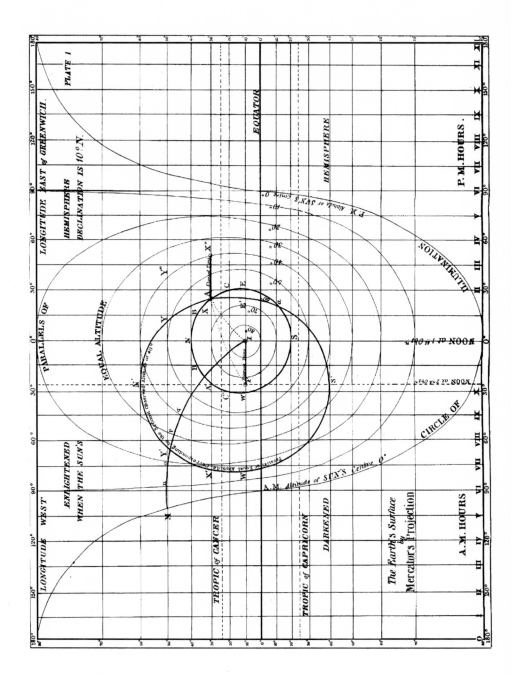

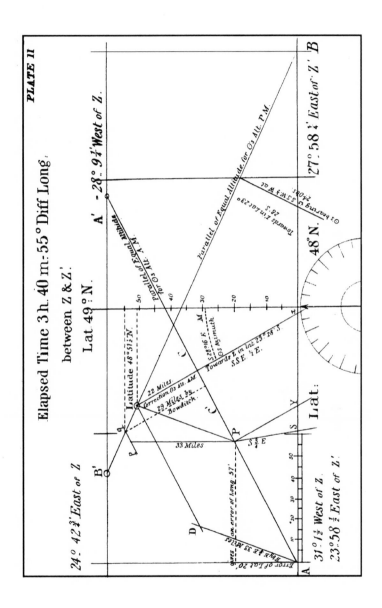

PLATE 11

Elapsed Time 3 h. 40 m. = 55° Diff Long.
between Z & Z'.
Lat 49° N.

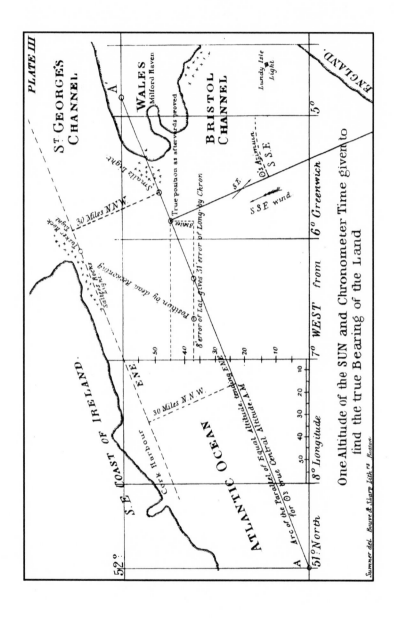

PLATE III

ST GEORGE'S CHANNEL

WALES

Milford Raven

BRISTOL CHANNEL

Lundy Isle Light

ENGLAND.

⊙'s Azimuth S.S.E.

S.E.

S.S.E. wind.

True position as afterwards proved

Smalls Light.

30 Miles N.N.W.

Quaker Rock

True position or error by Long by Chron

8 error of Lat gives 31 miles

Position by dead Reckoning

Saltee's Races

S.E. COAST OF IRELAND.

Cork Harbour

ENE

30 Miles N.N.W.

ATLANTIC OCEAN

Arc of the Parallel of Equal Altitude, tending ENE

Altitude of Equal Central Altitude A.M

A

51° North

52°

A'

5°

6° Greenwich

7° WEST from

8° Longitude

Sumner del.   Bouve & Sharp lith rs Boston.

One Altitude of the SUN and Chronometer Time given to find the true Bearing of the Land

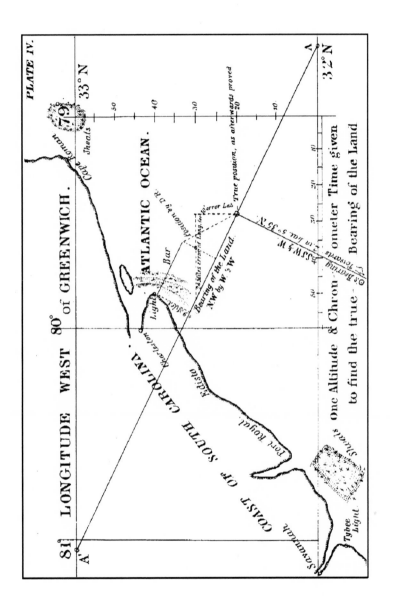

PLATE IV.

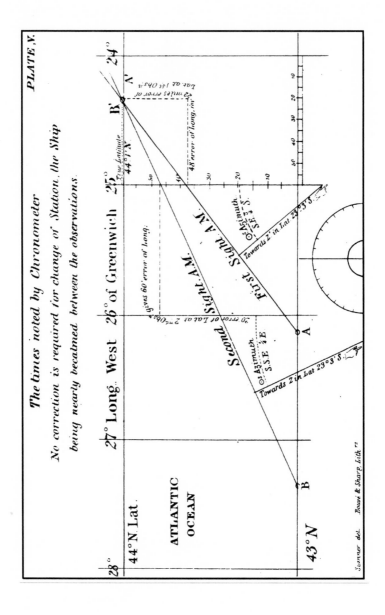

PLATE V.

The times noted by Chronometer

No correction is required for change of Station, the Ship
being nearly becalmed between the observations.

ATLANTIC
OCEAN

44° N. Lat.

28°

43° N

27° Long. West   26° of Greenwich   25°   24°

Sumner del.   Bouvé & Sharp, Lith'd.

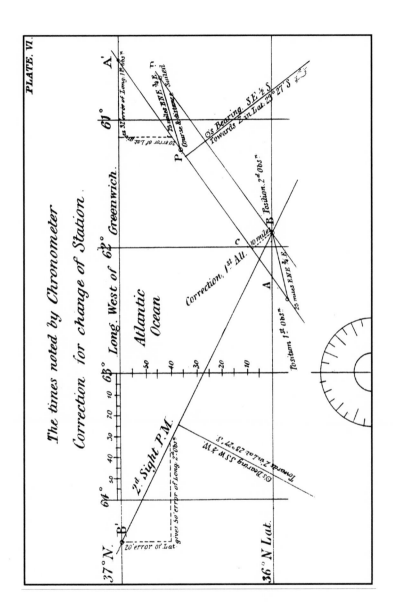

PLATE. VI.

The times noted by Chronometer
Correction for change of Station.

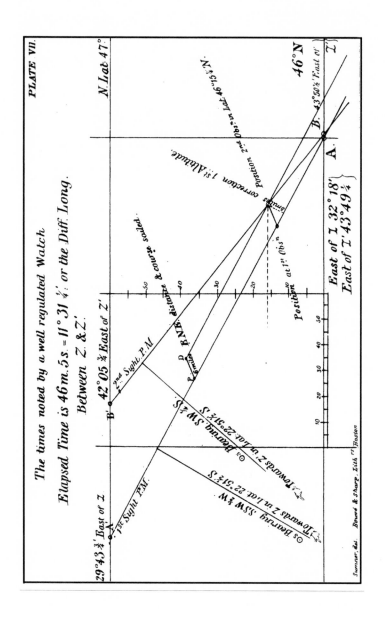

PLATE VII.

The times noted by a well regulated Watch

Elapsed Time is 46m.5s. = 11° 31¼′; or the Diff. Long.

Between Z. & Z′.

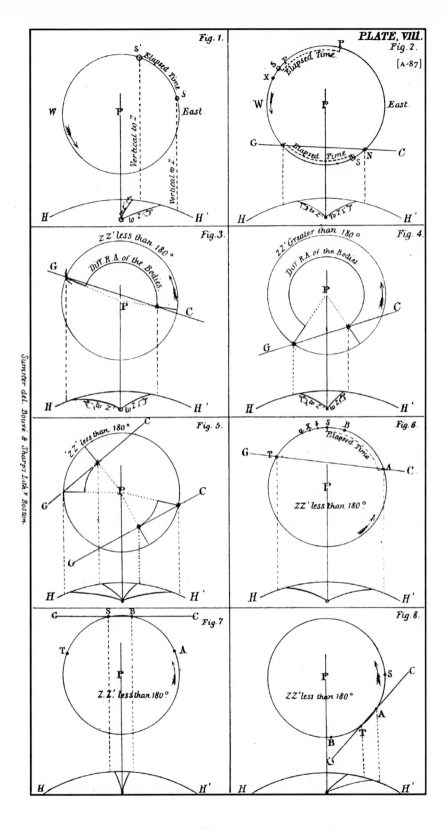

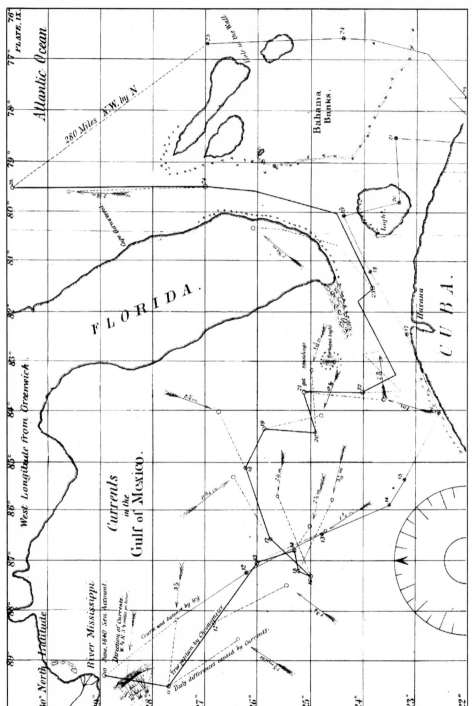

PLATE IX.

Atlantic Ocean

West Longitude from Greenwich.

North Latitude

FLORIDA.

CUBA.

Bahama Banks.

Currents
in the
Gulf of Mexico.

River Mississippi.

Havana

Light

Hole in the Wall.

280 Miles. N.W. by N.

Cape Canaveral

Qo. June, 1840 Sea Account.
Direction of Currents
W. S. N. 3 ¼ miles per hour.

Course and distance by log.

True position by Chronometer.

Daily differences caused by Currents.

Appendix B Part 1

Capitaine A. Marcq Saint-Hilaire
NOTE SUR LA DETERMINATION DU POINT
Revue Maritime et Coloniale
Pages 41-58, *Mar – Octobre* 1873

INTRODUCTION

APPENDIX B contains a translation of two key publications by Marcq-Saint-Hilaire, *Capitaine de frègate*, in the 1870's. The first paper, *Note sur la Détermination du Point*[15] (Appendix B Part 1) contained the basic concepts that Marcq Saint-Hilaire would synthesize into his intercept method, the "Nouvelle Navigation". At the end of the first paragraph on the first page he states:

> ...the declination or latitude also being known, one can mark on a graduated sphere a point **A** which is the position of the star at the moment of the observation. A small circle drawn around this point, **A**, as the center; with the observed zenith distance **N** as the radius, is the line of position of the observation. *For any position inside or outside of this small circle, one will observe at the moment the star was at point **A**, a zenith distance smaller or larger than **N*** [editor's emphasis] (Fig. 1).

The first part of this paragraph is simply a restatement of Sumner's Line of Position concept (Appendix A).

The sentence italicized here was not an original idea with Saint-Hilaire. It was commonly taught in navigation texts of the time. Nonetheless, this concept is the basis for his new method.

Twelve pages into the text, while discussing how to identify a star knowing its compass bearing and altitude, Saint-Hilaire observes:

> Notice in passing that if the readings of the compass as well as the determination of the variation could be sufficiently exact, the observation of the height of a star and the compass reading [i.e. the azimuth of the star] would give the means to determine immediately the position.

Again, this is a restatement of Sumner's method (Appendix A).

On the same page in the section dealing with correction of errors in the observed altitude:

> Therefore, if one notices after the calculation and the construction of an altitude, that a certain, more considerable error was committed in this altitude, one corrects the resultant one by taking a parallel to the line already drawn at a distance in miles equal to the expressed error in minutes in the direction of the star or to the opposite, according to whether the employed altitude was too small or too large.

Thus we have the basic elements of Saint-Hilaire's intercept method of finding position: determine the altitude and azimuth of the star from an estimated position at the time of the observation; determine whether the observed altitude is greater or less than the calculated altitude; convert minutes of difference in altitudes to miles; place a line perpendicular to the azimuth **m** miles toward the geographic position of the star from the calculated position if the observed altitude is greater than that calculated or **m** miles away from the calculated position if the observed altitude is less than that calculated. Saint-Hilaire was to combine these elements into a simple, coherent procedure that ultimately was adopted as the worldwide method of preference.

A short time later, in Marcq Saint-Hilaire's second publication, *Revue Maritime et Coloniale*, August, 1875[16] (Appendix B Part 2) he solidifies these concepts into an unified theory that came to be known as the "intercept" method:

From these formulae, one derives the value of H_e and Z and finally that of EE' which is equal to EA-E'A or to H_o - H_e: this arc of the great circle EE' is always small but it is at least equal to the distance from the **DR** position E to the true position which is found on **CC**. One may consider **EE'** as identical to the rhumb line tangent to E; since the angle **PEE'** or **Z** is known, one simple calculation based on the estimated position will be the distance from point E to the point E'.

If one has only this single observation without information about the causes of alterations to the estimate, one has to adopt E' as the position, as of all the positions on the geometric path **CC**, it is this one that is closest to point E.

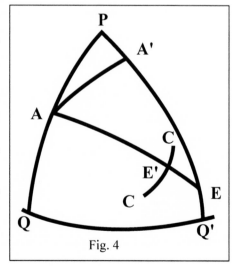

Fig. 4

...In summary, to calculate an observation, make the calculation of the altitude and the azimuth of the star for the **DR** position and the time of observation, add or subtract the estimated altitude from the observed altitude, consider this difference as a path given by the calculated azimuth and correct the **DR** position along this path.

This summary statement is essentially what we do today to find our position on a chart. The only difference is that we use an Assumed Position rather than the DR in order to simplify the calculation.

The second part of Saint-Hilaire's 1875 paper, not reported here, deals with the mathematics of estimation of the errors that could arise in using the intercept method. As Saint-Hilaire himself suggests, this paper provides more detailed mathematics than will be of interest to the average navigator! However, this paper amply illustrates the depth of Saint-Hilaire's competence in navigational mathematics.

NOTE

Appendix C gives a list of Definitions and Conventions used in translation of Saint-Hilaire's original publications. Appendix C also provides extensive Technical Notes that explain many of the calculations as well as the mathematical derivation of some of the key equations Saint-Hilaire used without his giving a detailed explanation.

NOTE

Bracketed page numbering in Appendix B follows the original articles closely.

NOTE

ON

THE DETERMINATION OF POSITION

––––––––

I. The altitude of a star, taken while noting the time on a chronometer, determines a geometric path containing the position of the observation.

The time on the chronometer gives the average time at Paris and, from the relation: average time at Paris + sidereal time = (longitude + right ascension of the star), one determines the star's longitude, that-is-to-say, the angle of the star's meridian with that of Paris, at the time of the observation. The declination or latitude being also known, one can mark on a graduated sphere a point **A** which is the position of the celestial body at the time of the observation. A small circle drawn around this point, **A**, as the center, with the observed zenith distance, **N**, as the radius, is the line of position of the observation. For any position inside or outside of this small circle, one will observe at the moment the celestial body was at point **A**, a zenith distance smaller or larger than **N** (Fig. 1).

Note. – **A** being the center of the small circle (called the circle of points of equal illumination), at each of its points, **Z**, this circle makes a right angle with the vertical **ZA**.

II. Two altitudes are necessary and sufficient to determine the position.

The altitude of another celestial body taken at the same time as the first gives a second geometric path that, by its intersection with the first one, determines the position from which the observations were taken.

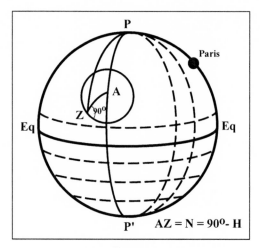

Figure 1

Note. – The two circles at their point of intersection are respectively perpendicular to the verticals of the two observed stars and make the same angle between them as the angle between their verticals.

III. Plot on the chart the geometric position given by an altitude.

An acceptable approximation is impossible with the forced reduction of dimensions obtained when plotting on a sphere. One may not employ the construction described above that does not require calculation. One must plot on the chart itself the projections of the two circles that, by their intersection, determine the fix.

In each of the **PAZ** triangles formed at the pole that contain the celestial body and the different points **Z** on the circle, two elements, **PA** and **AZ**, are constant and are respectively equal to the polar distance of the celestial body and to the observed zenith distance. By giving a value to one of these elements, **PZ** or angle **APZ**, one can calculate the other by the resolution of the triangle. Now **PZ** is the colatitude of point **Z** and angle **APZ** is equal to the longitude of the position minus the longitude of the star; it follows, taking one of the coordinates, latitude or longitude of the different **Z** points as one chooses, one can calculate the other. Then, carry the points thus obtained to the chart and plot point by point the curve that is the projection of the desired circle.

It is necessary to make this projection long enough to obtain an intersection at the observation position.

IV. The two geometric paths given by two altitudes intersect on the chart at an angle equal to the angle between the verticals of the observation.

Obviously, this flows from the properties of the projection, adapted to Mercator projection charts, so as to preserve the values of the angles (§ 2).

Note. – For each of these points, the projection of the small circle is perpendicular to the corresponding vertical.

V. The choice between calculation of the latitude or of longitude.

We have seen that to trace the curve point by point, one uses as one wishes, one of the coordinates, latitude or longitude, from different positions, Z, and then one calculates the other. The choice of the coordinate that one uses is not inconsequential. That part of the curve that one wishes to plot has a north-south direction if the observation has been made to the east or the west, that-is-to-say, from the prime vertical. That part of the curve deviates from the north-south direction by the amount that the observation itself deviates from the prime vertical and it deviates in the east- west direction when one has observed at the meridian.

If, for an observation done in the vicinity of the prime vertical, one takes the estimated longitude to derive the latitude, the point that one obtains will be the intersection of the meridian of the adopted longitude with the derived line that directs itself almost North and South. The intersection would take place at a very sharp angle and the position found would deviate considerably from the exact position even with the smallest difference between the true longitude and the one calculated.

It is necessary therefore, in the case of an observation in the vicinity of the prime vertical, to assume the latitude and calculate the longitude. The inverse is the case if one takes the observation in the vicinity of the meridian.

In summary, for the observations closer to the meridian than to the prime vertical, make the calculations of latitude; for the observations closer to the prime vertical than the meridian, then calculate longitude.

The longitude calculation, being more ordinary, can be used up to 30° from the meridian without inconvenience.

The meridian, the circummeridians of a celestial body, the altitude of the pole star can be used to determine a parallel of latitude. The calculation is simplified, but is only approximate for the circummeridians and the pole star.

VI. Practical plots of an altitude.

In practice, one is content to calculate two points that determine a chord of the curve of the desired projection that one can consider as the curve itself. One can even calculate only one point and the corresponding azimuth and draw a line passing through that point perpendicular to the azimuth. This line, tangent to the curve at this point, can be considered as the curve itself.

In the first case, with two latitudes including the true latitude, one makes two longitude calculations. One plots the two obtained positions that one then joins together by a straight line. If the altitude is near the meridian, one calculates two latitudes with two longitudes that comprise the true longitude.

In the second case, with the latitude or the estimated longitude, one calculates the longitude or the latitude as well as the azimuth, and at the point thus obtained, one plots a perpendicular to the azimuth.

VII. Formulae to employ.

Here are the formulae that appear to be the simplest:
1° For a calculation of longitude and azimuth:
[See Technical Note I, Appendix C.]

$$2S = L + \Delta + H$$

$$\mathrm{Sin}^2\, \frac{1}{2}\, P = \frac{\cos S \sin(S - H)}{\cos L \sin \Delta}, \mathrm{Sin}^2\, \frac{1}{2}\, Z = \frac{\sin(S - H)\, \sin(S - L)}{\cos L\, \cos H}.$$

2° For a calculation of latitude and azimuth:
[See Technical Note II, Appendix C.]

$$\mathrm{Sin} Z = \frac{\sin P \sin \Delta}{\cos H} \qquad (1)$$

$$\mathrm{Tan}\varphi = \tan\Delta\cos P, \mathrm{tg}\varphi' = \cotan H \cos Z \qquad (2)$$

$$\varphi = PK, \qquad \varphi' = ZK;$$

$$L' = 90° - (\varphi + \varphi').$$

(1) Pay attention to the value of **Z** which is given only by its sine and which always must be measured from the superior pole.

(2) Pay attention to the signs of φ and of φ' that are negative when **P** or **Z** > 90.°

VIII. The use of the chord or the tangent gives a sufficiently good approximation.

In different cases, one should be aware that an exact curve results from the plot of three or four points. One may always draw the complete curve if the greatest exactness is required.

If the estimated position is very wrong, one will recognize it at once because the point of intersection is very distant from that which was used for the plot and one repeats the calculation with the point found as a new estimated position.

When the zenith distance that results from the plot is small, the circle will be described with a small radius and with a more pronounced curvature. In this case, one does well to calculate three points if one wants a great exactness [A]

IX. To plot the result of an altitude close to 90.°

A zenith distance of 1° or less can be traced on a map just as on a sphere. One determines on the chart the position of the celestial body. Using the point obtained as the center, with the zenith distance measured on the scale of latitude as the radius, one draws a circle that is the desired projection. In the vicinity of the equator where the minutes of longitude vary imperceptibly, this construction may be extended to zenith distances a little larger than 1°.

[A] **[See Technical Note III, Appendix C.]** The tangent or the chord itself deviates so much from the exact projection of the circle that the variation $d\mathbf{Z}$ of the azimuth of the calculated position is considerable for the same displacement, **m** miles, from this point to the circle. Thus **Z** is the calculated position, **Z'** is the position at a distance of **m** miles from the circle (Fig. 2).

One has $\mathbf{Z'R} = d\mathbf{L} = \mathbf{ZZ'} \sin\mathbf{RZZ'} = \mathbf{m}\sin.\mathbf{Z}$.

[footnote [A] continues on the next 2 pages]

X. Reducing the result of an altitude to a given time.

Two simultaneous observations give the position by the intersection of the lines that they establish. If the altitudes are not simultaneous one reduces the results obtained to the time where one wants the position.

One has $\cos L \cos H \cos Z = \cos \Delta - \sin L \sin H$, from which differentiate by the ratio of Z to L. Since Δ and H are constant, one has:

$$dZ (\cos L \cos H \sin Z) = dL (\cos L \sin H - \sin L \cos H \cos Z),$$

now

$$\cot P \sin Z = \tan H \cos L - \sin L \cos Z,$$

where

$$\sin H \cos L - \sin L \cos H \cos Z = \cot P \sin Z \cos H;$$

substituting in the value of dZ and simplifying, one has

$$dZ \times \cos L = dL \times \cot P$$

where

$$dL = m \sin Z.$$

Therefore

$$dZ = \frac{m}{\cos L} \times \frac{\sin Z}{\tan P} = \frac{m}{\cos L} \times \frac{\sin \Delta}{\cos H} \times \cos P.$$

Figure 2

From this last value of dZ, one concludes that the variation of the azimuth, for the same displacement of Z on the circle, is thus much smaller when L and H are small and when P comes close to 90°. For the hourly altitudes, P is generally large and H is small so that the projection of the circle approaches a straight line. For the altitudes taken in the vicinity of the meridian, P is generally small and H is large. This is the one circumstance where one must take into account the variations in the azimuth by doing another calculation or by employing the following construction:

[footnote continues]

One transports the lines parallel to each other according to the course made good in the interval between where one was before and the place where one now wants the position. Example:

Take H and H', two altitudes plotted using the two points M, M' with azimuths Z, Z' and determine the position O. One wants to compute the curve of the projections of the two circles that are tangent to the lines M and M'.

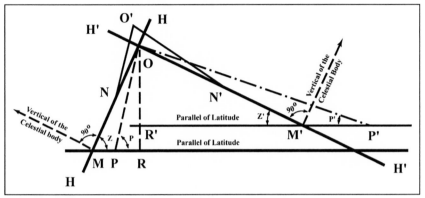

Figure 3

MO represents the displacement of the position M; OR is equal to dL, and measured on the scale of longitudes, is equal to $\dfrac{d\mathbf{L}}{\cos \mathbf{L}}$. In making the angle OPR equal to P, one has: $\mathbf{PR} = \dfrac{\mathbf{OR}}{\tan \mathbf{P}} = \dfrac{d\mathbf{L}}{\cos \mathbf{L} \tan \mathbf{P}} = d\mathbf{Z}.$

PR, measured on the scale of longitudes, gives the variation in minutes of the angle Z. That is to say, the curve of the projection cuts the parallel passing through O by the angle dZ+Z. Taking a line through N, the midpoint of MO, the line NO' makes an angle with NO of dZ minutes. Thus, one obtains a second element of the curve. Proceeding the same for the second altitude, one determines the corrected position O'.

One cannot be mistaken about the direction of dZ which has the same sign as dL or the opposite sign, according to whether P < or > 90°.

When P is equal to 90°, the curvature changes direction and this is the point of inflection of the curve where it approaches a straight line.

Instead of constructing the angle OPR = P, one can use the Traverse Tables in which one enters with OR in minutes of longitude as the departure and the angle P as the course. The difference in latitude gives dZ in minutes.

In the case where the straight lines H and H' are chords instead of being tangents one can employ an analogous construction, and trace the two elements of the curve at the two points that determined the chord.

[end footnote]

One has made observations at 10:30 o'clock in the morning and at 1 o'clock in the afternoon; one wants the position at noon. From 1030 hours until noon, made 12 miles to the NNE; from noon to 1 o'clock made 5 miles to the north.

The figure is self-explanatory. If at 10 ½ hours one was on the line **A**, at noon one evidently is on the line **A'**.

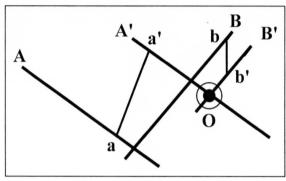

Figure 4

Signs: **A** Observation at 10 ½ hours.
       aa' = 12 miles to the N-N-E.
       A' Observation of 10 ½ hours brought forward to noon.
       B Observation at 1 hour.
       bb' = 5 miles to the South.
       B' Observation at 1 hour brought forward to noon.
       O = Position at noon.

Note. – The altitudes are considered as simultaneous any time that the movement of the ship in the interval between the observations is negligible. If it is otherwise, it is necessary to take this movement into account.

XI. The Case of several altitudes.

When one observes the altitude of several celestial bodies, either simultaneously or at different instants, one advances them to the time where one wants the position. If all the lines do not cross at the same position, which is generally the case, one makes an estimate, using his feelings, just as one does when several bearings do not cross, while taking into account the relative exactness of the altitudes, the celestial body observed, etc.

XII. To have a good position.

The only condition to fulfill consists of obtaining two lines, themselves crossing at a sufficiently large angle and approaching 90°.

For simultaneous observations, it suffices to choose two stars whose verticals satisfy this condition. (See § 4.)

For the observations at intervals, the same right angle condition must be fulfilled between the verticals of the observed celestial bodies or by the same celestial body observed from two different positions. Furthermore, the altitudes must be plotted in the least possible interval so as to avoid as much as one can, the errors arising from the dead reckoning in the interval.

It is often preferable to have a smaller angle between the verticals compensated by a smaller interval between the altitudes, especially if one is concerned about the errors in the dead reckoning and in the current.

The conditions to obtain a good position are obviously the same whether one constructs geometrically or whether one has recourse to calculation. Therefore, one must always put oneself in the positions that have just been enunciated.

If one prefers calculation, the Pagel method is better. One will be able to avoid some chances of error in the signs of the corrections by observing that, for an observation taken between the north and the east, for example, a latitude more north displaces more to the west and a latitude more south displaces more to the east, since the path of the points given by the altitude itself moves from the north-west to the south-east.

XIII. To obtain a good position at a given moment.

Observe as near as possible to the desired time so that everything needed satisfies the condition between the verticals as described in the preceding paragraph.

In the morning and evenings, altitudes of stars or planets combined with that of the Sun give an excellent position. At night, the uncertainty of the observations of stars makes it necessary to take a number of altitudes of different stars that one then combines with the altitude of the moon, if one is able.

During the day, employ the combined observations of the moon and the sun as much as one can.

At noon, with only the sun, two observations taken on each side of the meridian between 30° and 45° of the azimuth gives the best possible position. Thus, one has two observations intersecting at an angle of 60° to 90° and as close together in time as possible.

XIV. Taking only one altitude.

A single altitude, giving a geometric path containing the position, determines the position itself by its intersection with another geometric path obtained by a bearing, a depth sounding, the distance to the coast, or by any other means. To have a good position, these two geometric paths must intersect at a suitable angle.

1st EXAMPLE: One estimates oneself to be 10 miles off a coast and one takes an observation:

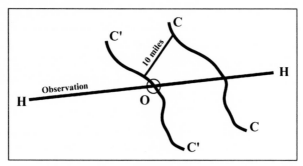

Figure 5

HH Line of Position from an altitude observation.
CC Line of the coast.
C'C' Parallel to the coast at 10 miles.
O is the Position.

2nd EXAMPLE: One has a bearing to point A and observed an altitude:

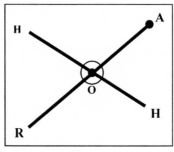

AR Bearing of A
HH Line of position from an altitude observation.
O is the Position

Figure 6

3rd EXAMPLE: One has made a sounding of 50 meters and taken one altitude:

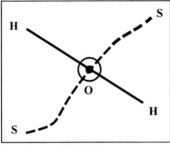

Figure 7

HH Line of Position from an altitude
SS Line of soundings of 50 meters.
0 is the Position

Note. – The result of one sounding, that of one observation, etc., can be brought forward to a given time by a parallel transportation as we have seen for an altitude. This is as good as two observations. One observation and a sounding taken together or at an interval, two such soundings in certain localities, serve to determine the point that is always given by the intersection of two geometric paths.

A single altitude aided by the knowledge of currents or of the causes of the errors in the estimated position makes it easy to have the position.

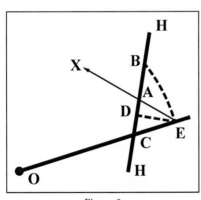

Figure 8

EXAMPLE: Set **O** as the last known position. **E** is the estimated position at the moment of the observation **H**. If the direction of the current is known, **EX** for example, and if the estimated position is good, one places oneself at **A**. If the error in the estimate originates with the compass and not from the log, one draws an arc of the circle **EB** with point **0** as the center that determines the point **B** on the line **H** where one must place oneself. If, on the other hand, the error originates from the estimate of speed and not from the heading, one must place oneself at **C**. Finally, if one has no information, neither about the causes of the error of the dead reckoning nor of the currents, one places oneself on the line **H**, as near as possible to **E** at the foot of the perpendicular **D**. One clearly can not be certain when using this manner of plotting, but it is the probabilities on which one must depend. This is the only way to use concurrently all the data that one possesses to get the most probable knowledge of the position.

A single altitude can permit one to make a landfall. EXAMPLE: Set A as the destination. Line **H** the result of the altitude observation.

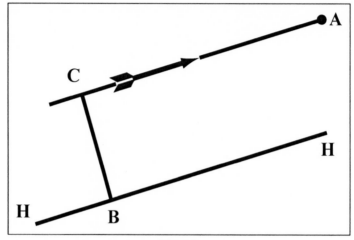

Figure 9

Construct a line through **A** parallel to **H**. Join this parallel line by any transverse route such as **BC**, and find the course to the destination. The observation must be made in a direction coming close to the perpendicular to the presumed bearing to the destination in order to avoid a long transverse route. At the moment of entering a straight or a narrow passage, etc., an observation taken in a perpendicular direction to the direction of the straight, allows, by a similar operation to the preceding one, to follow the middle of the passage.

An altitude taken either ahead or astern will inform you as to which position one has advanced on the course and whether one has current with or against oneself. An altitude taken across-wise will determine if one is set to right or to the left of the course, whether by error of the compass, or by force of the current. The first observations could be called altitudes of speed and the second altitudes of direction.

XV. To identify an observed star.

It sometimes happens that one does not know the star that one has observed because the condition of the sky prevents seeing the constellations. In this case, and this is a good precaution always to take, it is necessary to sight it with the compass. With the estimated position and the true azimuth of the star, construct a crude position triangle in which **PZ, ZA** and **Z** are known and derive an approximate value for the right ascension and declination of the observed star. Then one sees in the *Connaissance des temps* which is the star or the planet for which the elements themselves match those of the one observed. For a small azimuth angle, a simple graphic construction is sufficient. Naturally, it is necessary to have observed a brilliant star so that she finds data for herself in the *Connaissance des temps*.

Notice in passing that if the readings of the compass as well as the determination of the compass variation could be sufficiently exact, the observation of the altitude of a celestial body and the compass reading would give the means to determine the position immediately.

XVI. Correction of an error committed in the employed altitude.

An altitude that is too large diminishes the zenith distance and approaches the observed celestial body. That is say that if the celestial body is in the NNE, and if the altitude used in the calculation is too large by just 10', the line WNW by ESE that one determines is displaced to the NNE by 10 miles. Therefore, it is easy to correct the altitude by plotting on a sphere. The inverse occurs for an altitude that is too small. Therefore, if one notices after the calculation and the construction of an altitude, that a certain small error was committed in this altitude, one corrects the resultant altitude by taking a parallel to the line already drawn at a distance in miles equal to the expressed error in minutes in the direction of the celestial body or to the opposite, according to whether the employed altitude was too small or too large.

XVII. The result of an altitude having been plotted, plot an altitude observed with the same celestial body without another calculation.

Given **H** as the altitude plotted; **t**, the seconds in time between the first altitude and the altitude that is now to be plotted and which one has taken after the first, and larger than the first by **m** minutes.

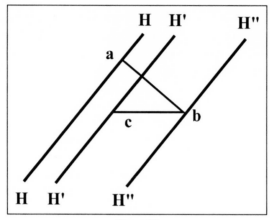

Figure 10

If, after time **t**, the celestial body is considered as having remained immobile, the second altitude will determine a line of points parallel to H but nearer the celestial body by **m** miles. That is to say, it will give H", assuming **ab** = **m** miles and directed towards the celestial body. However, during the interval **t**, the celestial body, neglecting its true movement, has moved to the west during **t** seconds. The line of position will be displaced to the west by the same difference in longitude and it moves on the parallel of longitude **bc**=**t** seconds [of time] = $^t/_4$ minutes [of longitude]. The parallel plotted at **c** is the result of the second altitude. In this fashion one may, by a single calculation, have the mean value of several sights on the same body taken at a short interval of time.

XVIII. Incorrect altitudes.

When one has observed an altitude incorrectly by about 4', for example, in one direction or the other, it is sufficient to give a passage four miles on each side of the line obtained, with the result of a large band eight miles wide that certainly contains the position. If the other altitude also is dubious, one makes the same construction. Thus, one obtains a space containing the position and enlarged all the more by the errors in altitude as the angles between these altitudes diverge from a right angle.

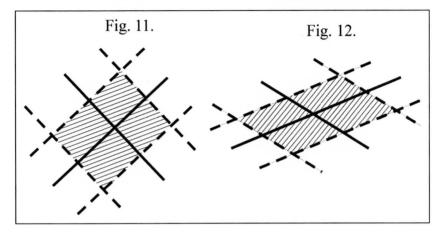

Fig. 11.

Fig. 12.

XIX. Error due to the error of the chronometer.

All that has been said thus far assumes that the chronometer is well regulated. If its estimated daily error is incorrect, the results given by the astronomical observations will be exact only in latitude and erroneous in longitude due to the error in the chronometer. For the results given by an altitude and by a terrestrial observation, such as a sounding, survey, etc, it is easy to see how these measurements will be influenced by the error of the chronometer by transferring the line given by an altitude to the east or to the west by an amount equal to the error in the chronometer. The results of an altitude are thus less influenced by the error of the chronometer if the altitude is more distant from the prime vertical and approaching the meridian. At the meridian, the influence is zero.

XX. Limit to the error in position.

Those elements that come together to determine the position are not perfectly exact. All are subject to a certain error and thus give an approximate position. By assuming a limit in these errors, one may determine a limit to the error in the position, that is to say, an area that will contain the position with certainty.

A position obtained by two altitudes at an interval is subject to errors of dead reckoning during the interval, to the errors of altitudes and to the error of the chronometer.

Suppose that the error in speed in the interval is estimated at 1/20 and the error in the course at 3°. The error in the first altitude taken is about 1½ minutes, the second is about 1 minute, and the error of the watch correction is about 5 seconds.

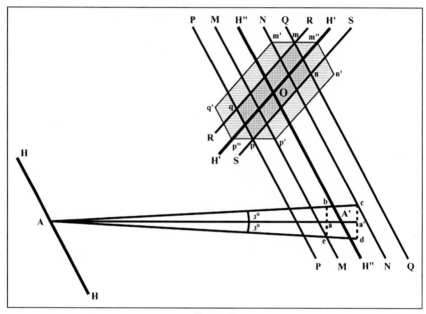

Figure 13.

Make **A** the position on the line of position derived from the first altitude **H**, not brought forward to the time of the second observation. **AA'**, equal to 20 miles, is the resultant track made good in the interval. The line **H"** parallel to **H** would be the line of position from the first altitude brought forward without taking account of any errors. The distance **AA'** was assumed to be equal to 20 miles and was estimated to an accuracy of about 1/20. The position **A** brought forward to **A'** finds itself confined by the limits **a,a'** at 19 and 21 miles. The course being not exact to about 3°, the surface **bedc** defines the limits of position **A** brought forward to the estimated time of the second altitude.

The parallels to **H** drawn at the corners **e** and **c** of the surface **bedc** determine a band **MN** that is the result of the first altitude while taking the possible dead reckoning errors into account. Since this altitude could to be erroneous by 1½ minutes, it is necessary to increase the width of this band by 1½ miles on each side. Thus, one has the band **PQ** for the final result of the first altitude. **H'**, the second altitude, has an error giving it the width of 1 mile of each side so that one has the band **RS** for the result of this altitude.

The two bands **PQ** and **RS** give the surface **mnpq** as limits to the position. It suffices to transport this area to the east and to the west by 5 seconds of time or 1'15" of longitude to take the chronometer error into account. Thus, one has as the final limit of the position, the surface **m'm"n'p'p"q'**.

In the chosen example where all the errors are admittedly within very ordinary limits, the exact position could be at **p"**. Since **0** is the sought for position, it could be in error by about 4 miles. This is the maximum error. So, for the maximum error to occur, it is necessary that the errors in each of the different elements attain their limits and accumulate themselves so as to falsify the position in the same direction, something that is not very probable, but possible.

A position given by two simultaneous altitudes is subject only to the errors of altitude and chronometer. Thus, it is necessary to have recourse to simultaneous altitudes or at least to observe the altitudes as close together as one can.

XXI. Conclusion.

The theory that has just been exposed is not new. Many officers certainly employ the graphic constructions, but they are far from being generalized. Nevertheless, the methods offer great advantages especially in the circumstances where the determination of the position presents some difficulties. They allow one to realize the limit of error and to do the earthly and astronomical observations concurrently. They offer the resource to take the observation, calculate and trace each altitude by a different person so as to divide the work and accelerate the result. Last, and very important, a single graphic construction gives the means to tie together all the possible parts of an isolated altitude.

This theory avoids certain practices that are not very logical into which one is led to fall. What can one do with a single altitude taken outside the meridian? With doubtful latitude, one calculates a longitude that one considers as good. Otherwise, one plots the resulting position that one considers as doubtful and to which one grants hardly any confidence. In the first case, one acts on a false hypothesis, sometimes dangerous, exact only for an observation done strictly on the prime vertical. In the second case, one neglects or one does little with the unique observation that one possesses. Is it not preferable to plot the line of position given by the altitude? One uses everything that one can take from a single observation.

Sometimes one seems to believe that an altitude cannot give good results because a slight difference in latitude induces a considerable difference in longitude. All the altitudes taken to the same exactness are equally good. An observation to the N.E. is as valuable as an observation to the North, sometimes better. It is the combination of the two altitudes that must satisfy certain conditions since it is the combination of the two observations that determines a good position.

It also happens with a doubtful horizon, or with a cloudy sun that one deprives oneself of observations because they would not be sufficiently exact. What one realizes is that an error in the altitude itself of 10' produces a line, determined by this altitude that passes within 10 miles of the exact position. Thus, in all circumstances, one should not hesitate to take altitudes doubtful to 5', 6' or even more, that can be precious, despite their uncertainty.

Today the great speeds of steam ships as well as the often-doubtful deviations of the compass require more frequent determination of position. Thus, it can be useful to propagate a method that, we do believe, returns a prompter and easier determination. For a long time, this method has given us great service, not only in ordinary times where all is good, but also in those circumstances where the ordinary methods that usually are good, are otherwise insufficient, slower and less certain.

MARCQ SAINT-HILAIRE,
Captain of Frigates.
[October 1873]

Appendix B Part 2

Capitaine A. Marcq Saint-Hilaire
CALCUL DU POINT OBSERVÉ
Revue Maritime et Coloniale
Pages 341-376, *Mar – Aout* 1875

CALCULATION OF THE OBSERVED POSITION

Method of Estimated Altitudes.

We will recount succinctly below the principles upon which rests the determination of a ship's position by the altitude of celestial bodies and the chronometer.

Convention. For clarity, we will call the *terrestrial position*, or simply *projection*, of a celestial body at the given moment, the point on the surface of the earth where, at that moment, the celestial body is at its zenith.

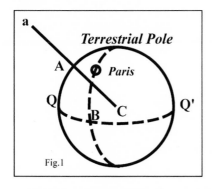

Fig.1

Thus, (Figure 1) the point A is the terrestrial projection of the celestial body *a*; the latitude and longitude of A will be called the terrestrial latitude and longitude of the celestial body. It is evident that the terrestrial latitude **AQ** of the celestial body is equal to its declination and that the terrestrial longitude, **BQ**, is equal to the hour angle of the celestial body from the meridian of Paris. The terrestrial longitude of the sun is the true time at Paris.

§1. *With an accurate chronometer, one may know at each instant the terrestrial projection of the celestial bodies given in the Nautical Almanac.*

Example. The 24th of October 1874, at $3^{hr}43^m32^s$ by the chronometer, what is the terrestrial position of Vega? The chronometer is $4^{hr}45^m58^s$ slow on Paris mean time.

	h m s		
Chronometer Time	3 43 32		
Chronometer slow	4 45 58		
Paris Mean Time	8 29 30		
[See Technical Note IV, Appendix C.]			
Sidereal time 24 Oct. at 0^{hr}	14 10 51		
Correction for $8^h29^m30^s$	1 24		
Sidereal time at Paris	22 41 45		
Right Ascension of Vega	18 32 41	Declination	38° 40' 13" S
Hour angle Vega from Paris	4 09 04		
Terrestrial Projection, G_a 62°16'00"W		L_a 38° 40' 13" N	

At the moment the chronometer shows $3^h43^m32^s$, Vega will be at its zenith over the point described by the latitude and longitude above.

§2. *The complement from 90° of the altitude of a celestial body, alternatively called the Zenith Distance, measures the distance on the earth from the point of observation to the terrestrial projection of the celestial body.*

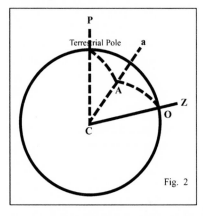

Fig. 2

Example: One sees (Figure 2) that the Zenith Distance of the celestial body **a**, measured from point **O**, is the angle **aCZ**. This angle is measured by the arc of a great circle, **OA** that joins the point of the observation to the projection of the celestial body. Suppose that at the time used in the first paragraph, one has obtained for the true altitude of Vega 48°51'. In this case, the Zenith Distance, that is, the arc OA equals 41°09' and the point of observation will be at a distance of 41°09' or 823 leagues or 2,469 miles from the projection of Vega, that is to say, at the position situated at 62°16'00" longitude West and at 38°40'13" latitude North.

Thus, taking the altitude of a celestial body is equivalent to measuring the distance from the point of observation to another point on the earth, a point which itself can be established if one notes the time on the chronometer. It is this two-fold operation, taking the altitude and noting the corresponding time that constitutes an *observation*.

Remark. - The angle at **O** on the surface of the earth, made by the meridian, **OP,** and the arc **OA** is the same as the azimuth angle of the celestial body, since the plane **PCZ** is the meridian of the place and that a**CZ** is the vertical plane of the celestial body. It follows that if, at the moment of observation, the celestial body bears N70°W, the arc of the great circle **OA** also is directed from point **O** towards N70°W.

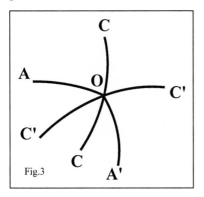

Fig.3

*§3. On a sphere (Figure 3), all the points situated at a given distance from point **A** will be on a circle **CC** having point **A** as its center and **OA** as the radius that is equal to the given distance.* At any point, such as point **O**, the circle **CC** is perpendicular to the corresponding arc **OA**. Thus:

One observation determines a geometric path on the earth of the point of observation. This path is a circle having for its center the terrestrial projection of the celestial body and for its radius the complement of 90° of the measured altitude. At the point of observation, the geometric path is in a direction perpendicular to the azimuth of the celestial body. (See the remark in §2.)

§ 4. On a surface, two geometric paths from the same point establish this position by their intersection. Thus:

Two observations are necessary and sufficient to determine the point of the observation. This point is found at the intersection of two circles on the earth, having respectively for centers the terrestrial projection of the observed celestial bodies and for radii, the complement to 90° of their observed altitudes. At their point of intersection, the two geometric paths are respectively perpendicular to the verticals of the observations and it follows that they cross at an angle equal to those of the verticals.

Example: Let **C'C'** (Figure 3) be the second geometric path with **A'** as the center. It will determine the position of the observation, **O**, by its intersection with **CC**. The angles **AOC** and **A'OC'** are right angles and the angle **COC'** is equal to **AOA'**.

In summary, the position given by two *observations* is determined by their distances from two points on earth in exactly the same fashion that a position is determined on a plane by the distances from two given points on the plane. The same very simple construction, where one would draw two circles with a compass, may be employed on a sphere, if it were possible to obtain a sufficient accuracy by doing so. We will not speak of the two solutions given by the intersection of two circles. In practice, any uncertainty about which point to use is not possible.

Important remark: The point obtained by the intersection of two lines is much better determined when the angles at which the lines cross is near 90°. Thus, for the two observations, choose two celestial bodies whose verticals cross as close as possible to a right angle. The direction of these verticals is unimportant; it is sufficient that they cross conveniently. This is the only condition with which to be concerned, exactly as in the case where one determines the position by the bearings of two points on the earth.

We have just made a geometrical statement of the problem of determination of position by observations. We believe that the following treatise will be preferable to the method in which the problem consists of separately finding the latitude by a meridian altitude or otherwise and then finding the longitude by the difference in time between Paris and the local time. Thus, one looses the proper goal of the problem and one must be aware of the consequent errors. In the traditional approach, what one determines are the latitude and the time and not the position. Many people are persuaded that it is *indispensable* to observe at the meridian and the prime vertical, or as near as possible to these two directions but this is not at all necessary. Whatever the position of the celestial body in the sky, the chronometer determines its terrestrial position with an exactness that depends only on the chronometer error. On the other hand, the exactness of the altitude measurement depends neither on the direction of the celestial body nor on its movement, more or less large, in azimuth and in altitude, but only on exterior circumstances such as the condition of the sky, the horizon, etc. It follows that all times are equally good for taking an observation and that, in all cases, this observation determines the path of a point with an exactitude that depends only on the accuracy of the chronometer and that with which the altitude has been determined. It is well understood that we eliminate the case of altitudes so small that the refraction is uncertain.

Meridian altitude. – The observation of the meridian altitude at sea differs from the observations as we have defined them, in the sense that, instead of noting the time, one assures that the measured altitude is the maximum altitude and one simply accepts that this altitude corresponds to the passage of the celestial body across the meridian.

The determination of the declination of a celestial body does not require knowing the time exactly. One obtains, with sufficient accuracy, the distance between the terrestrial pole and the terrestrial projection of the celestial body. The complement of the altitude gives the distance of this projection to the point of observation. Addition or subtraction gives the distance of this latter point to the pole. The geometric plot is a circle having its center at the earth's pole, that is to say, a parallel of latitude.

The maximum altitude of a celestial body corresponds rigorously to its passage through the meridian of the observer only if the movement in declination of the celestial body and the movement of the observer in latitude are equal and in the same direction.

The Calculations

The calculation of the position given by two observations comes from the intersection of two circles determined by their centers and their radii. Except in the specific case where one of the circles is a parallel of latitude, that is to say, when one of the altitudes is determined at the meridian, the direct and rigorous calculation of the position depends on the resolution of a spherical quadrangle in which one knows one angle and the four sides. This calculation is long and cannot be started until the two observations are completed, which delays the result. One will generally abandon the effort, even though this is the only means to have a fix in complete rigor. One has recourse to different methods to determine the position based on the approximate knowledge of the position given by dead reckoning. One will then correct this DR position by an approximate method, but by one that is sufficiently accurate in practice. The procedure we are going to explain is of this type and it follows naturally from that which has been explained above.

First, we shall consider a single observation.

Calculation of a Single Observation.

Let **A** (Figure 4) be the terrestrial projection of the celestial body; **E** is the estimated position at the time of the observation; **P** is the earth's pole; and **QQ'** is the equator. Let **CC** be the geometric path given by the observation and **E'** its point of intersection with the arc **AE**. **AE'** is equal to the complement of the observed altitude which will be designated H_o. The angle at **E'** is a right angle.

Call **D** = **AQ**, the terrestrial latitude or the declination of the star; L_e = **EQ'**, the estimated latitude; and **P** = **APE**, the difference between the terrestrial longitude of the celestial body and the estimated longitude. [See Technical Note V, Appendix C.]

In the triangle **APE**, where one knows two sides and the included angle, we will calculate the complement of **EA** and the angle **PEA**. To accomplish this, draw the arc of a great circle **AA'** perpendicular to **PE**. The two right triangles **PAA'** and **EAA'** give:

$$\tan \mathbf{PA'} = \tan \mathbf{PA} \cos \mathbf{P}; \quad \cos \mathbf{EA} = \frac{\cos \mathbf{PA}}{\cos \mathbf{PA'}} \cos(\mathbf{Q'A'} - \mathbf{Q'E});$$

$$\cos \mathbf{PEA} = \tan \frac{(\mathbf{Q'A'} - \mathbf{Q'E})}{\tan \mathbf{EA}},$$

from which one derives $\mathbf{A'Q'} = \mathbf{D'}$, $90°-\mathbf{EA} = H_o$ and $\mathbf{PEA} = \mathbf{Z}$. Substituting one obtains:

$$(1)\ \tan \mathbf{D'} = \frac{\tan \mathbf{D}}{\cos \mathbf{P}};\ (2)\ \sin H_e = \frac{\sin \mathbf{D}}{\sin \mathbf{D'}} \cos(\mathbf{D'}\text{-}L_e);$$

$$(3)\ \cos \mathbf{Z} = \tan(\mathbf{D'}\text{-}L_e)\tan H_e.$$

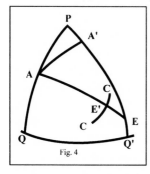

Fig. 4

From these formulae, one derives the value of H_e and $\mathbf{Z}$ and finally that of **EE'** which is equal to **EA-E'A** or to $H_o\text{-}H_e$. This arc of the great circle **EE'** is always small since its maximum value is equal to the distance from the estimated position **E** to the true position **E'** on **CC**. One may consider **EE'** as identical to the rhumb line tangent at **E**. Since the angle **PEE'** or **Z** is known and knowing the coordinates of point **E**, one simple dead reckoning type calculation will give the coordinates of point **E'**.

If one has only this single observation without information about the causes of alterations to the dead reckoning, one must adopt **E'** as the position, since, of all the positions on the geometric path, it is this one that is closest to the estimated position **E**.

H_e and **Z** are obviously the altitude and the azimuth of the celestial body that one should measure at the estimated position **E** at the time of the observation. For this reason we give the name *estimated altitude* to H_e.

One must be very careful to give the longitudes G_a and G_e and their algebraic difference $(G_a\text{-}G_e) = \mathbf{P}$ the appropriate designation East or

West. **D'** always has the same name North or South as **D** because **D'** is the projection on the meridian of the estimated position. The algebraic difference, $(D'-L_e)$, also must carry the name North or South as appropriate. The angle **Z** must always be smaller than 90°. The direction of this azimuth is indicated by the sign of $(D'-L_e)$ and of **P.** The difference (H_o-H_e) must be oriented in the direction of the angle **Z**, that is to say, towards the celestial body if it is positive and the opposite if it is negative.

In summary, to calculate an observation, make the calculation of the altitude and the azimuth of the celestial body for the estimated position and the time of observation. Subtract the estimated altitude from the observed altitude. Consider this difference as a displacement of the ship. The course is given by the azimuth and the distance by the difference in altitude. Correct the position along this track.

One could dispense with the calculation of the azimuth of the celestial body by measuring the celestial body's bearing but it is more accurate to make the calculation. Besides, the calculation is so short that to take a reading from the compass and to correct it perhaps takes a little more time.

Construction of an Observation on the Chart.

To obtain the projection **e'** of the point **E'** on the chart, it is sufficient to carry, starting from the estimated position **e** (Figure 5), the distance **ee'** equal to the difference (H_o-H_e) measured on the latitude scale, in the

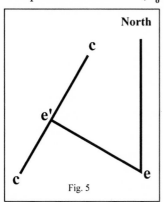

Fig. 5

direction of the celestial body or the opposite, depending on whether this difference is positive or negative. The angle at **E'** on the sphere is a right angle. Since the angles are plotted on the chart at their true size, the perpendicular **cc** to **e'e** will be the tangent to the projection of **CC**. This is the tangent that one may consider as conforming, within certain limits, to the projection itself and representing on the chart the geometric path of the position given by the observation. This line will be called, according to common usage, the *droite d' observation* or the *line of position*.

Numerical example. – On 24 October 1874, at 8 o'clock in the evening, at the estimated position L_e = 35°30' N and G_e = 9°30' W, one obtains the corrected altitude of Vega, H_o = 48°51'00". The terrestrial coordinates of Vega, determined by the chronometer, will be L_a or D = 38°40'13" N, and G_a = 62°16'00" W.

$$\tan D' = \frac{\tan D}{\cos P}$$

$$\cos Z = \tan(D'-L_e)\tan H_e$$

$$\sin H_e = \frac{\sin D}{\sin D'}\cos(D-L_e)$$

Latitude	Longitude		
D= 38° 40' 13"N	G_a= 62° 16' 00" W	tan D= $\bar{1}$.90325	sin D= $\bar{1}$.79577
L_e = 35° 30' 00"N	G_e= 9° 30' 00" W		
	P= 52° 46' 00" W	C cos P 0.21820	
D'= 52° 54' 30"N		tan D' 0.12145	Csin D' 0.09818
D'-L_e= 17° 24' 30"N		tan (D'-L_e) $\bar{1}$.4963	cos (D'-L_e) $\bar{1}$ .97964
		tan H_e 0.0512	sin H_e $\bar{1}$ .87359
		cos Z $\bar{1}$.5475	H_e = 48° 22' 15"
	ε 26.9^miles		H_o = 48° 51' 00"
λ = 10' 10"N	g 33' 06" W	Z =N69°20' W	
L_e'= 35° 40' 10"N	G_e'= 10° 03' 06"W		H_o-H_e= +28' 45"

[See Technical Note VI, Appendix C]
[λ = dLatitude; g = dLongitude; ε = Departure, miles east or west.]

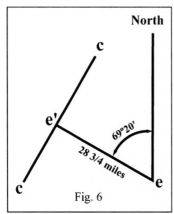

Fig. 6

The azimuth Z is NorthWest because (D-L_e) and P are respectively named North and West. The correction (H_o-H_e), equal to 28¾ miles, must be carried in the direction of the azimuth, that is to say, N69°20'W since it is positive. If the correction were negative, it would be necessary to carry it in the direction opposite the azimuth, that is to say, S69°20'E. The correction, made by using the Traverse Tables, gives a corrected position more exact than the estimated position - the position e' situated at L_e 35°40'10"N, G_e 10°03'06"W.

For plotting the line of position on the chart, it is sufficient to carry, starting from the estimated position **e** (Figure 6) 28 ¾ miles to N69°20'W, and from the position *e'* to draw *cc* perpendicular to **ee'**. *cc* is the line of position.

Calculation of the Position Given by Two Observations.

Suppose now that two observations have been made at the same place, or if not exactly the same, the displacement of the ship in the interval between the two observations is negligible.

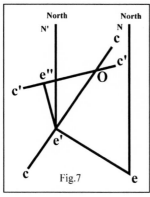

Fig.7

Calculate one of the observations as has been described; (Figure 7) on the chart given **e** the **DR** position, **e'** the position corrected by calculation, **cc** the line of position perpendicular to **ee'**. The angle **Nee'** is equal to the calculated azimuth Z.

Calculate the second observation in the same manner, considering the corrected position **e'** as the new **DR** position.

Take $(H'_0 - H_e)$ and **Z'** as the difference of altitudes and the azimuth obtained by this calculation. Place the point **e''** in relation to **e'** just as the latter is related to **e**, making the angle **N'e'e''** = Z' and making **e'e''** = $(H'_0 - H_{e'})$. The perpendicular **c'c'** to **e'e''** is the line of position of the second observation. The point **O**, at the intersection of the two lines of position, is the observed position that one must calculate.

In the triangle **e'e''o** that is right at **e''**, **e'e''** is equal to $(H'_0 - H_{e'})$. The angle at **O** is equal to that of the two verticals of observation **ee'**, **e'e''** or (Z-Z'). Thus, one has $e'O = \dfrac{e'e''}{\sin O} = \dfrac{H'_0 - H_{e'}}{\sin O}$. The Traverse Tables will give the value of **e'O** without calculation. This line has a known direction since it is perpendicular to the vertical of the first observation. A new dead reckoning calculation will pass from the corrected point **e'** to the observed position **O**.

To find the course derived in this latter dead reckoning calculation, one must take care to choose between the two sides of the perpendicular to the first azimuth, the one that makes a sharp angle with the second azimuth. Thus, this will be the direction in which the correction $\dfrac{H'_0 - H_{e'}}{\sin O}$ must be carried. If this distance is negative, it will be obvious to carry it in the opposite direction. In the end, a simple sketch in the nature of Figure 7 will eliminate all risks of error.

If the angle of the two verticals is a right angle, **e'e"** will coincide with **cc** and the point **e"** will be the same as the observed position **O**. It will suffice in this case to make the **DR** calculations for the distance $(H'_o - H_e)$ and the course **Z'**, from which one will obtain the observed position.

If the ship has moved in the interval between the observations, one calculates the first observation as has been described. In Figure 8, **e'** is the corrected position and **cc** is the line of position given by this calculation. Carry the line **e'e₁'** forward starting from point **e'**, representing the displacement of the ship during the interval. Line **c₁c₁**, parallel to **cc** and passing through **e₁'**, obviously is the line of position from the first observation brought forward to the time of the second.

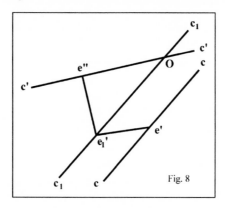

Fig. 8

In calculating the second observation with the point **e₁'** as the estimated position, one obtains the second line of position **c'c'** which determines, by its intersection with **c₁c₁**, the observed position **O**. One sees that in this case, it is sufficient to advance the corrected position, obtained in the first calculation by taking account of the course and speed in the interval and to continue the calculation as has been described in the preceding.

In summary, calculation of position based on two observations consists of:

1st. With the estimated position and the first observation, calculate the corrected position;

2nd. Correct this position by the course and speed in the interval;

3rd. Calculate the second observation with the position thus obtained;

4th. Correct this position by a track perpendicular to the azimuth of the first observation and equal to the difference in the altitudes of the second calculation divided by the sine of *the angle of observation*.

Thus, one will obtain the observed position for the time of the second observation.

We will call the angle between the verticals of the two celestial bodies observed *the angle of observation*. In the best circumstances, this angle should approach 90°, and that is the only condition with which we need be concerned.

Numeric example. - Suppose that in the same place where one has made the observation on Vega given above, one also has obtained a corrected altitude of Capella 15°32'30", and for the terrestrial projection of this star the point L_a' or $D = 45°52'10"$N. G_a' = 96°06'00"E).

Second Calculation

[See Technical Note VII, Appendix C.]

Latitude		Longitude		Calculation of **D'** and **Z**		Calculation of **H$_{e'}$**	
Corrected position first observation:							
$L_{e'}$=	35° 40' 10"N	$G_{e'}$=	10° 03' 06"W	**Z**= N69° 20' W			
D=	45° 52' 10"N	G_a=	96° 06' 00"E	log tan **D**	0.01318	log sin **D**	$\overline{1}$.85598
		P =	106° 09' 06"E	cologcos **P**	-0.55567		
D'=	105° 06' 10"N			log tan **D'**	-0.56885	colog sin **D'**	0.01526
(**D'**-$L_{e'}$)	69° 26' 00"N			log tan (**D'**-$L_{e'}$)	0.4257	log cos(**D'**-$L_{e'}$)	$\overline{1}$.54568
				log tan **H$_{e'}$**	$\overline{1}$.4323	log sin **H$_{e'}$**	$\overline{1}$.41692
						H$_{e'}$ = 15°08'24"	
				log cos **Z'**	$\overline{1}$.8580	**H'$_0$** = 15°32'30"	
						(**H'$_0$** - **H$_{e'}$**) = +24'06"	
λ =	25'00"N	ϵ 9^{m}4		**Z'** = N46°10'E			
		g =	11'36"E	**V** = N20°40'E		(**H'$_0$** - **H$_{e'}$**) = + 26'07"	
L_0=	36° 05' 10"N	G_0=	9° 51' 30"W	**Z'-V** = 25°30'		sin **O**	

[λ = dLatitude; g = dLongitude; ϵ = Departure, miles east or west]

After having calculated (**H'$_0$**-**H$_{e'}$**) and **Z'**, we have drawn from **Z'** the azimuth perpendicular to that of the first observation and making an acute angle with that of the second. Thus, we have obtained the course **V** from the final dead reckoning calculation. The number of miles from this calculation has been obtained by searching the Traverse Tables with the number of minutes of longitude corresponding to (**H'$_0$**-**H$_{eve}$**) miles at the latitude (**Z'-V**).

In working thus, one will avoid making a mistake in the direction of **V** because (**Z'-V**) must always be less than 90°.

See Figure 9 corresponding to the above calculations.

e is the estimated position from the first calculation.
ee' = 28 ¾ miles N69°20'W.
e' is the corrected position used in the second
  calculation.
e'e" = 24.1 miles N46°10'E.
Oe'e" = 25°30', and **e'O** = 26.7 miles N20°40'E.
O is the observed position.

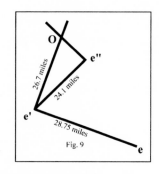

Fig. 9

2nd example. The estimated position is
58°47'N, 2°39'E and one has:

Givens:

	Corrected Altitude	Corresponding Declination	Corresponding True Time in Paris
1st observation	30°30'	1°09'00"South	$22^h53^m25.3^s$
Estimated travel in the interval 11 miles to N63°W true.			
2nd observation	31°00'	1°10'40"South	$0^h31^m56.6^s$

Required: the position of the 2nd observation.

1st	Formulae	Latitude	Longitude	$\tan D' = \dfrac{\tan D}{\cos P}$ $\cos Z = \tan(D'-L_e)\tan H_e$	$\sin H_e = \dfrac{\sin D}{\cos P}\cos(D'-L_e)$
		Estimated. position.		[Logarithms]	[Logarithms]
C		58° 47' 10" N	2° 30' 00" E		
a	θ	1° 69' 00" N	16° 38' 40" E	$\overline{2}$.30263	$\overline{2}$.30255
l	P		14° 08' 40" E	0.01337	
c	D'	1° 11' 10" N		$\overline{2}$.31600	1.68409
u	(D'-L_e)	57° 35' 50" S		0.1975	$\overline{1}$.72905
l	H_e			$\overline{1}$.7840	$\overline{1}$.71569
a	Z			$\overline{1}$.9815	H_e 31° 18' 27"
t			ε 13m,8		H_o 30° 30' 00"
i	λ	46' 24" N	g = 27' 00" W	Z= S16° 35' E	- 48' 27"
o		Corrected Position			
n		59° 33' 24" N	2° 03' 00" E		
			ε 9.8m		
	DR in the interval				
	λ	5' 00"N	g = 19'06"W	N63°00' W	11.0^{miles}

2nd		Position corrected to second time.			
C		59° 38' 24" N	1° 43' 54" E		
a	θ	1° 10' 40" N	8° 44' 09" W	$\overline{2}$.31300	$\overline{2}$.31291
l	P		10° 28' 03" W	0.00729	
c	D'	1° 11' 52" N		$\overline{2}$.32020	1.67981
u	(D'-L_e')	58° 26' 32" S		0.2117	$\overline{1}$.71880
l	H_e'			$\overline{1}$.7783	$\overline{1}$.71152
a	Z'			$\overline{1}$.9900	H_e' 30° 58' 30"
t			ε 3m,0	Z'= S12° 15' W	H'_o 31° 00' 00"
i	λ	54" S	g = 5' 54" W	V'= S73° 25' W	+ 1' 30"
o		Observed Position at second time		Z'-V' 61° 10'	+ 3^m .1
n		59° 37' 20" N	1° 38' 00" E		

Figure 10, adjacent, illustrates the preceding calculation.

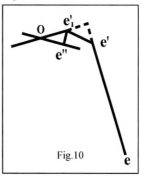

Fig.10

e is the estimated position that was used in the first calculation.

ee' is the first correction - 48.6 miles N16°35'W.

e'e'$_1$ is the track in the interval - 11 miles N63°W.

e'$_1$e'' = 1.5 miles to S12°15'W.

e'$_1$o is the second correction, 3.1 miles S73°25'W.

O is the observed position.

The direct, rigorous calculation will give as the observed position L_o = 59°37'30", G_o = 1°37'54". One sees that the result that has been obtained is one of perfect exactness. One may not always expect to obtain exactness this great. It happens in this special case with such fortunate circumstances that the azimuth calculated in the first observation is very nearly equal to the angle between the bearing of the two points estimated and observed. The observations are in the worst conditions for the determination of position. The angle of observation of only 29° is too small. An error of 1' in the measurement of altitudes would falsify the position by a little more than two miles. The error in latitude would be small but the error would be almost entirely in longitude.

The Case Where One of the Observations Is Made Near the Meridian.
[See Technical Note VIII, Appendix C.]

For an observation made at the meridian, the difference G_a-G_e or **P** is zero, and the formulae are as follows:

$$D = D'; \sin H_e = \cos(D-L_e) \text{ or } H_e = 90°-(D-L_e); \cos Z = 1 \text{ or } Z = 0.$$

Thus, one has H_e and **Z**. The rest of the calculation is made in the same fashion.

First example – Suppose that one has made an observation in the morning and an altitude of the sun at noon; take 50°00' as the meridian altitude and 15°S as the corresponding declination of the sun.

Position obtained from the estimated position corrected to noon.

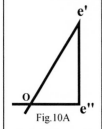

Fig.10A

$\begin{cases} \text{e' morning position corrected to noon; e'e''} = 30^{\text{miles}} \text{ S;} \\ \text{e''e'o} = 30°; \underline{e}\text{''o} =17.4^{\text{miles}} \text{ or } 19'18"W \\ \text{o observed position} \end{cases}$

Observation

Morning	$L_{e'}$	25° 30' 00"N	$G_{e'}$	40° 20' 00"W	Z=S60°E
At noon	D θ	15° 00' 00"			
	$D-L_{e'}$	40° 30' 00"			
	$H_{e'}$	49° 30' 00"			
	H_o	50° 00' 00"	ε = 17.4^{mi}		Z'= South
$H_o-H_{e'}$ or λ		+30' 00"S	g	19' 18" W	V=S30°W
	L_o	25° 00' 00"N	G_o	40° 39' 18"W	

To derive **e''o**, it is sufficient to take from the Traverse Tables the departure corresponding to the course angle of 30° and difference of latitude of 30 miles, without using the distance **e'o**.

The calculated position was prepared before noon and it takes only an instant to complete it.

Second example – One has taken an altitude of the sun at noon and another observation at night.

Given at the time of the night observation, L_o = 25°00'N; the latitude derived from that at noon, and $G_{e'}$ = 40°10'E as the estimated longitude. With this position, calculate the second observation. $(H'_o - H_{e'})$ = - 25'30" and Z' = S48°W are the results obtained.

End of the calculation

1st observation
L_0 = 25°00' N
$G_{e'}$ = 40°10' W
Z north or south

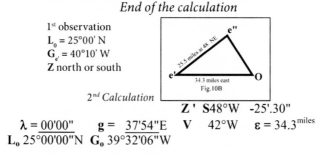

Fig.10B

2nd Calculation

Z' S48°W -25'.30"

$\lambda = \underline{00'00"}$ $g = \underline{37'54"E}$ V 42°W $\varepsilon = 34.3^{miles}$
L_0 25°00'00"N G_0 39°32'06"W

It is evident that in the preceding case there is no advantage to utilize the estimated altitude. Since one knows the latitude from the first observation, it will be much more rigorous to calculate the longitude directly by the usual method. The example has been given to show how one may proceed if one always wishes to use the kind of calculation which has been given here and which consists of finding the distance and the great circle route from one point to another on a sphere.

Comments on the Method.

We do not think that anyone still uses this method to calculate approximately one point on a sphere given by its distances from two known points when one has previously determined a position near the sought after position. This method of calculation is applicable to the same problem on a plane. A numerical example will make the idea perfectly understandable.

We will assume rectangular coordinates and we will use the same notations, **L** and **G**, North or South, East or West as they were given on the sphere.

Derive (Figure 11) the point **x** situated at 43 meters from point **a** and at 58 meters from point **a'**. The coordinates of **a** and **a'** are (L_a = 63 meters N, G_a = 17 meters W). ($L_{a'}$ = 22 meters N, $G_{a'}$ = 50.4 meters E) and knowing the approximated point **e** (L_e = 35 meters N, G_e = 4.1 meters E.)

By means of the coordinates of **e** and of **a**, with the table of right triangles [Traverse Tables] one has calculated the length and direction of **ea**, from which one may derive that of **ee'** and the coordinates of **e'**. Using the same method one has calculated the points **e'** and **a'**, the length and direction of **e'e''**. From this one has derived, by means of the right triangle **e''e'o**, the length and direction of **e'o** and the coordinates of **o**. The point **o** at the intersection of two tangents to the circles at **e'** and at **e''**, may be considered as the point **x** itself if the point **e** is sufficiently near.

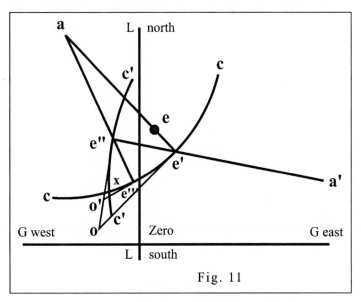

Fig. 11

L.		G.	Azimuth	Distances
e	35.0N	4.1E		35= ea
a	63.0N	17.0W		42= e'a
(a - e)	28.0N	21.1W	Z = N37°W	8= ee'
(e' - e)	6.4S	4.8E		
e'	28.6N	8.9E		
a'	22.0N	50.4E		
(a'-e')	6.6S	41.5E	Z' = S81°E	42= e'a
				58= e''a'
				-16= e'a''
o-e'	13.8S	18.4W	V N52°E	-23= e'o
o	12.8N	9.5W	46°	

In the case where one wishes a better approximation, after having obtained **e'e''**, one calculates the coordinates of **e''**, similarly the length and direction of **e''e'''** and one determines the point **o'**, and so on. One may also start the calculation again with the point **o** considered as the estimated position.

It is clear that if one wishes a perfectly exact solution, it will be preferable to make a direct calculation that consists of the solution to the equations for two circles:

$$(L-63)^2 + (G+17)^2 = 43^2; \ (L-22)^2 + (G-50.4)^2 = 58^2.$$

The approach that has been followed in the preceding calculation for a plane is precisely that which has been adopted for the analogous calculation on a sphere. It is only that the altitudes are used in place of the zenith distances, which amounts to the same and avoids the simple operation of taking the complement of the altitudes. Applied to the determination of a position at sea, having a reasonably good approximation, this method will give a sufficiently exact position. However, if the errors in the advancement of the line of position are so great that they become unacceptable, then it will be necessary to make a second approximation in the same fashion as we did on the plane. Very small zenith distances or very unfavorable angles of observation also may make a second approximation necessary even with only an ordinary error in the estimated position. In addition, one should note that, all other data being equal, the more the angle between the two circles, that is to say, the angle of observation, will approach a right angle, the more point *o* will approach point **x**, because the second tangent, that at **e''**, then becomes smaller and smaller. This is one more reason if one uses this method of calculation, to be sure that the angle between observations approaches 90°.

The method of calculation ordinarily used consists of making, *in every case*, two calculations of longitude with the estimated latitude. Thus, obtain a point on each geometrical path and construct two tangents at these points, from which one calculates the point of intersection, generally by the method of Pagel. In this fashion, the estimated longitude is completely neglected. It will certainly be more logical if one would use only one of the elements of the estimated position, the one believed to be the least erroneous. Or better, without knowing which one is the most likely in error, it is better to follow the procedure given before in a *Note sur le point observé, (Revue maritime, October 1873)* where it is thus formulated: "For the observations closer to the prime vertical than to the meridian, make a calculation of longitude with the estimated latitude. For the observations closer to the meridian than the prime vertical, make the calculation of latitude with the estimated longitude. Afterwards, correct the position." We have not gone into the details of the calculation. A figure illustrating a specific case will help in understanding the importance of this. Let **cc** and **c'c'** (Figure 12) be the projections on the chart of two circles where their intersection determines **x** that we want to determine. Take **e** as the estimated position. Construct the parallel through **e** that cuts the two curves at **b** and **b'**. By the usual method, these are the two positions that one determines and the position of the observation is the point of intersection **o"** of the tangents at **b** and **b'**. If one of the observations is made close to the meridian, be aware that if there is an error in the estimated latitude, the point **o"** will be considerably distant from point **x**, since one of the tangents starts from a very distant point[1].

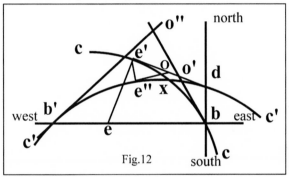

Fig.12

---

[1] Different methods have been proposed to correct for the inexactness in the usual method when the altitudes are taken close to the meridian. One can find at the end of the work of *M.le lieutenant de vaisseau* Hilleret, about the curves of altitude (*Revue maritime, May 1874*) the example noted above calculated with five different methods, the observations are made close to the meridian, one is at 16° to the East [of the meridian] and the other at 13° to the West [of the meridian].

In this specific case, the calculation by Pagel usually employed, gives 10 miles of error in the result; the three following methods give a position with an exactness of 2.8 to 3 minutes but requires the use of second differences or the use of geographic constructions and of special tables. These four methods use the estimated latitude and neglect the longitude, and even with this complicated calculation, they do not arrive exactly at the correct result.

[Footnote continues, next page]

If one follows the procedure given above, with the first observation, which is closer to the prime vertical than the meridian, one calculates a longitude with the estimated latitude that will give point **B**. The second observation, to the contrary, being nearer to the meridian than to the prime vertical, is calculated with the estimated longitude. That is to say, with the longitude of point **B**, one calculates a latitude that will give point **d**. Correcting the position in the usual manner and replacing the coefficient $\frac{d\mathbf{G}}{d\mathbf{L}}$ with the coefficient $\frac{d\mathbf{L}}{d\mathbf{G}}$ calculated by the logarithmic differences or by the azimuth or otherwise, one will obtain as the position the point **o'**, most likely more exact than **o"** and with no additional calculation. This procedure seems to us like progress compared to the way the calculation usually is made. It presents, it is true, the inconvenience of having to change the calculation according to the direction of the observation. The method we propose today avoids this inconvenience (in the case of Figure 12, the position that one will obtain, in practice, will be the position **o** obtained after having determined **e'** and **e"**). In all probability, the results will be more exact and this offers another advantage and that is to determine immediately the position that one should adopt if one does not have another observation. The calculation is simple because it always consists of calculating the distance and the direction from one point to another, and we are convinced that one could become comfortable with it as easily as one has become comfortable with the hour angle, and without the need of a special table. The calculation of the correction, which is a Dead Reckoning calculation currently used in navigation, is made very easily. Perhaps we should add that from the moment that one gives up the direct calculation as too

---

The fifth method, called the curves of altitude by Mr. Hilleret himself, gives an exact position by an ingenious calculation that makes use of meridional parts or Naperian logarithms instead of common logarithms; but the precision obtained has nothing to do with the method of calculation. It functions uniquely from the use of estimated longitude to calculate the latitude, totally neglecting the estimated latitude. By doing so, one also has followed the method given above. One will obtain the same result identically and more simply by calculating two latitudes and the coefficients $\frac{d\mathbf{L}}{d\mathbf{G}}$ by the usual method with the two altitudes and the estimated longitude and then correcting the estimated position as one usually does with the two calculated longitudes and the coefficients $\frac{d\mathbf{G}}{d\mathbf{L}}$.

long and that one takes recourse to calculation of an assumed position, the method of estimated altitudes is the most reasonable. From this it is well understood that taking an altitude is exactly the same as measuring the distance from a point given by the time on the chronometer. What is more natural than to verify if the estimated position is found at the calculated distance, and if you cannot find it there, to correct it as a consequence?

Simplification of the Calculations.

We have seen that, when using the method of estimated altitudes, in every case one must calculate the direction Z and the complement of 90°, H_e, from the distance from point e situated at latitude L_e, to point a situated at latitude D. The difference in the longitude of the two points is equal to P. The simplified calculations arranged according to the specific values that P, D, and L might have, will be presented very briefly.

To start, we remark that H_e must be derived sufficiently accurately since one will calculate the number of miles that it has to be carried in a certain direction. On the contrary, it is sufficient in practice to have the value of Z that determines this direction to ± one-half degree.

If the angles P and Z are quite small, one may accept the ratios $\frac{Z}{P}$ and $\frac{\sin Z}{\sin P}$ as equal. One will calculate Z by the formula $Z = P\frac{\cos D}{\cos H_e}$, which can be done without logarithms by means of the Traverse Tables. One may calculate in this manner so long as Z and P do not exceed 25°. One will know this in advance since P is given and one will always know approximately the direction in which one has made the observation.

Example: P = 14°30', D = 30°00', H_e = 60°00'. With the Traverse Tables one finds:

$$\frac{14.5}{\cos 60°} = 29;\ 29 \times \cos 30° = 25.1 \text{ from which } Z = 25°06'.$$

The exact value of Z will be 25°42' with a negligible difference of 36'.

If P = 0 (meridian altitude) one has: $H_e = 90°-(D-L)$, Z = 0.

If D = 0, one has: $\sin H_e = \cos L \cos P$.

$$\cos Z = \tan L \tan H_e \text{ where } \sin Z = \frac{\sin P}{\cos H_e}$$

If L = 0, one has $\sin H_e = \cos D \cos P$.

$$\cos Z = \frac{\sin D}{\cos H_e} \text{ where } \sin Z = \tan P \tan H_e.$$

If **D** is small and at the same time **P** is such that **D'** also is small, take them as identical and accepting the ratios $\dfrac{\tan D'}{\tan D''}; \dfrac{D'}{D}$ and $\dfrac{\sin D'}{\sin D}$ as equal, the general formula for triangles can then be written:

(1) $D' = \dfrac{D}{\cos P}$; (2) $\sin H_e = \cos P \cos(D'-L_e)$; (3) $\cos Z = \tan H_e \tan(D'-L_e)$.

Formula (1) is calculated with the Traverse Tables. One may use these formulae when **D'** does not exceed 3°.

If P = 90°, one has: $\sin H_e = \sin D \sin L_e$ $\begin{cases} \cos Z = \dfrac{\tan H_e}{\tan L_e} \\ \sin Z = \dfrac{\cos D}{\cos H_e} \end{cases}$

When **D** differs little from 90°, as is the case with the pole star, call **Δ** the complement of **D**. Then one will have $H_e = L_e + \Delta \cos P$; $Z = \Delta \dfrac{\sin P}{\cos H_e}$. These formulae can be calculated with the Traverse Tables. *Example*:

Calculation of an Observation of the Pole Star.
[See Technical Note IX, Appendix C.]

At the estimated position 59°30' N and 15°00' W, one has observed H_0 of the pole star as 59°50', the terrestrial coordinates of the star being $\Delta = 1°21'24''$, $G_a = 80°00'E$.

L_e	59°30'00"N	G_e	15°00'00"W	$\Delta \sin P$	81'
Δ	1°21'24"	G_a	80°00'00"E		
$\Delta \cos P$	-7'06"	P	95°00'00"E		
H_e	59°22'54"			$\Delta \dfrac{\sin P}{\cos H_e}$	161'
H_0	59°50'00"	ε	1.3^{miles}		
$H_0 - H_e$ or λ	+27'06"	g	2'30"E	Z	N2°41'E
L_e	59°57'06"	G_e	14°57'30"W		

We do not think that one should consider in every case, the observation of the pole star as having been made at the meridian and to neglect its azimuth, which may be as large as 3° at a latitude of 60°. If, for the determination of position, this observation is combined with another which itself has been made at less than 30° to 40° from the meridian, it may result in a measurable error from the exact position.

When **P** is included in the limit of circummeridian altitudes (this limit is given in the tables. One knows that it depends on the values of L and D and of the accuracy desired), one calculates the correction **C** to make to the altitude where the angle is **P**, and one will have:

$$H_e = 90°-(D-L_e)-C; \quad Z = P\dfrac{\cos D}{\cos H_e}. \; \textit{Example:}$$

Calculation of a Circummeridian Observation.

At an estimated position (EP) of 25°00' S and 30°00' W, one has obtained $H_o \theta$ = 54°20', the terrestrial coordinate of θ being 10° N and 25° W.

Calculation.

Latitude		Longitude	αP^2 and $Z = P\dfrac{\cos D}{\cos H_e}$		$H_e = 90° - (D - L_e) - \alpha P^2$	
			3.06"			
Est.Posit. (EP)	25°00'00"S	30° 00'00" W	× 400			55°00' 00"
Celestial body	10°00'00"N	25° 00'00" W	1224	or		-20' 24"
Difference	35°00'00"	5° 00'00" E			H_e	54°39' 36"
		or 20.0^{minutes}	$P \cos D$ 4.9°		H_o	54°20' 00"
		ε 2.9^{miles}				
λ	19'24"S	g 3' 12"W	Z 8.5° N E		$H_o - H_e$ -19' 36"	
Correct Position	25°19'24"S	30° 03'12" W				

The exact calculation will give H_e 54°39'00" and Z = 8°34'.

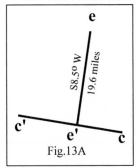

Fig.13A

S8.5° W
19.6 miles

One was satisfied with the first term, αP^2, of the correction. If the approximation is not sufficient with the first term, it will be simpler to make the usual calculation than to attempt the calculation of the second or third terms. The result has been, as for the other observations, the corrected position and the azimuth with which one will calculate the exact position with a second observation.

There will be several other specific cases to examine. One will easily see the simplifications that result with these calculations. We are going to apply the simplifications we have just seen to the calculation of the position determined by the two observations given on page [B2-352].

Example: [See Technical Note X, Appendix C.]

At estimated position 58°N and 1°00'E, one has taken:

	$H_o \theta$	$D \theta$	$G_a \theta$
1st observation	30°30'00"	1°09'00"N	16°38'40"E
In the interval, made 11 miles on course N63°W true.			
2nd observation	31°00'00"	1°10'40"N	8°44'09"W

Calculation

Fig.13B

Le	58' 30" 00" N	Ge 1° 00' 00" E		$CosP* = \overline{1}.98362$
D	1° 09' 00" N	Ga 16° 38' 40" E		$cos(D'-Le) = \overline{1}.73251$
D'	1° 11' 36" N	P 15° 38' 40" E		$sin He = \overline{1}.71613$
D'-Le	57° 18' 24" S	ε 15.8^{miles}		He 31° 20' 33"
First				Ho 30° 30' 00"
correction λ 48' 00" N	g 30'36"W	Z S18.2°E		- 50' 33"
	ε 9.8^{miles}		
Interval λ 5' 00" N	19'06" W	N63°W	11^{miles}
Le' 59° 23' 00" N	Ge' 0° 10' 18" E	1270	90°-(D-Le') 31° 47' 40"
		1"18	
		1016	
		127	
		127	
D 1° 10' 40" N	Ga 8° 44' 09" W	1499" or	24' 59"
D-Le' 58° 12' 20" S	P 8° 51' 27" W		He 31° 22' 41"
	or 35.6^{miles}		Ho -31° 00' 00"
	ε 45.0^{miles}	Z' S10.4°W	-22' 41"
Second			
correction λ 14' 48" N	g 1° 28' 42" E	V S71.8°W	-47.4^{miles}
Lo 59° 37' 48" N	Go 1° 39' 00" E	61.4°	

[*The notation cosP = $\overline{1}$.98362 indicates the value minus 1. See Appendix C Page [C-1].]

The position thus obtained is only one-half mile from the exact position whereas the estimated position was in error by 70 miles.

In the first calculation one has followed what has been said for the case where **D** and **D'** are sufficiently small. The second observation has been calculated as circummeridian. In the two calculations the azimuth has been taken from the Traverse Tables by the formula $Z = \dfrac{P}{\cos H}$ neglecting cosD

One sees that the method of determining position is always the same and that the method given above is only a simplification in the calculation of the distance and direction from one point to another. We have made the calculations in the manner we believe to be most clear - by leaving aside the calculations of the terrestrial coordinates of the celestial body and of corrections of altitude which have to be made first and which we think are preferable to set aside.

Order of calculations: If the two observations are made at an interval, it is always normal practice to calculate the first, to correct that which is erroneous about that position and then do the second calculation to determine the exact position. When one makes the calculations all at the same time, without being forced to calculate the observations in the order in which they have been made, it is advantageous to start with the observation that is closest to the direction of the suspected error in the dead reckoning.

Thus, if the two observations are made, one to the North-East and the other to the East-South-East, and that one knows to have been driven to the South-South-West or to the North-North-East, it will be preferable to calculate first that to the North-East and follow with that of the East-South-East. If one has been displaced in the direction one has estimated, the first corrected position approaches the true position and the definitive position will be very exact.

If one has no indication of the probable direction of the error of the dead reckoning, generally it will be preferable to start with the observation where the angle P is the closest to 90°. Finally, the order in which the calculations are made has little importance. The two points obtained by starting with one or the other observation are different from each other but both are sufficiently exact.

Observations Near the Zenith.

[See Technical Note XI, Appendix C.]

In this case, the zenith distance is small. One will make the calculation in the following manner, more exactly and more simply than in the preceding method. If one calls $\varphi(x)$ the function of x equal to $\dfrac{2\sin^2 \frac{x}{2}}{\sin 1''}$, one finds by a simple transformation that the general formula

$\cos N = \sin L \sin D + \cos L \cos D \cos P$ may be written

$\varphi(N) = \varphi(D-L) + \cos L \cos D \times \varphi(P)$.

This formula can be calculated from Table XLI of Caillet which gives $\varphi(x)$ for the angles x less than 7°45'. One derives the estimated zenith distance from which one will subtract the observed zenith distance. The azimuth will be given by the formula $Z = \dfrac{P \cos D}{N}$ which resolves with the Traverse Tables. The rest of the calculation continues in the usual fashion[1].

---

[1] The formula that follows can be used to calculate the hour angle P, knowing the three sides such that **N** and **P** are found within the limits of the table. It would be desirable that this table be extended like Table XLII, that gives the logarithm of the function φ.

Example: At a estimated position 10°20'N and 40°05'W, one has obtained:

G	H₀θ		Dθ	Gθ or **Paris True time**
i	1ˢᵗ observation	83°37' 00"	14° 22' 15"N	35° 53' 45" W
v	Route in the interval	{ before noon 2.4ᵐⁱˡᵉˢ toward N13°W		
e		{ after noon 1.6ᵐⁱˡᵉˢ toward N13°W		
n	2ⁿᵈ observation	84°14' 30"	14° 22' 54"N	43° 40' 24" W

Required, the position at noon.

Calculation
[See Technical Note XII, Appendix C.]

$$\begin{cases} \varphi(N_e) = \varepsilon(D-L) + \cos L \cos D \times \varphi(P) \\ \sin Z = \dfrac{P \cos D}{N_e} \quad [\text{Distances}] \end{cases}$$

	Latitude		Longitude			
Estimated Position	10° 20' 00"N		40° 05' 00"W	$\varphi(P)$	555.0	
				× cos L	546.2	
1ˢᵗ celestial body	14° 22' 15"N		35° 52' 45"W	× cos D		529.1 2ⁿᵈ term
						.....511.9 φ(D – L)
						1041.0 φ(Nₑ)
Difference	4° 02' 15"N		4° 12' 15"E	23ᵐⁱⁿ02ˢᵉᶜ−	5° 45' 30" (Nₑ)
				$\sin Z = \dfrac{4.1}{5.8}$		
	or 16ᵐⁱⁿ09ˢᵉᶜ	or	16ᵐⁱⁿ49ˢ			6° 23' 00" Nₒ
1ˢᵗ Correction	26' 36"S		26' 48"W	Z N45°E		- 37' 30"
Before noon	2' 24"N		0' 36"W	N13W	2.4ᵐⁱˡᵉˢ	
Noon corrected	9° 55' 48"N		40° 32' 24"W			
Afternoon	1' 36"N		24"W	N13W	1.6ᵐⁱˡᵉˢ	
2ⁿᵈ position corrected	9° 57' 24"N		40° 32' 48"W		307.0	293.0
					302.4	614.8
2ⁿᵈ Celestial body	14° 22' 54"N		43° 40' 24"W			907.8
Difference	4° 25' 30"N		3° 07' 36"W	21ᵐⁱⁿ30.6ˢᵉᶜ−	5°22' 39" Nₑ
	or 17ᵐⁱⁿ42ˢᵉᶜ		or 12ᵐⁱⁿ30.4ˢᵉᶜ	$\sin Z' = \dfrac{3.0}{5.4}$	5° 45' 30" Nₒ
						22' 51"
				Z ' N34°W		
2ⁿᵈ correction	16' 14"S		16' 42 E	V N45°W	-23.2ᵐⁱˡᵉˢ
Noon observed	9° 39' 24"N		40° 15' 42"W	11°	

The factor $\varphi(P)$ multiplied by cosL and then by cosD has been taken from the Traverse Tables. The calculation by logarithms would be a little longer.

The estimated position was in error by 44 miles; the corrected position by the first observation in error by less than 23 miles, the final position is exact to about 6/10 mile. This trivial error derives from the fact that since the distances are small, the circles of observation are accentuated curves (see page [B2-373] if one wishes to have a more correct approximation.) The observations are made under very good conditions – they strike an angle of 79° and are separated by less than one-half hour, thus avoiding even the smallest errors in dead reckoning.

Use of the Traverse Tables to resolve spherical triangles: One has seen that frequently the azimuth has been obtained from the Traverse Tables without calculation. Thus, one should do this every time when one wishes to have an angle when great precision is not needed. *Examples:*

1st. Find Z knowing $P = 45°30'$, $D = 17°00'$, $H = 40°30'$, one has $\sin Z = \frac{\sin P \cos D}{\cos H}$. Take any radius, 100 for example. The Traverse Tables give:

$100 \sin P = 71.4$; $71.4 \cos D = 68.3$; $\frac{68.3}{\cos H} = 89.9 = 100 \sin Z$;

$Z = 64°$; or exactly $63°45'$.

2nd. $\sin x = \sin 3° \frac{\sin 75°}{\sin 50°}$. x being small, one may assume $\frac{\sin x}{\sin 3°} = \frac{x'}{180'}$ and one will have $180' \sin 75° = 174'$; $\frac{175'}{\sin 50°} = 227'$; $x = 3°47'$, the exact value.

3rd. $\sin x = \frac{\sin 3°20'}{\sin 7°10'} \cos 40°$, where approximately $\sin x = \frac{200 \cos 40°}{430}$, $200 \cos 40° = 153.2$ $\sin x = \frac{153.2}{430}$ $x = 20°50'$, or exactly $20°55'$.

It is precisely this last case that has been used in the preceding calculation to get the azimuths. All these calculations were made by eye without having anything in writing.

4th. Find the azimuth of a celestial body having two adjacent observations of the celestial body. [**See Technical Note XIII Appendix C.**]

With the formula $\sin H = \sin L \sin D + \cos L \cos D \cos P$, differentiating H with respect to P, L and D being constant, gives:

$\sin Z = \frac{-dH}{dP \cos L}$ from which one takes the value of Z. *Example:*

Being at $40°00'$ latitude one has obtained:

	Time by Chronometer	Altitude
First observation	3^h25^m	$36°20'$
Second observation	3^h27^m	$36°30'$
from which	-0^h02^m so that $dP = -0°30'$ $H = 0°10'$	

and $\sin Z = \frac{10}{23}$ and $Z = 25°45'$.

5th. Calculate the direct course from a position situated at 15° S and 160° E, to the position situated at 60° S and 56° E. [**See Technical Note XIV, Appendix C.**]

Formula: $\cot Z = \dfrac{\tan 60° \cos 15°}{\sin 104°} - \dfrac{\sin 15°}{\tan 104°}$

The Transverse Tables give on sight:

First term × 50^{miles} = 86.2

Second term × 50^{miles} = –3.2 South-West

$\cot Z = \dfrac{89.4}{50}$, $Z = $ S29°15'W to ± one-half degree

One sees that this method uses the natural values instead of the logarithms.

6th. Calculate the change, dP, in the value P for a given change, dL, in L, H and D being constant and knowing Z. One uses the relation $dP = \dfrac{dL \cot Z}{\cos L}$ derived from the formula $\sin H = \sin L \sin D + \cos L \cos D$ cos P, differentiated with respect to L and to P, given L = 30°, Z = N40°W, $dL = 9'$N. The Traverse Tables give without calculation $dP = 12.4'$E. (The Pagel correction is the same as dP in seconds of time for $dL = 1'$; it is equal to $\dfrac{4 \cot Z}{\cos L}$ and in this case, to 5.5^{seconds}). In the same way, one can find dP knowing dL.

Conversely, knowing dL, dP, and L, find Z.

Given L = 30°, $dL = 1'$N; $dP = 5.5''$ or 1.375'E, one has $\cot Z = 1.375$ cos 30°, from which Z = N40°W or S40°E.

It is useless for us to extend any more the examples of what one may take from the tables of right rectangular triangles for the calculations at sea. They may replace the many small, specific tables that one has taken the pain to calculate.

Similarly, a table of spherical right triangles calculated from the formula $\cos x = \cos z \cos y$, giving one of the three angles x, y, or z, knowing the other two, permits the rapid resolution of the spherical triangles. This table could replace the tables of amplitude, of rising and setting of celestial bodies, and the tables made to compute the time under favorable circumstances.

Average value of several observations made on the same celestial body. We think that at sea one must take three sights for an observation to avoid the errors of the readings from the chronometer and the sextant, but it is useless to take more observations. The calculations will be made with the average of three times and three altitudes. One may obtain a separate result from each of the three observations in the following manner:

Make **h** the time and **H** the altitude from the first observation. d**h** is the difference in time, and d**H** is the difference in altitude between the first and the second observation. The first observation will be calculated as usual, giving H_e and **Z** for results.

The second estimated altitude, H'_e will be given by the formula $H'_e = H_e + d$hcosLsinZ, taken from the previously cited relation dH = $-d$PcosLsinZ, and neglecting the true movement of the celestial body, that of the observer and the rate of the chronometer. (d**h** must be given a sign: minus when the celestial body is in the west.)

The correction given by the first observation is H_o-H_e. The second correction is H'_o-H'_e or $H_o + d$H-H_e-$d$hcosLsinZ. The average will be $(H_o\text{-}H_e) + \dfrac{d\text{H} - d\text{hcos Lsin Z}}{2}$. The Traverse Tables can be used to calculate d**h** cos **L** sin **Z**. One will do the same for three or more calculations.

Example: One has made three observations, latitude = 35°.

	Time				Apparent Altitude	
			Difference	Difference x cosL		Difference
First Observation	3^{hr} 35^{min} 20^{sec}				40° 20'00"	
Second	3^{hr} 35^{min} 45^{sec}		25^{sec}	20.5^{sec}	40° 25'00"	5'00"
Third	3^{hr} 36^{min} 25^{sec}		65^{sec}	53.2^{sec}	40° 31'15"	11'15"

Calculation of the first observation gives these results:
H_o = 40°31'00", H_e = 40°40'30", and Z = N60°E.

The two other observations will be dealt with properly as follows:

		Second Observation		Third observation	
			17.8^{sec}	46.1^{sec} $\Big\}$	dh cos L sin Z
	H_e	40° 40'30"	+4'27"	+11'31"	
	H_o	40° 31'00"	+5'00"	+11'15"	
Z N60°E		-9'30"	+33"	-16"	
			+6"	+17"	
Average		-9'24"			

The corrections 4'27" and 11'31" to make to the first estimated altitude to determine the two others are obtained by multiplying the differences 25^{sec} and 65^{sec} by cos L and then by sin Z, and then transforming them to minutes. They are positive because the celestial body is in the east.

The corrections to make to the position are: -9'30" for the first observation; -9'30"+33" for the second, and -9'30"-16" for the third, which gives the average correction of -9'24" to apply in the direction N60°E.

It is obvious that the two observations can be made and calculated at the same time by two different persons; in this case, one will

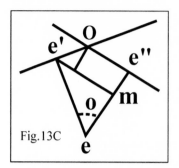

Fig.13C

obtain the position in the following manner: (Fig 13C) **e** is the estimated position that will serve in the two calculations. **ee'** and **ee"** are the two corrections obtained and **O** is the observed position. Construct **e'm** perpendicular to **ee"**.

One has: $\mathbf{e'o} = \dfrac{\mathbf{me''}}{\sin o} = \dfrac{\mathbf{ee''} - \mathbf{ee}\cos o}{\sin o} = \dfrac{\mathbf{ee''}}{\sin o} - \dfrac{\mathbf{ee'}}{\tan o}$ from which one can derive **e'o**. The position **O** can be obtained as usual.

Example: Given 30°10'N and 15°25'E as the estimated position; + 15 miles to N25°E, and 17 miles to S45°E are the two corrections found.

Calculation

Estimated Position	30° 10' 00"N	15° 25'00"W				
First correction	13' 36"N	7' 18"E	**Z**	N25°E+15^{mi}	$\dfrac{15}{\tan o} =$	- 5.5^{mi}
			Z'	S45°E-17^{mi}		
			o	= 110°	$\dfrac{-17}{\sin o} =$	-18.1^{mi}
Second correction	5' 18"N	12'54"W	**V**	S65°E		-12.6^{mi}
Observed position	30° 28' 54"N	15° 30'36"W				

When the angle of observation **o** is equal to 90°, the two corrections being made to the position are similarly given by the calculations. A sketch will avoid the errors of sign.

Approximations Given by the Calculation.

It seems to us necessary to determine, at least roughly, the approximations that one obtains by the calculations and thus to know if it is necessary to make a second calculation to obtain a more correct position[1].

---

[1] [**See Technical Note XV, Appendix C.**] One has assumed in the preceding that the curve corresponding to the observation is identical, within the limits of the calculation, to the tangent at the position. This hypothesis is acceptable in practice. However, in the case where the zenith distance is small and the curve is pronounced, this will need to be taken into account.

Given (Figure [14], on a sphere) **a** and **a'**, the projections of two celestial bodies, then **cc**, **c'c'**, the two circles corresponding to the

---

We are now going to determine the center and the radius of curvature at a point on the curve. We will then comment on how one will have to take these into account in the calculation.

Determination of the Center and the Radius of Curvature of a Given Point on a Curve of Observation.

Given on the chart (Figure A.) **cc** the curve, **z** the given position and **a** the terrestrial position of the celestial body. Construct the vertical of the celestial body **za**, the meridian and the parallel at **z**. The angles are projected in their true size. **Nza** is equal to the azimuth, **Z**, of the celestial body. The angle **cza** is a right angle, and **zn** on the scale of longitudes, is equal to the hour angle **P**. The tangent **zω** to **za** is perpendicular to the curve. Make the same for a point infinitely near, **z'**. The point **ω** is the point of intersection of the two infinitely close perpendiculars and is the center of curvature. The radius ρ is equal to **zω**. The angle **ω** is evidently the difference, dz, between the two azimuths at **z** and at **z'**. **zm** is the difference dP between the two hour angles.

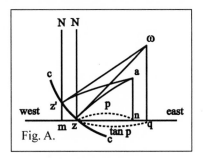

Fig. A.

The two triangles **zz'ω** and **zz'm** give:

$$zz' = \omega z \times \omega; \quad zz' = \frac{zm}{\cos z};$$ from which ωz or $\rho = \frac{dP}{dZ} \times \frac{1}{\cos z}$. In the triangle **PZA** on the sphere, one has $\frac{\sin P}{\sin Z} = \frac{\sin N}{\sin \Delta}$ and in this case, ω is constant; from which by differentiating, $\cos P \sin Z dP = \cos Z \sin P dZ$ or $\frac{dP}{dZ} = \frac{\tan P}{\tan Z}$; from which by replacement: $\rho = \frac{\tan P}{\sin Z}$. It is well understood that ρ must be measured on the scale of longitudes. One will have the value of the radius measured in radians, remembering that the radius is very approximately equal to the arc of 57.3°, which will give $\rho^\circ = \frac{57.3^\circ \tan P}{\sin Z}$.

The figure makes clear that the coordinates of ω will be given by the formulae:

$$(L_\omega)_c = (L_z)_c + 57.3^\circ \frac{\tan P}{\tan Z} \; ; \; G_\omega = G_z + 57.3^\circ \tan P.$$

If one deals with azimuth angles greater than 90°, one must always pay attention to the denomination of P and to the sign of tan P; the same for Z and tan Z. If P = 90°, the radius is infinite and the point Z is a point of inflection of the curve. If P is equal to 0° or to 180°, it is the same as Z; in place of the indeterminate ratios $\frac{\tan P}{\sin Z}$ and $\frac{\tan P}{\tan Z}$, one takes the following ratios as equal and determinable:

observations that determine the true position **x**. **o** is the observed position obtained using the points **e'**, **e"** and the tangents **e'o**, and **e"o**. The error in the position is measured by **ox** and will be called **E**. Draw the arcs **oa** and **oa'** which determine the points **m** and **m'** on the circles. [**See Technical Note XVI, Appendix C.**]

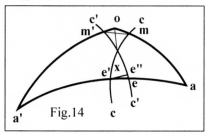

Fig.14

By considering the small spherical quadrangle **omxm'** as planar with right angles at **m** and **m'**, one has **ox** or $E = \dfrac{mm'}{\sin mom'}$,

$$(1)\quad E^2 = \frac{om^2 + om'^2 - 2om \times om' \times \cos mom'}{\sin^2 mom'}.$$

Consider the rhumb line arc **e'o** as identical to the arc of a great circle joining the two points. The triangle **oe'a** with a right angle at **e'** gives:

$$\frac{\cos H}{\cos D \cos P} \text{ and } \frac{\cos H}{\cos D} \times \frac{\cos Z}{\cos P}; \text{ both of which reduce to } \frac{\cos H}{\cos D}.\;{}^{\bullet}$$

Numeric example

Take 25°30'N and 15°25'W as the given position; also take **P** = 62°E, **Z** = S44°E.

				Latitudes	Meridional Parts	Longitudes
				Z 25°30'N	1583.2'N	15°25' W
The Traverse Tables give:	57.3°	tan 62° =	107.7°=			107°42' E
		$\dfrac{107.7°}{\tan 44°}$ =	111.5°=		6690.0S	
		$\dfrac{107.7°}{\sin 44°}$ =	155° = ρ	ω 64°29'S	5106.8'S	92°17' E

[The primary footnote continues]

${}^{\bullet}$ What we have just said is only a repetition in a little different form of that which we have said in a preceding note. One will find in the work of M. Hilleret, cited before, a more complicated demonstration, we think, of the value of the radius, based on the equation of a curve and the general formulae for the radii of curves. We believe the construction of the center that we have just given, to be very much simpler.

$$\tan\frac{(oa - e'a)}{2} = \frac{\tan^2\frac{e'o}{2}}{\tan\frac{oa + e'a}{2}}$$ where one makes $e'o = t$ and $e'a$ or $ma = N$,

$$\tan\frac{mo}{2} = \frac{\tan^2\frac{t}{2}}{\tan N}$$ and as t and om are small, $om = \frac{t^2}{2\tan N}$ (t is that which

has been called the second correction in the calculations.)

Similarly, one will have $om' = \frac{(e''o)^2}{2\tan N'}$ and, as one has $e''o = e'o\cos o =$

$t\cos o$, o being the angle of observation $ae'a'$ obtained as the difference

in the calculated azimuths of the two celestial bodies, it follows that

$om' = \frac{t^2\cos^2 o}{2\tan N'}$. If one calls r the ratio $\frac{\tan N}{\tan N'}$, the value of om is de-

rived from $om = \frac{t^2}{2r\tan N'}$. The angle mom' which is the corrected

angle of observation, may differ notably from $ae'a'$ or o. Never the

less, it will be a sufficient approximation to consider the two angles as

One will construct the center either by means of its coordinates or by drawing a line towards S44°E and with a length of 155° measured on the longitude
scale, or finally by taking the point on this line found at 92°17' East longitude.
This latter procedure is the most expedient, the line will be thus traced as one
knows, and the Traverse Tables will give the lon-
gitude on sight.

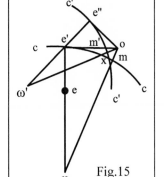

Fig.15

Calculation of a second approximation

Given (Figure 15) cc, and c'c', two curves of
observation that determine the exact position
x. o is the position obtained by the intersection
of the two tangents at e' and at e''. t miles is the
length of e'o and t' the length of e''o, equals tcoso.
ω and ω' are the centers of curvature of the two
curves, the radii ωo and ω'o will determine on
their curves the points m and m'. The triangle
e'ωo gives $\tan\omega = \frac{oe'}{\omega o'} = \frac{t}{\rho\cos L}$; a very approximate value of om in miles. $\alpha = \frac{t}{2}\sin\omega$. Similarly,
one will have in the triangle e''ω'o

$$\tan\omega' = \frac{t'}{\rho'\cos L} = \frac{t\cos o}{\rho'\cos L}\text{ and }\alpha' = \frac{t\cos o}{2}\sin\omega'.$$

With ω and ω' one corrects the azimuths z and z' from the two observations which will give the directions z and z' of oω and oω'. Knowing the
length and the direction of om and om', one will calculate the point of intersection of the tangents at m and m', as has been indicated for the case where
the two observations have been calculated with the same estimated position.
If the angle of observation o is convenient, most often t will be small and thus
α' will be negligible.

equal. Replacing **om, om'** and the angle **mom'** by their values in the formula (1), it follows;

$$E = \frac{t^2}{\tan N'} \times \frac{\sqrt{1 + r^2 \cos^4 o - 2r\cos^3 o}}{2r \sin o} = \frac{t^2}{\tan N'} \times K.$$

The following table gives the coefficient **K** for different values of **r** and **o**. For the values of **r** smaller than one, the coefficient has been multiplied by **r** in such a way that one must always take the ratio of **t²** to the tangent of the smallest zenith distance. In practice, the ratio $\frac{\tan N}{\tan N'}$ will be replaced by $\frac{N}{N'}$ and one can make the estimate by sight. Similarly, in place of $\frac{t^2}{\tan (N \text{ or } N')}$, one will take $\frac{t^2}{N \text{ or } N'}$, the zenith distance being expressed in minutes because **t** is expressed in miles; **E** will be given in miles. Never forget that **N** is the true zenith distance from the first calculation and **N'** that of the second calculation.

That which has been said assumes that one wants an exactitude that is not necessary in practice.

If by chance one wants a perfectly correct position, the simplest will be to renounce the calculations of an assumed position and make the direct calculation. In this case, one knows that one takes forward the first altitude to the time of the second along the course made good in the interval and the bearing from the first celestial body, observed or calculated. Subsequently, one resolves the spherical quadrangle **Paa'x** in which **a** and **a'** are the projections of the two celestial bodies, **P** is the pole and **x** is the true position. **ax** and **a'x** are

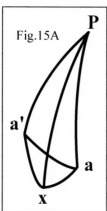

Fig.15A

equal to the two distances observed. The angle **P** is equal to the difference in the terrestrial longitudes of the two celestial bodies. The triangle **Paa'** gives **aa'** and one of the angles at **a** and at **a'**. The triangle **aa'x** gives the angle corresponding at **a** or to **a'**. Finally, one of the two triangles, **Pxa** or **Pxa'**, gives the co-latitude **Px** and one of the angles at **P** from which one derives the longitude. One has imagined various simplifications to this calculation that one generally calls, wrongly we think, the computation of the latitude by two altitudes and the interval. That is the calculation of position in all its generality. The interval in time between the observations has not to be considered except in the specific case where the sun has been observed two times and where the angle **P** is equal to the interval in true time.

Table of approximation: $E = \dfrac{t^2}{N \text{ or } N'} \times K.$

Angle of Observation O.

$\dfrac{\tan N}{\tan N'}$ or $\dfrac{N}{N'}$	15°	30°	45°	60°	75°	90°	105°	120°	135°	150°	165°
0	19.	10	7	6	5	5	5	6	7	10	19
1/8	17	9	»	5.	»	»	»	»	7.	11	21.
1/4	15	8.	6.	»	»	»	»	»	»	11.	23
1/3	13.	8	»	»	»	»	»	»	8	12	25
1/2	11	7	6	»	»	»	»	»	8.	13.	28
2/3	8.	6	5.	»	»	»	»	6.	9	14.	31
1	5	5	5	5	»	»	»	»	10	17	37
3/2	6.	4	3.	3.	3.	3.	3.	4.	7.	13.	31
2	9	»	2.	2.	2.	2.	2.	4	6.	12	27.
3	12	5	»	2	1.	1.	1.	3	5.	10.	24.
4	13.	5.	»	1.	»	1	»	2.	5	9.	22
8	15	6.	3	»	0	0.	0.	2	4.	8.	20.
∞	18	7.	»	»	»	0	»	»	3.	7.	18

The coefficient K is given in tenths. A dot following a number indicates that one must add half-tenth more. The sign » indicates that one may use the number above in the same column.

Example: Make N = 7°20', N' = 2°10', O = 130° and t = 30 miles; the table gives K = 4, from which $E = \dfrac{30^2}{130} \times 0.4 = 2.7$ miles.

Second example: Calculation from page [B2-362]. N = N' = 60°, O = 29°, t = 47.4 miles. In this case $\dfrac{N}{N'} = 1$. The table gives K = 5, from which $E = \dfrac{(47.4)^2}{3600} \times 0.5 = 0.3$ miles; the exact error is one-half mile.

Third example: Calculation from page [B2-364]. N = 6°23', N' = 5°45', O = 79°, t = 23.2 miles. $\dfrac{N}{N'}$ is a little greater than one; the table gives K = 4, from which $E = \dfrac{(23.2)^2}{345} \times 0.4 = 0.6$ miles which is the same error as calculated.

Examination of the table shows what one should find from the remainder of the discussion of the formula:

1st That the most favorable angle of observation for the calculation is 90°;

2nd That an acute angle of observation is preferable to an obtuse angle. That is to say, that it would be better to have an angle of 30° than an angle of 150°.

3rd That it is preferable to calculate the large zenith distance first and finish with the small one.

The table also shows that **K** increases rapidly if the angle of observation is smaller than 45° or larger than 135°. Thus it would be best, as much as possible, to keep it between these limits.

It is well understood that the error **E** that we just calculated only represents the error of the position arising from the calculation and in no way that which could derive from errors in the altitudes. One knows that, due to errors in the altitudes, the most favorable angle of observation also is 90°.

Second approximation: When the approximation obtained by use of the preceding table does not prove sufficient, it is recommended to make a new calculation with the position obtained as the estimated position. The second calculation will be necessary only when one or both of the two zenith distances is small or in the case of a very unfavorable angle of observation. *Example:*

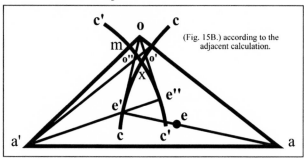

(Fig. 15B.) according to the adjacent calculation.

e is the estimated position			
ee' is the first correction	= - 40.9 miles to	S 72°	E
ee"	= - 42.5 miles to	S 63.5°	W
e'o is the second correction	= - 60.6 miles to	S 18°	W
o is the observed position			
oo' is the first correction	= 7.4 miles to	W 58°	E
o'o"	= 6.8 miles to	S 54°	W
o'x is the second correction	= 7.3 miles to	S 32°	W

x is the observed position. The position actually obtained is the crossing point of the tangents at **o'** and **o"**.

Calculation of a Double approximation.

[See Technical Note XVII, Appendix C.]

At an estimated position of 11°00' N and 25°42' W, one has observed:

		Zenith distance θ	Declination θ	G θ or the true time at Paris
Given	1st observation	3°54'18"	10°00'00"	22°35'00"
	2nd observation	3°25'24"	10°00'18"	28°50'00"

[St Hilaire lost accuracy by interpolating roughly in the traverse table (correct interval after noon is 1'34"N and 22"W) but we kept his values as they came straight from the tables. Concerning the azimuth he does not give any rule to determine the orientation. In this case, as the sun is north of the observer, the azimuth is NxyE before noon and NvwW after noon.]

Calculation

	Latitudes	Longitudes	$\varphi(N) = \varphi(P)\cos L \cos D + \varphi(D - L)$; $\sin Z = \dfrac{P \cos D}{N}$	Distances
	Est. position 11°00.0'N	25°42.0 W	$\varphi(P)$ 305.1 = 294.8 = $\varphi(P)\cos L \cos D$ × cos L 299.5	
1st A p p r o x	1st body 10° 00.0N	22°35.0' W	$\varphi(D - L)$ = 31.4	
	Difference 1°00.0'S	3°07.0' E	$\varphi(N_e)$ = 326.2	3° 13.4'= N_e
				3° 54.3'= N_o
	1st correction 12.7'N	39.6' W	Z S72°E	40.9'= N_o
	Corrected Posit 11°12.7'N	26°21.6' W	192.2 185.7 188.6	
	2nd body 10°00.3'N	28°50.0' W	45.7	
	difference 1°12.4'S	2°28.4' W	231.4	2° 42.9'= N'_e
				3° 25.4'= N'_o
			Z' S63.5°W	- 42.5'
	2nd correction 57.6'N	19.1' E	V S18.0°W	- 60.6'
	Observed Posit 12°10.3'N	26°02.5' W	45.5° E = $\dfrac{3670}{208}$ .x0.9= 16^{mi}	
2nd A p p r o x	Diff. 1st body 2°10.3'S	3°27.5'E	375.6 361.7 367.2 148.1 509.8	4° 01.7'
	1st Correction 3.9'S	6.5'E	Z_1 S58°W	+ 7.4'
	Corrected posit 12°06.4'N	25° 56.0'W	264.2 254.3 258.2 138.5	
	Diff 2nd body 2°06.1'S	2° 51.0'W	392.8	3° 32.2'
			Z'_1 S54°W	+ 6.8'
	2nd correction 6.2'S	4.0'W	V_1 S32°W	+ 7.3'
	Observed Posit 12°00.2'N	26° 00.0'W	22°	

As the calculation of the approximation has given 16 miles for the error **E**, one has done a second calculation which has given a position only 2/10 miles from the exact position, 12°N and 26°W. The table has given a correction too large, since the true angle of observation is but 112° while the same angle obtained by the two first azimuths is 135°.

In the case of small zenith distances, one may easily obtain a second approximation just as one would do on a plane. One calculates the change ΔZ in the first azimuth between the position **a** and the position **o** (Figure 15) this change is equal to the angle **oae'**, and is given by the formula $\tan \Delta Z = \dfrac{oe'}{e'a} = \dfrac{t}{N}$.

By applying this correction, one will obtain the corrected first azimuth $Z_1 \cdot$ **oo'** or α will be given by the formula $\alpha = \dfrac{t}{2} = \sin\Delta Z$. In the same manner, one can obtain the change, $\Delta Z'$, of the second azimuth as well as **om'** or α' by the formulae $\tan\Delta Z' = \dfrac{oe''}{a'e''} = \dfrac{t\cos o}{N'}$ and $\alpha' = \dfrac{t}{2} \cos o \sin\Delta Z'$. Knowing **om'** and **oo'** in length and direction, one will calculate the point of intersection of the tangents at **o'** and at **m'** as has been said on page [B2-368]. These calculations may be taken by sight from the Traverse Tables. Applying this method to the preceding:

		Latitude	Longitude			N_o 3° 54'
1st A				**Z**	S72.0° E	
p						N'_o 3° 25'
p				**Z'**	S63.5° W	
r				**V**	S18.0° W	-60.6 miles = **t**
o	Observed position	12° 10.3 N	26° 2.5' W		45.5°	
x				ΔZ	15.0°	
2nd A	1st correction	4.2' S	6.6' E	Z_1	S57.0° E	$\alpha=7.8^{mi}$ $\dfrac{\alpha}{\tan O'} = -2.5^{mi}$
p				$\Delta Z'$	S12.5°	$\alpha'=4.5^{mi}$ $\dfrac{\alpha'}{\sin O_1} = +4.7^{mi}$
p						
r				Z'_1	S51° W	
o				O_1	108°	
x	2nd correction	6.0' S	4.0' W	V_1	S33° W	difference $+7.2^{mi}$
	Observed Position	12° 00.1'N	29° 59.9'W			

The directions of the changes ΔZ and $\Delta Z'$ are easily seen from that of the second correction, **t**.

MARCQ SAINT-HILAIRE,
Capitaine de frégate.

(The conclusion in the next issue)
[*Revue maritime* March-August 1875]
[Not reproduced here]

Appendix C

TECHNICAL NOTES

Symbols and Definitions Used in Translations of Saint-Hilaire's Publications of October 1773 and August 1875.

Symbols

A - the geographic position of the star.

C - the Complement - in a log sin or log cos function indicates 1 minus the log of the function.

D - declination.

E - the ship's estimated position.

G_a - the longitude of the celestial body.

G_e - the longitude of the estimated position; $(G_a - G_e)$ = angle **P**.

H_o - observed altitude, the corrected sextant altitude.

H_e - altitude from the estimated (DR) position.

L_e - latitude of the estimated (DR) position.

O - the ship's true position.

P - the angle at the pole; the angle **APE,** or sometimes the angle **APZ**.

QQ' - the equator.

Z - the azimuth of the celestial body.

$\overline{\text{T}}$ - used with logarithms to indicate that, in modern usage, the value should be subtracted from 10 before adding or subtracting the logarithm.

α - corrected altitude of a celestial body.

λ - a correction to latitude.

φ - departure - distance made good East or West. Sometimes used to indicate **PK** and as φ' to indicate **ZK** when the celestial triangle is divided into two triangles.

g - a correction to longitude.

θ - the symbol for the sun; θ̲ - the symbol for the lower limb of the sun.

t - the second correction in the calculations.

aust. - austral - indicates Declination or Latitude South.

bor. - boreal indicates Declination or Latitude North.

dead reckoning position or **DR position** - position corrected for course and speed but not corrected for wind and current.

estimated position – **DR** position corrected for wind and current.

track - course steered during the interval.

Definitions

Astre - a celestial body, not limited to star.

chemin - track or course.

chronomètre - translated as "chronometer", the ship's principal time keeper. Records Astronomical Time (the Mean Time at Paris, TMP) in hours, minutes and seconds for 24 hours starting at noon Civil Time. Civil Time is recorded with the symbol "M" before the time as in M $7^{hr}47^m56^s$.

circonférence inscrite - inscribed circle.

compteur - translated as "counter", the time keeper used to carry time of the observation to the chronometer for comparison. Recorded with the symbol "C" before the hours, minutes, seconds as in C$5^{hr}30^m00^s$.

Connaissaissance des temps - the French celestial almanac or ephemeredes, their *Nautical Almanac*.

droite d'observation - line of position.

journal - the ship's log book.

lieu géométrique - a line composed of points, in this case, part of a circle

l'angle d'observation - the angle between the verticals of the two stars observed.

Latitudes Croissantes - Meridional parts.

log - the device thrown overboard to measure the ship's speed.

montre - sometimes the binnacle watch, sometimes the ship's chronometer.

montre d'habitacle or *montre de bord* - translated as "binnacle watch" or the "deck watch". Set to local civil time in hours and minutes, no seconds. Recorded with "M" for morning (*Matin*) or "S" for afternoon (*Soir*) written after the time as in 8ʰ25ᵐ M.

point - position or fix.

point approché - An approximate position based on a **DR** if current and wind are not known; on an **EP** if the **DR** position is corrected for wind and current.

point estimé - an Estimated Position (**EP**) except when it is clear that the position has not been corrected for wind and current. In these cases, Dead Reckoning (**DR**) position is used.

point observé - position established by an observation.

projection terrestre de l'astre - the geographic position (**GP**) of the star on the surface of the earth.

Registre du Chronomètre - the record of the state of the chronometer.

table de point - Traverse Tables.

Technical Notes to Appendix B-1, Part 1. The Determination of Position.

Technical Note I. Section VII. Formulae to use.

from page [B1-44]

    The following provides the derivation of the formulae Saint-Hilaire recommends for the computation of longitude and azimuth, knowing <u>latitude</u> and the observed altitude.

    In spherical triangle **PZA** one has for the perimeter $2S' = PA + AZ + ZP$: or for the ½ perimeter: $S' = \dfrac{PA + AZ + ZP}{2}$.

One computes

$$S'-PA = \frac{AZ + ZP - PA}{2}$$

$$S'-ZP = \frac{AZ + PA - ZP}{2}$$

$$S'-AZ = \frac{ZP + PA - AZ}{2}$$

The geometric formula for the ½ perimeter gives:

$$\sin^2 \frac{P}{2} = \frac{\sin(S'-PA)\,\sin(S'-ZP)}{\sin PA\,\sin PZ}$$

Saint-Hilaire uses:
$$2S = L + \Delta + H = (90° - ZP) + PA + (90° - AZ) \quad \text{where}$$

$$S = 90° - \frac{AZ + ZP - PA}{2} = 90° - (S'-PA).$$

From which one derives:

$$S - H = 90° - \frac{AZ + ZP - PA}{2} - H = 90° - \frac{AZ + ZP - PA}{2} - (90° - AZ) =$$

$$-\frac{AZ + ZP - PA}{2} + \frac{2AZ}{2} = S - H = \frac{AZ + PA - ZP}{2} = S'-PZ.$$

Using these values, the formula for the ½ perimeter becomes:

$$\sin^2 \frac{P}{2} = \frac{\cos S \sin(S-H)}{\sin\Delta \sin PZ} = \frac{\cos S \sin(S-H)}{\sin\Delta \cos(90° - PZ)} = \frac{\cos S \sin(S-H)}{\sin\Delta \cos L}.$$

One can compute Z in the same way:

$$\sin^2 \frac{Z}{2} = \frac{\sin(S'-ZP) \sin(S'-AZ)}{\sin ZP \sin AZ}.$$

$$S-L = 90° - \frac{AZ + ZP - PA}{2} - (90° - ZP) = \frac{ZP + PA - AZ}{2} = S'- AZ.$$

$$\sin^2 \frac{Z}{2} = \frac{\sin(S-H) \sin(S-L)}{\sin ZP \sin AZ} = \frac{\sin(S-H) \sin(S-L)}{\sin(90° - L) \sin(90° - H)} = \frac{\sin(S-H) \sin(S-L)}{\cos L \cos H}$$

from page [B1-44]

The following provides the derivation of the formulae Saint-Hilaire recommends for the computation of latitude and azimuth, knowing <u>longitude</u> and the observed altitude.

Applying the sine formula:

$$\frac{\sin Z}{\sin PA} = \frac{\sin P}{\sin AZ} = \frac{\sin P}{\sin(90° - H)} = \frac{\sin P}{\cos H} \quad \text{or} \quad \sin Z = \frac{\sin PA \sin P}{\cos H} = \frac{\sin \Delta \sin P}{\cos H}$$

From Napier's rules applied to the spherical triangle **PAK** one derives:

$\cos P = \cot(90° - PK)\cot\Delta$ or $\tan\varphi = \tan\Delta\cos P$.

In triangle **AKZ**, one has:

$\cos Z = \cot(90° - KZ)\cot ZA$ or

$\tan\varphi' = \cos Z\tan ZA$.

$\tan\varphi' = \cos Z\tan(90° - H) = \cos Z\cos H$.

In the above calculations:

S = half the sum of Latitude, polar distance of the body and altitude of the body.

$$S = \frac{L + \Delta + H}{2} = \frac{(90° - ZP) + PA + (90° - AZ)}{2}$$

S' = half the perimeter of the celestial triangle **PZA**.

K = the point on arc **PZ** where a perpendicular arc through point **A** falls.

H = the observed altitude 90 - H = **AZ**.

Δ = the polar distance of the celestial body, PA in the celestial triangle.

φ = PK.

φ' = ZK.

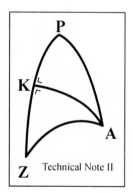

Technical Note II

[c-6]

from page [B1-45]

In this extensive footnote, Saint-Hilaire addresses the errors that can result from using chords or tangents of the circle of equal altitude rather than the curve of the circle itself. See the Figures in the Footnote for the derivation of the terms **M**, **m**, and **R**.

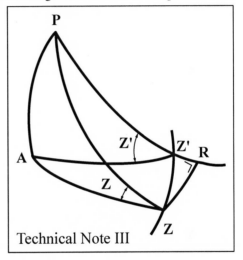

With **P** as centre and **PZ** as radius, draw the arc of circle **ZR**.

The angles **ZRZ'** and **ZP** are right angles.

ZZ' is perpendicular to **AZ** and **ZR** is perpendicular to **PZ**. Thus **Z'ZR** is equal to **Z**.

The small triangle **ZZ'R** may be considered as a plane triangle and one has:

Z'R = **ZZ'** sinZ = **M** sinZ.

Z'R is an arc of meridian **PZ'** and is thus equal to dL, the difference in latitude between **Z'**. and **R**. As **Z** and **Z'** have the same latitude, this is also the difference in latitude between **Z** and **R**. dL = **m**sinZ

Applying the fundamental formula to **PAZ**:

cosΔ = cosAZcosPA + sinAZ sinPAcosZ.

or: cosΔ = cos(90° - H)cos(90° - L) + sin(90° - H)sin(90° - L)cosZ.

cosΔ = sinHsinL + cosHcosLcosZ.

cosLcosHcosZ = cosΔ - sinLsinH.

Considering Z and L as variables, let us compute the differentials of both terms: $\cos L \cos H(-\sin Z)dZ + (-\sin L)dL\cos H\cos Z = -\cos L dL\sin H$ or: $dZ(\cos L x \cos H \sin Z) = dL(\cos L\sin H - \sin L\cos H\cos Z)$. (1)

Applying the rule of the four consecutive parts to the spherical triangle **PZA**:

$\cot P\sin Z = \cot AZ \sin PZ - \cos PZ\cos Z$.

$\cot P\sin Z = \cot(90° - H)\sin(90° - L) - \cos(90° - L)$.

$\cos Z\cot P\sin Z = \tan H\cos L - \sin L\cos Z$.

Multiplying both factors by $\cos H$:

$\cot P\sin Z\cos H = \sin H\cos L - \sin L\cos Z\cos H$.

The second factor is the multiplier of dL in equation (1) which becomes:

$dZ\cos L\cos H\sin Z = dL\cot P\sin Z\cos H$ or

$dZ\cos L = dL\cot P$. (2)

$$dZ = \frac{dL\cot P}{\cos L} \text{ but } dL = m\sin Z \text{ and thus } dZ = \frac{m\sin Z}{\cos L\tan P}.$$

One can also write:

Applying the sine rule to triangle PZA, one has:

$$\frac{\sin Z}{\sin AP} = \frac{\sin P}{\sin ZA} \text{ or } \frac{\sin Z}{\sin\Delta} = \frac{\sin P}{\cos H} \text{ or } \sin Z = \frac{\sin P\sin\Delta}{\cos H} \text{ and thus}$$

$$dZ = \frac{m\sin P\sin\Delta}{\cos H\cos L\tan P} = \frac{m\sin\Delta\cos P}{\cos H\cos L}.$$

In the continuation of Footnote A on Page [B1-47] in Figure 3 and the related text, Saint-Hilaire provides the method to be used in establishing the corrected position **O'** given the observation of the altitudes of two celestial bodies. The following equations give the basis for the constructions Saint-Hilaire uses to find **O'**.

Let **A** be the celestial body and **M** the point where one has computed the tangent **MO** at the curve of equal altitude. Saint-Hilaire draws the tangent to the curve of equal altitude at **V** that is the point on the curve having the same latitude as the calculated position **O**. Draw the bisector of angle **MAV** that intersects tangent **MO** at **S**. The angles **SMA** and **SVA** are right angles. Thus, angle **VSO** is equal to angle **VAM** that is the difference in azimuth dZ between the points **M** and **V**.

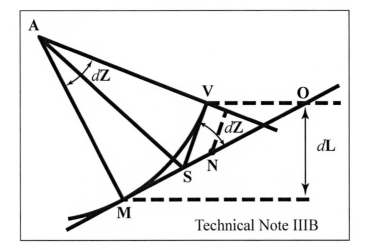

Technical Note IIIB

Saint-Hilaire constructs a parallel to the tangent **VS** through point **N**, the midpoint of **MO**. This is acceptable so long as *dZ* is a small angle.

Saint-Hilaire computes the angle *dZ* in the following way: draw a line through **O** making an angle **P** with the parallel of **M**. The perpendicular to the parallel originating from **O** determines point **R. OR** is the difference in latitude between **M** and **O.**

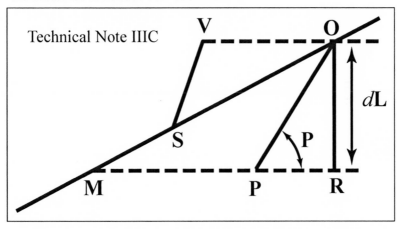

The following explains how Saint-Hilaire might have used Traverse Tables to convert the observations to a position on a chart. On a Mercator chart the distance on the latitude scale is equal to the distance on the longitude scale divided by the cosine of the latitude. Make **K** the length corresponding to a distance of one minute measured on the scale of latitude at latitude L. This same length K measured on the scale of longitude corresponds to K/cosL minutes of longitude.

Similarly, if one measures dL on the scale of longitude, one will obtain dL/cosL minutes.

The distance PR equals $\dfrac{d\,L}{\tan P}$. PR, measured on the longitude scale, equals $\dfrac{d\,L}{\tan P \cos L}$.

From equation (2) one derives $d\mathbf{Z} = \dfrac{d\,L \cot P}{\cos L} = \dfrac{d\,L}{\tan P \cos L}$. This means that PR measured in minutes on the scale of longitude represents the measure of $d\mathbf{Z}$ in minutes.

If one prefers to use the traverse table, one will first measure, on the chart, the value of OR (that is, dL) on the scale of longitude. One obtains thus dL /cosL = A.

In the traverse table, one takes P as a course and A as departure.

If D is the distance sailed, the departure A equals D sinP and the difference in latitude (as used in the departure tables, $d$lat) equals D cosP.

$$\mathbf{D}\cos P = \frac{\mathbf{D}\cos P \sin P}{\sin P} = \frac{\mathbf{D}\sin P}{\tan P} = \frac{\mathbf{A}}{\tan P} = \frac{d\mathbf{L}}{\cos L \tan P}\ .$$

In the "Departure" column one looks for the value of A. The corresponding difference in latitude represents the value of $d\mathbf{Z}$.

Technical Notes to Appendix B Part 2, Calculation of the Observed Position.

Technical Note IV. Example of Calculations.

from page [B2-342]

Saint-Hilaire appropriately corrects the mean time given by the chronometer to sidereal time of the observation at Paris. The following gives the derivation of the correction.

The sidereal day is four minutes shorter than the mean solar day. A time difference of 8h29min induces a correction of

$$\frac{4\text{min} \times 8\text{h}29\text{min}}{24\text{h}} = \frac{240\text{sec} \times 30540}{86400} = 84\text{sec} = 1\text{min}24\text{sec}.$$

TECHNICAL NOTE V.

CALCULATION OF AN OBSERVATION.

from page [B2-346]

Saint-Hilaire cites the fundamental equations for sight reduction to obtain the parameters needed to work his calculated the estimated position, H_e; the distance of the true position from the estimated position, H_o - H_e; and the azimuth of the celestial body, Z. The following provides the derivation of these critical elements of the intercept method.

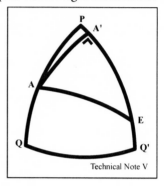

Technical Note V

Applying Napier's rule to the spherical triangle **PAA'** one obtains:

$\cos P = \cot(90° - PA')\cot PA = \cot A'Q'/\tan PA$.

Or: $1/\cos P = \tan PA/\cot A'Q' = \tan PA \tan A'Q'$.

Or: $\tan A'Q' = \dfrac{1}{\tan PA \cos P} = \dfrac{\tan(90° - PA)}{\cos P} = \dfrac{\tan AQ}{\cos P}$ where **AQ** is the declination **D** of the celestial body.

Name the arc **A'Q'** as **D'**: $\tan D' = \dfrac{\tan D}{\cos P}$. (1)

Applying the fundamental formula to **PAA'**:

$\cos PA = \cos AA' \times \cos PA' + \sin PA \sin PA' \times \cos 90° = \cos AA' \cos PA'$

from which one derives:

$\cos AA' = \cos PA/\cos PA'$. (a)

Applying the fundamental formula to **EAA'**:

$\cos EA = \cos AA' \times \cos A'E + \sin AA' \sin A'E \cos 90° = \cos AA' \cos A'E$.

Replacing $\cos AA'$ by its value (a), one finds:

$\cos EA = \dfrac{\cos PA}{\cos PA'}\cos A'E = \dfrac{\cos PA}{\cos PA'}\cos(Q'A' - Q'E)$.

$\sin(90° - EA) = \dfrac{\sin(90° - PA)}{\sin(90° - PA')}\cos(Q'A' - Q'E) = \dfrac{\sin AQ}{\sin A'Q'}\cos(Q'A' - Q'E)$.

(90° - **EA**) is the altitude of the body, H_E, observed from point **E**. **Q'A'** is **D'**. **AQ** is **D**.

Q'E is the latitude of the observer, L_E. One has:

$$\sin H_E = \frac{\sin D}{\sin D'} \cos(D' - L_E) \quad (2)$$

Applying Napier's rule to the spherical triangle **EAA'**:

$\cos PEA = \cot EA \cot(90° - A'E) = \tan(90° - EA)\tan A'E =$

$\tan(90° - EA)\tan(Q'A' - Q'E).$

PEA is the azimuth **Z**. 90° - **EA** is H_E. **Q'A'** is **D'**. **Q'E** is the latitude of the observer, L_E.

$$\cos Z = \tan H_C \times \tan(D' - L_E). \quad (3)$$

PLOTTING AN OBSERVATION ON THE CHART.

from page [B2-348]

Saint-Hilaire provides a table to illustrate how the factors in his intercept method are calculated. He used the arithmetic and Traverse Tables notations that would be familiar to the navigators of his time. The following table is a reconstruction of Saint-Hilaire's table with explanations of the calculations.

	A	B	C	D
1	D = 38° 40'13"N	G_a=62° 16'00"W	tan D = $\overline{1}$.90325	sin D = $\overline{1}$.79577
2	L_e=35° 30'00"N	G_e = 9° 30'00"W		
3		P =52° 46'00"W	C cos P= 0.21820	
4	D'= 52° 54'30"N		tanD' = 0.12145	C sin D' = 0.09816
5	D'-L_e= 17° 24'30"N		tan (D'- L_e)= $\overline{1}$.4963	cos (D'-L_e) = $\overline{1}$.97964
6			tan H_e 0.0512	sin H_e = $\overline{1}$.87359
7			cos Z = $\overline{1}$.5475	H_e = 46° 22'15"
8		ε 26ᵐ9		H_o = 48° 51'00"
9	λ = 10'10"N	g 33'06"W	Z=N69°20'W	H_o-H_e = + 28'45"
10	$L_{e'}$ 35° 40'10"N	$G_{e'}$ =10° 03'06"W		

1. **C1** $\overline{1}$.90325 is the logarithm of tangent D. $\overline{1}$.90325 is equal to 0.90325 - 1, it is the same as 9.90325 in other tables. The same remark applies to all logarithms.
2. **D1** $\overline{1}$.79577 is the logarithm of sinD.
3. **B3** P is the difference (C1 - C2), between G_a and G_e.
4. **C3** CcosP is the logarithm of (1/cosP) or -log sinP.
5. **C4** is the sum of C1 and C3 and thus 0.12145 is the logarithm of tanD'. From this value, one derives the value of D'(A4) and the value of log (1/sinD')(D4).
6. **A5** is the difference (A4-A2). From this value, one derives the logarithms of tan(D' - L_e) (C5) and of cos(D' - L_e)(D5).
7. **D6** is the sum (D1 + D4 + D5) and thus the logarithm of sinH_c. From this value, one derives the value of H_c (D7) and of log tanH_c (C6)
8. **C7** is the sum (C5 + C6) and thus $\overline{1}$.5475 is the logarithm of cosZ. From this value, one derives Z (C9)

9. **D9** is the difference (**D8** - **D7**) and is the intercept, 28′45″ or 28.75 miles.
10. **B8** is the intercept (**D9**) multiplied by the sine of the azimuth (**C9**) and is thus the departure.
11. **A9** is λ, the difference in latitude that is obtained by multiplying the intercept by the cosine of the azimuth.
12. **B9**, the difference in longitude, is obtained by dividing the departure (**B8**) by the cosine of the latitude.
13. **A10** is the final latitude obtained by adding (**A9**) and the estimated latitude (**A2**).
14. **B10** is the final longitude obtained by adding (**B9**) and the estimated longitude (**B2**).

SECOND CALCULATION - A NUMERIC EXAMPLE.

from page [B2-351]

The following table is a reconstruction of Saint-Hilaire's table with an explanation of the calculations:

	A	B	C	D
1	$L_{e'}$= 35° 40'10"N	G_e= 10°03'06"W	Z=69°20'W	
2	D= 45° 52'10"N	$G_{a'}$ = 96°06'00"W	tan D= 0.01318	sin D = $\overline{1}$.85598
3		P = 106°09'06"W	C cos P= 0.55567	
4	D'= 105° 06'10"N		tanD' = 0.56885	C sin D' = 0.01526
5	D'-$L_{e'}$= 69° 26'00"N		tan (D'- $L_{e'}$)= 0.42570	cos (D'-L_e) = $\overline{1}$.54568
6			tan $H_{e'}$ = $\overline{1}$.4323	sin $H_{e'}$ = $\overline{1}$.41692
7				$H_{e'}$ = 15° 08'24"
8			cos Z'= $\overline{1}$.85800	H'$_o$ = 15° 32'30"
9				H'$_o$-$H_{e'}$= + 24'06"
10		ε 9.4^m	Z' =N46°10'E	
11	λ = 25'00"N	g 11'36"W	V =N20°40'E	(H'$_o$-$H_{e'}$)/sinO= + 26'07"
12	L_e 36° 05'10"N	$G_{e'}$ = 9°51'30"W	Z'-V= 25°30'	

1. **A1** is the latitude corrected after the first position line, $L_{e'}$.
2. **B1** is the longitude corrected after the first position line, $G_{e'}$.
3. **C1** is the azimuth of the first observation.
4. **A2** is the declination D, of Capella.
5. **B2** is the hour angle $G_{a'}$, of Capella.
6. **C2** is the logarithm of tanD.
7. **D2** is the logarithm of sinD.
8. **B3** is the difference (B2 - B1). P = 106°09'06" is thus the local hour angle.
9. **C3** is the logarithm of (1/cosP). 0.55567 is thus -(log cosP).
10. **C4** is the sum (C2 + C3) and also is the logarithm of tanD', from which one derives D' (A4) and log(1/sineD') (D4).
11. **A5** is the difference(A4 - A1). 69°26'00" is thus (D' - $L_{e'}$) from which one derives log tan(D' - $L_{e'}$) (C5) and log cos(D' - $L_{e'}$)(D5).
12. **D6** is the sum (D4 + D5). $\overline{1}$.41692 is thus the logarithm of sinHe', from which one derives log tanH$_e$'(C6) and H$_e$' (D7).

13. **C8** is the sum (**C5** + **C6**). T̄.85800 is thus log cos**Z'**, from which one derives **Z'** (**C10**).

14. **D8** is the observed altitude of Capella, H'_o.

15. **D9** is the difference (**D8** - **D7**) and represents the intercept, 24'06" or 24.1 miles.

16. **D11** is **E'O**, that is to say, the intercept (**D9**) divided by the sine of the acute angle **O** between the two verticals of observation (**C1** and **C10**) or between the two position lines. In operational notations **C1** =290°40' and **C10** =046°10'. The acute angle between those two directions, **O**, is thus equal to (290°40' - 180°) - 46°10' = 64°30'. **O** can also be deduced from (**C12**): **O** = 90° - (**Z'** - **V**) = 90° - 25°30' = 64°30'.
E'O = 24.1/sin64°30'= 26.7miles which is erroneously written as 26'07"(26.12 miles) in the original computation. Figure 9 and the other computations use the correct value.

17. **C11** is **V**, the direction of the first position line (**E'O**). In this case (290°40' + 90°) = 20°40'.

18. **C12** is the direction of **E'O**: (**Z'** - **V**) or (**C10** - **C11**).

19. **A11** is the difference of latitude corresponding to **E'O**, i.e., **E'O** multiplied by the cosine of **V**. 26.7cosine20°40' = 25 miles or 25 minutes.

20. **A12** is the sum (**A1** + **A11**) and is the latitude of **O**, 36°05'10'N.

21. **B10** is the departure corresponding to **E'O**, i.e., **E'O** multiplied by the sin of **V** = 26.7 x sin20°40' = 9.4 miles.

22. **B11** is the difference of longitude corresponding to a departure of 9.4 miles at a latitude of 36°, i.e., 9.4/cos36° = 11.6' or 11'36".

23. **B12** is the sum (**B1** + **B11**) and is the longitude of **O**.

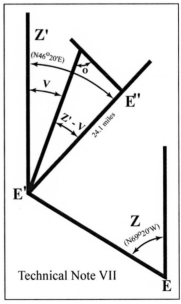

Technical Note VII

The figure provides a plot of the above calculations.

Technical Note VIII. The case where one of the observations is near the meridian.

from page [B2-353]

The computations are similar to the preceding ones from pages [B2-348] and [B-2-351]. After the first computation giving a position E' of 59°33'24"N 2°03'00"E, Saint-Hilaire calculates the transfer of this position for a ship's displacement of 11 miles in the direction N63°W. The difference in latitude is 11 minutes x cos63° = 5minutes. The departure is 11 x sin63° = 9.8 miles. The difference in longitude corresponding to 9.8 miles at a latitude of 59° 38' is 9.8/cos59°38' = 19.3'. Saint-Hilaire gets a slightly different result (19'06" or 19.1') as he is interpolating by sight in the Traverse Tables. Thus, he obtains an advanced position to start the second computation.

	A	B	C
1	$L_{e'}$ = 25°30'00"N	$G_{e'}$ = 40°20'00"W	Z=S60°E
2	D = 15°00'00"S		
3	D - $L_{e'}$ = 40°30'00"S		
4	$H_{e'}$ = 49°30'00"		
5	H_o = 50°00'00"	ε 17.4^{mi}	Z' South
6	H'_o- $H_{e'}$ = λ = 30'00"	g 19'18"W	V S30°W
7	L_o = 25°00'00"N	G_o=40°39'18"W	

1. A1 is the estimated latitude.
2. B1 is the estimated longitude.
3. C1 is the azimuth of the first observation.
4. A2 is the declination of the sun.
5. A3 is the zenith distance of the sun.
6. A4 is the estimated altitude, 90° - A3.
7. A5 is the observed altitude of the sun.
8. A6 is the intercept (e'e") = A5 - A4.
9. A7 is the corrected latitude : A1 + A6.
10. C5 is the azimuth, Z' of the second observation.
11. C6 is V, the direction of the first position line, e'o : **90° + Z = 90° + C1.**

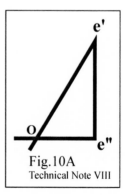

Fig.10A
Technical Note VIII

12. **B5** is **e"o**, the departure corresponding to a course of 30° and a difference in latitude of 30'. It is equal to **e'e"** x tan30°. It is taken from the Traverse Table.
13. **B6** is the difference in longitude corresponding to a departure of 17.4 miles at a latitude of 25°: **B5**/cos25° = 19.3'.

Technical Note IX.
Calculation of a Polar Observation.

from page [B2-360]

For his calculation of the observation of the Pole star, Saint-Hilaire uses simplified formulae and resolves them using the Traverse Tables. The computations are easy to follow. We shall illustrate below how the entries in the Traverse Tables were used. In Saint-Hilaire's time the Traverse Tables did not use the specific terminology "$d$lat" and "departure". The columns of the page used to solve a triangle for an angle of "C°" were labeled as follows:

Distance: **a.**

$d$lat = **b** = **a** cosC.

departure = **c** = **a** sinC

The symbols for departure and $d$lat were respectively ε and λ.

Given Δ = 1°21'24' or 81.4".

Δ cosP = 81'4" x cos95 = - 7.1' = - 7'06".

From the Traverse Tables on the page for 95°, Distance 81.4, $d$lat 7.1.

Δ sinP = 81'4" x sin95 = 81'.

From the Traverse Tables, page for 95°, Distance 81.4, departure 81'.

H_e = L_e + ΔcosP = 59°30' - 7'06" = 59°22'54".

H_c = 59°50'.

Intercept = H_c - H_{ze} = 27'06".

$$Z = \Delta \frac{\sin P}{\cos H_e} = \Delta \sin P \frac{1}{\cos H_e} = \frac{81'}{\cos 59°22'54"} \cdot$$

From the Traverse Tables, interpolation between pages for 59° and 60°:

$d$lat 81, distance 161' = 2°41' = 2.7°. λ = 27'06" x cosZ = 27.1' x cos2.7°.

From the Traverse Tables, interpolation between pages 2° and 3°, λ = 27.1' = 27'06".

Latitude = L_e + λ = 59°30' + 27'06" = 59°57'06".

ε = 27'06" x sinZ = 27.1' x sin2.7°.

From the Traverse Tables, interpolation between pages 2° and 3°,
$\varepsilon = 1.27' = 1.3'$.
$g = 1.27'/\sin \text{Lat} = 1.27'/\sin 59°30'$.
From the Traverse Tables, interpolation between pages 59° and 60°,
$g = 2.5' = 2'30''$.

Technical Note X. Calculation of a Circummeridian Observation.

from page [B2-361]

In this section Saint-Hilaire illustrates his method of sight reduction using the two calculated positions determined in the previous example. The original Table of Calculations on page [B2-362] has been corrected, expanded and rearranged for ease in following the calculations. The modern symbols, *d*lat, *d*lon, and departure, have been substituted for λ, **g**, and ε, respectively.

Calculation

L$_e$ 58' 30" 00" N	**Ge** 1° 00' 00" E		CosP* = $\overline{1}$ 98362
D 1° 09' 00" N	**Ga** 16° 38' 40" E		cos(D'-Le) = $\overline{1}$ .73251
D' 1° 11' 36" N	**P** 15° 38' 40" E		sin H$_e$ = $\overline{1}$ .71613
D'-L$_e$ 57° 18' 24" S	Departure 15.8^{miles}		H$_e$ 31° 20' 33"
1st Correction			H$_o$ -30° 30' 00"
*d*lat 48' 00" N	*d*lon 30'36"W	**Z** S18.2° E	- 50' 33"
Interval 11 miles	Departure 9.8^{miles}		
*d*lat 5' 00" N	*d*lon 19'06" W	N63°W	11^{miles}
L$_{e1'}$ 59° 23' 00" N	**G$_{e1'}$** 0° 10' 18" E	1270	90°-(D-L$_{e1'}$) 31° 47' 40"
		1"18	
		1016	
		127	
		127	
		1499" or	
D 1° 10' 40" N	**G$_a$** 8° 44' 09" W		24' 59"
D - L$_{e1}$ 58° 12' 20" S	**P** 8° 51' 27" W		H$_e$ 31° 22' 41"
	or 35.6^{miles}		H$_o$ -31° 00' 00"
2nd Correction	Distance 47.4^{mile}	**Z'** S10.4°W	-22' 41"
*d*lat 14' 48" N	Departure 45.0^{miles}	**V** S71.8°W	
	*d*lon 1° 28' 42" E	61.4°	
Observed L$_o$ 59° 37' 48" N	**G$_o$** 1° 39' 00" E		

λ = *d*lat = *d*Latitude; **g** = *d*lon = *d*Longitude; ε = Departure, miles east or west.

The following expands and illustrates the details of the calculations Marcq Saint-Hilaire used to determine the Observed Position in the table.

$$\mathbf{D'} = \frac{\mathbf{D}}{\cos \mathbf{P}} = \frac{1° 09'}{15°38'40"} = 1°11'36".$$

Since **D** and **D'** are small, use the simplified formula

$\sin H_e = \cos P \times (D' - L_e)$. Calculate using logarithms.

The azimuth, Z, is obtained from $\cos Z = \tan H_e \times \tan(D - L_e) = \tan 31°20'33'' \times 57°18'24''$.

$Z = S18.2°E$.

$H_o - H_e = 31°20'33'' - 30°00'00'' = -50'33''$.

The first correction is $-50'33''$ or 50.55 miles in the direction S18.2E that converts to 50.55 miles in the direction N18.2W. From this,

$\lambda = 50.55^{\text{miles}}\cos 18.2° = 48'$;

$\varepsilon = 50.55^{\text{miles}}\sin 18.2° = 15.8$ miles;

$g = \dfrac{15.8}{\cos 58°30'} = 30'36''$.

The course made good in the interval is 11 miles to N63°W which from this, $\lambda = 11^{\text{miles}}\cos 63° = 5'$;

$\varepsilon = 11^{\text{miles}}\sin 63° = 9.8^{\text{miles}}$;

$b = \dfrac{9.8}{\cos(58°30'+48')} = 19'06''$.

Since the second altitude is circummeridian, differentiating the general formula:

$\sin H_e = \sin L \sin D + \cos L \cos D \cos P$

and taking L and D as constant, gives

$\cos H_e\, dH_e = \cos L \sin P\, db$.

Close to the meridian $dP = P$ and as P is small, $\sin P = P$, then $\cos H_e \times dH_e = -\cos L \cos D\, P^2$ and

$dH_e = \dfrac{-\cos L \cos D}{\cos H_e\ P^2}$.

Close to the meridian $H_e = 90° - (L - D)$, or taking the absolute values in the parentheses, as Saint-Hilaire does,

$dH_e = -\dfrac{\cos L \cos D}{\cos(90 - (D - L))}P^2$.

The factor $\dfrac{\cos L \cos D}{\cos(90 - (D - L))}$ is what Saint-Hilaire calls α. It is a function of only L and D and its value can be taken from a circummeridian table. In this example the value is $1.18''$. The actual altitude equals the meridian altitude minus αP^2.

If one expresses P in minutes of time instead of in degrees, ($1° = 4$ minutes), dH_e becomes the change in altitude per minute of time during a meridian pass.

From the table $P = 8°51'27''$ which is equivalent to 35.6 minutes (after meridian pass in this case) so that $P^2 = 1270$.

$\alpha P^2 = 1.18'' \times 1270 = 1499'' = 24'59''$ to be subtracted from the meridian altitude which is given by $90° - (D - L_{e1'})$.

$H_e = (90° - (1°10'40''N - 59°23'00''N)) - 24'59'' = 31°22'41''$.

$H_e - H_o = 31°22'41'' - 31°00'00'' = 22'41''$ or 32.7 miles for the intercept.

In the figure, the angle between $e_1 e''$ at N10.4°E and $e_1'O$ at N71.8°E is 61.4°.

e_1O measures $\dfrac{22.7^{\text{miles}}}{\cos 61.4°} = 47.4^{\text{miles}}$ in the direction N71.8°E.

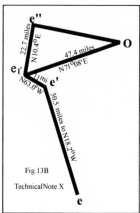

Fig. 13B

Technical Note X

47.4 miles to N71.8°E is equivalent to a change in latitude, λ, of $47.4^{\text{miles}} \times \cos 71.8° = 14.8'$; and a departure, ε, of $47.4^{\text{miles}} \times \sin 71.8° = 45^{\text{miles}}$.

At latitude 59°23', this corresponds to a change in longitude, g, of $\dfrac{45^{\text{miles}}}{59°23'} = 88.7'$ or 1°28'42''E.

The true position, O, is at $G_o =$

$G_{e1'} + g = 0°10'18''E + 1°28'42''E = 1°39'00''E$.

$L_o = L_{e1'} + \lambda = 59°23'00''N + 14'48''N = 59°37'48''N$.

Technical Note XI.

Observations made near the zenith.

from page [B2-363]

In discussing the calculation of observations near the zenith, Saint-Hilaire refers to a "simple transformation" when, in practice, the transformation relies on a complex sequence of formulae:

$\cos(D - L) = \cos L \cos D + \sin L \sin D$ or $\sin L \sin D = \cos(D - L) - \cos L \cos D$.

Replacing in the general formula: $\cos N = \sin L \sin D + \cos L \cos D - \cos P$, one obtains:

$\cos N = \cos(D - L) - \cos L \cos D + \cos L \cos D \cos P = \cos(D - L) + \cos L \cos D (\cos P - 1)$.

Now, $\cos x = 1 - 2\sin^2 x/2$. Using this formula for N, $(D - L)$ and P one gets:

$1 - 2\sin^2 N/2 = 1 - 2\sin^2(D - L)/2 + \cos L \cos D.(1 - 2\sin^2 P/2 - 1)$ or

$- 2\sin^2 N/2 = - 2\sin^2(D - L)/2 + \cos L \cos D.(- 2\sin^2 P/2)$ or

$\sin^2 N/2 = \sin^2(D - L)/2 + \cos L \cos D.(\sin^2 P/2)$.

Dividing by $\sin 1''$, one finally gets:

$$\frac{\sin^2 N/2}{\sin 1''} = \frac{\sin^2 (D-L)/2}{\sin 1''} + \frac{\cos L \cos D (\sin^2 P/2)}{\sin 1''}$$ i.e., the proposed

formula.

The azimuth has to be computed by dividing P by the estimated zenith distance and not by the actual zenith distance as the computations are based on the estimated position. Since the body is quite close to the zenith, a small variation in position produces important changes in azimuth. In the example at the end of the chapter, the difference is as large as 20°.

Technical Note XII. Calculation
of an Observation Made near the Zenith.

from page [B2-364]

Saint-Hilaire lost accuracy by interpolating roughly in the traverse table (correct interval after noon is 1'34"N and 22"W) but we kept his values as coming straight from the tables. Concerning the azimuth, he does not give any rule to determine the orientation. In this case, as the sun is north of the observer, the azimuth is NxyE before noon and NvwW after noon (where xy and vw are integers of degrees).

The Table of Calculations has been corrected, expanded and rearranged for ease in following the calculations.

G		$H_o\theta$		D θ	G θ or **Paris True time**
i	1st observation		83°37' 00"	14° 22' 15"N	35° 53' 45" W
v	Route in the interval	{ before noon	2.4^{miles} toward N13°W		
e		{ after noon	1.6^{miles} toward N13°W		
n	2nd observation		84°14' 30"	14° 22' 4"N	43° 40' 24' W

Calculation

	Latitude	Longitude	$\Big\{$ $\varphi(N_e) = \varphi(D-L) + \cos L \cos D \times \varphi(P)$ $\quad \sin Z = \dfrac{P \cos D}{N_e}$
Estimated Position	10° 20' 00" N	40° 05' 00" W	
1st celestial body	14° 22' 15" N	35° 52' 45" W	
Difference D-L	4° 02' 15" N	P = 4° 12' 15" E	$\varphi(P)$.... 555.0
	or 19^{min}09^{sec}	or 16^{min}49^{sec}	$\varphi(P) \times \cos L$ 546.2
			$\varphi(P) \times \cos L \times \cos D$ 529.1
			$\varphi(D - L)$ 511.9
			$\varphi(N_e)$. 1041.0
			$(N_e) = 23^{min}02^{sec} = 5°45'30"$
			$\sin Z = \dfrac{4.1}{5.8} = 0.7$
			Z = N45°E V = N45W
			$N_o = 90°-87°37'00 = \underline{6°23'00"}$
			-37'30"
dlat		26' 36" S departure ε=26.6^{miles}	
		dlon 26'48"W	
Interval Before noon λ			2.4 miles N13W
dlat		2'24" ε= 0.54^{miles}	
		dlon 0'33"W	
Corrected Noon Position	9° 55' 48" N	40° 32' 21" W	
Interval After noon λ			1.6 miles N13W
dlat		1' 36" N departure 0.36^{miles}	
		dlon 0'24"W	
Position after 2nd correction	9° 57' 24"	40° 32' 45" W	
2nd Celestial body	14° 22' 54" N	43° 40' 24" W	
Difference D - L	4° 35' 30" N	P = 3° 07' 39" W	$\varphi(P)$ 307.2
	or 17^{min}42^{sec}	or 12^{min}30.4^{sec}	$\varphi(P) \times \cos L \times \cos D$ 293.0
			$\varphi(D - L)$ 614.8
			$\varphi(N_e)$ 907.8
			$N_e = 21^{min}30.6^{sec}$ or 5°22'39"
			$N_o = 90°-84°14'30 = \underline{5°45'30"}$
			22'51"
			or 22.8^{miles}
			$\sin Z' = \dfrac{3.0}{5.4} = 0.56$
			Z' = N34°W V = N45°W
Corrected Noon Position	9° 55' 48" N	40° 32' 21" W	
			$Z'-V = \dfrac{11° 22.8}{\cos 11} = 23.2^{miles}$
dlat		16' 24" S departure 16.4^{miles}	
		dlon 16' 39" E	
Observed Noon Position	9° 39' 24" N	40° 15' 42" W	

λ = dlat = dLatitude; g = dLongitude; ε = Departure, miles east or west

Technical Note XIII. Using the Traverse Tables to resolve spherical triangles.

from page [B2-365]

The formula giving $\sin Z$ is obtained as follows.

Applying the sine rule in the navigation triangle one obtains

$$\sin Z = \frac{\sin P \cos L}{\cos H}.$$

Differentiating H with respect to P in the general formula:

$$\cos H \, d H = -\cos L \cos D \sin P \, d P \quad \text{or}$$

$$\frac{-d H}{d P \cos L} = \frac{\sin P \cos D}{\cos H} = \sin Z.$$

Technical Note XIV. Using the Traverse Tables to resolve spherical triangles.

from page [B2-365]

The following will explain the fifth example in more detail. Here Saint-Hilaire uses the Traverse Tables to determine the course from one geographic position to another.

First Saint-Hilaire chooses an arbitrary distance of 50 miles to enter the Traverse Tables:

50 x sin60 = 43.3 (departure corresponding to a track of 60°)

43.3/cos60 = 86.7 (distance corresponding to a *d*lat of 43.3 and a track of 60°)

This is the value of the factor 50 x tan60°.

86.7 x cos15 = 83.7 (*d*lat corresponding to a distance of 86.7 and a track of 15°)

83.7/sin104 = 83.7/sin76 = 86.2 (distance corresponding to a departure of 83.7 and a track of 76°)

This is what Saint-Hilaire writes simply as: "First term multiplied by 50 = 86.2."

He does the same for the second term, adds it to the first term and finally divides the sum by 50, the arbitrary distance used to enter the tables.

This is what Saint-Hilaire means when he says: "The Traverse Table gives on sight"!

Technical Note XV. Using the Traverse Tables to resolve spherical triangles.

from page [B2-368]

In this extensive footnote, Saint-Hilaire provides the method of calculation of the radius of curvature and the center for a point on the curve of equal altitudes. The following gives the derivation of the critical factors and equations in this calculation.

$zm = dP$

$\omega = dZ$

$zz' = \omega z \times \omega$

In the small triangle $zz' = zm/\cos Z$.

ωz or $\rho = zm/\omega.\cos Z = dP/dZ.\cos Z$.

Applying the sine rule in the position triangle gives $\sin P/\sin Z = \sin PZ/\sin\Delta$.

Calling N the colatitude of Z, $\sin P/\sin Z = \sin N/\sin\Delta$. (1)

$\sin P = \sin Z \times \sin N/\sin\Delta$,

$\cos P dP = \cos Z dZ \sin N/\sin\Delta$.

Replacing $\sin N/\sin\Delta$ by $\sin P/\sin Z$ (1)

$\cos P.dP = \cos Z dZ \sin P/\sin Z$ or $dP/dZ = \tan P/\tan Z$.

Hence $\rho = \tan P/\tan Z \cos Z = \tan P/\sin Z$.

All computations are based on the value of zn which, measured on the scale of longitude, represents P. Thus, any length resulting from computations using P must be measured on the scale of longitude. This is the case for the radius ρ. ρ, a length on the chart, is an arc on the surface of the earth and is expressed in radians. One will obtain its value in degrees by multiplying by 57.3. On a Mercator chart, the scale of latitude represents meridional parts: $(Lx)_c$.

The meridional part of ω equals the meridional part of Z increased by ωq which is equal to $\rho.\cos Z$.

$(L\omega)_c = (Lz)_c + \rho\cos Z = (Lz)_c + \cos Z.\tan P/\tan Z =$
$(Lz)_c + \tan P/\tan Z,$

Expressing ρ in degrees, one obtains $\rho = (Lz)_c + 57.3 \times \tan P/\tan Z$.
For the longitudes, one has

$G_\omega = .G_z + zq = G_z + \rho \sin Z = G_z + (\tan P/\sin Z) \sin Z = G_z + \tan P$

Thus, zq is equal to $\tan P$ (see Appendix B-2, page [B2-369], Figure A).
Degrees could be used instead of radians, which gives

$G_\omega = G_z + \tan P^{\text{ radians}} = G_z + 57.3 \tan P^{\text{ degrees}}$.

The limits of $\tan P/\sin Z$ (ρ) and $\tan P/\tan Z$ when P and Z are equal to zero is found in triangle **PZx**:

$\cos H/\sin P = \cos D/\sin Z$ or $\sin P/\sin Z = \cos H/\cos D$.

$\sin P/(\sin Z \times \cos P) = \tan P/\sin Z = \cos H/(\cos D \times \cos P)$.

When **P** equals zero, the limit of $\tan P/\sin Z = \cos H/\cos D \times 1 = \rho$.

One finds in a similar manner $\tan P/\tan Z = \cos H/\cos D \times \cos Z/\cos P$.

When **P** and **Z** are equal to zero, the limit is $\cos D/\cos H \times 1/1$.

The example is simple, one first computes $57.3 \times \tan P = 57.3 \times \tan 62 = 107.7°$ which is the longitude correction in an easterly direction (S44°E). Thereafter, the latitude correction is $107.7/\tan Z = 111.5°$ or 6690 minutes in southerly direction (S44°E). The corresponding meridional parts are to 5106.8 or 64°29'.

$\rho = 107.7/\sin 44 = 155°$.

TECHNICAL NOTE XVI.
APPROXIMATIONS GIVEN BY THE CALCULATIONS.

from pages [B2-370] to [B2-372]

In this section Saint-Hilaire deals with the magnitude of the errors produced by his suggested approximations and gives the procedure for determining whether further corrections are needed. The constructions are all spherical, **C'C'** and **CC** are the small circles of two observations. The radii **oa** and **oa'** drawn on the sphere are arcs of great circles. **e'o** and **e"o** are tangents to the circles of observation. Point **o** is determined on the Mercator chart by the intersection of the tangents **e'o** and **e"o**. **e'o** and **e"o** are straight lines on the Mercator chart and thus are rhumb lines. **a'e"** and **a'e'** are arcs of great circles.

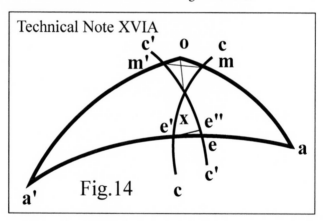

Technical Note XVIA

Fig. 14

The "plane" quadrilateral **omxm'** is inscribed in a circle having **ox** as diameter. The angle **om'm** is the same size as angle **oxm**. Sin **om'm** = sin **oxm** = **om/ox**. Or, by the sine rule **mm'/sin mom'** = **om/sin om'm** = **ox**.

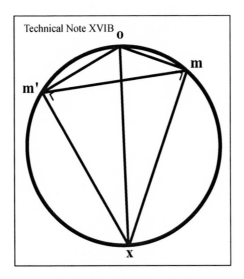

Technical Note XVIB

Page [B2-371] Continued

$$\tan(\frac{oa-e'a}{2}) = \frac{\tan^2\frac{e'o}{2}}{\tan(\frac{oa+e'a}{2})}.$$

oe'a is equal to 90°, thus cos **oa** = cos **e'a** cos **e'o**.

cos **eo** = cos **oa**/cos **e'a**.

$$\tan^2(\frac{e'o}{2}) = \frac{\sin^2(\frac{e'o}{2})}{\cos^2(\frac{e'o}{2})} = \frac{2\sin^2(\frac{e'o}{2})}{2\cos^2(\frac{e'o}{2})} = \frac{1-\cos e'o}{1+\cos e'o} = \frac{1-\frac{\cos oa}{\cos e'a}}{1+\frac{\cos oa}{\cos e'a}} = \frac{\cos e'a - \cos oa}{\cos e'a + oa}$$

Applying Simpson's rule one gets:

$$\frac{\cos e'a - \cos oa}{\cos e'a + \cos oa} = \frac{2\sin(\frac{e'a+oa}{2}).\sin(\frac{oa-e'a}{2})}{2\cos(\frac{e'a+oa}{2}).\cos(\frac{oa-e'a}{2})} = \tan(\frac{e'a+oa}{2}).\tan(\frac{oa-e'a}{2})$$

Thus:

$$\tan^2(\frac{e'o}{2}) = \tan(\frac{e'a+oa}{2}).\tan(\frac{oa-e'a}{2}) \quad \text{or} \quad \tan(\frac{oa-e'a}{2}) = \frac{\tan^2(\frac{e'o}{2})}{\tan(\frac{e'a+oa}{2})}.$$

Formula: $E = \dfrac{t^2}{\tan N'} \dfrac{\sqrt{1 + r^2 \cos^4 o - 2r \cos^3 o}}{2r \sin o}$

$om = \dfrac{t^2}{2 \tan N} = \dfrac{t^2}{2r \tan N'}$

$om' = \dfrac{t^2 \cos^2 o}{2 \tan N'}$.

$E^2 = \dfrac{om^2 + om'^2 - 2\, om \cdot om' \cos mom'}{\sin^2 mom'} = \dfrac{\dfrac{t^4 + t^4 r^2 \cos^4 o - 2t^2 \cdot rt^2 \cos^2 o \cdot \cos mom'}{4r^2 \tan^2 N'}}{\sin^2 mom'}$

$mom' = o$

$E^2 = \dfrac{t^4 \cdot (1 + r^2 \cos^4 o - 2r^2 \cos^3 o)}{4r^2 \tan^2 N' \cdot \sin^2 o}$

$E = \dfrac{t^2}{2r \tan N' \sin o} \cdot \sqrt{1 + r^2 \cos^4 o - 2r \cos^3 o} = \dfrac{t^2}{\tan N'} \cdot \dfrac{\sqrt{1 + r^2 \cos^4 o - 2r \cos^3 o}}{2r \sin o}$

Technical Note XVII.
Calculation by a double approximation.

from page [B2-374]

In the section Saint-Hilaire provides a method for improving the accuracy of a fix of position by repeating the calculations a second time. The following explains and expands Saint-Hilaire's calculations.

The zenith distances are very small and are computed as explained on pages [B2-363] and [B2-364] (see table XLI of Caillet).

The azimuth is computed from the estimated position and one has to use **Ne** in the formula $\sin \mathbf{Z} = \dfrac{\mathbf{P} \cos \mathbf{D}}{\mathbf{N}}$.

$\mathbf{D} - \mathbf{L} = 1°$, $\varphi(\mathbf{D} - \mathbf{L}) = 31.4$.

$\mathbf{P} = 3°07'$, $\varphi(\mathbf{P}) = 305.1$.

$\varphi(\mathbf{P}) \cos\mathbf{D} \cos\mathbf{L} = 305.1 \times \cos 10 \times \cos 11 = 294.8$.

$\varphi(\mathbf{P}) \cos\mathbf{D} \cos\mathbf{L} + \varphi(\mathbf{D} - \mathbf{L}) = \varphi(\mathbf{N}_e) = 294.8 + 31.4 = 326.2$ $\mathbf{N}_e = 3°13'4$.

$\sin \mathbf{Z} = \dfrac{\mathbf{P} \cos \mathbf{D}}{\mathbf{Ne}} = \dfrac{3.12 \times \cos 10}{3.22} = 0.952.$ $\mathbf{Z} = 72°$.

The sun is in the East (its longitude is 22°35'W and the observer's longitude is 25°42'W) and in the South (its northerly declination is smaller than the northerly latitude of the observer). The azimuth is thus S72°E or 108° in modern notations.

The difference between the observed and the computed zenith distance gives the intercept (**ee'**): - 40.9' in direction S72E (108°) or 40.9 in direction N72W.

$d$lat = 40.9 x cos72 = 12.6N.

$d$dep = 40.9 x sin72 = 38.89 that corresponds, at a latitude of 10°, to a $d$lon = 38.89/cos10 = 39.5W.

Saint-Hilaire's results are slightly different due to "on sight" interpolations in the Traverse Tables.

One determines a new estimated position (11°12'7N, 26°21'6W) from which one computes the second observation.

$\mathbf{D} - \mathbf{L} = 1°12.4'$.

$\varphi(D - L) = 45.7$.

$P = 2°28.4'$.

$\varphi P = 192.2$.

φP x cos10° x cos11.2° = 185.7.

$\varphi N_e = 45.7 + 185.7 = 231.4$. $N_e = 2°42.9'$

which in turn gives an intercept (e'e" and not ee") of - 42.5.

$$SinZ' = \frac{2.47 \times cos\, 10}{2.715} = 0.895.\ \ Z' = 63°6.$$

The azimuth is SW this time as the westerly longitude of the sun is more controlling than the westerly longitude of the observer S63.6W = 243.6. As the intercept is negative, the direction becomes 063.6. (See the figure below.)

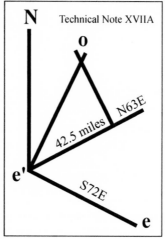

One computes the intersection of the two straight lines by the method of page [B2-368], remembering that the second line has been computed from point e'.

ee' = 40.9

The direction V, i.e., e'o is perpendicular to ee': 108 - 90 = 018.

o is the difference of the azimuths 108 - 063.5 = 44.5°.

t = e'o = e'e"/sin o = 42.5/sin44.5 = 60.1.

Saint-Hilaire finds 60.6 from the Traverse Tables.

60.6 miles in direction 018 corresponds to a $d$lat of 57.6 and a departure, φ, of 18.7 or a $d$lon of 19.1.

One gets a new estimated position of 12°10'3N and 26°02'5W.

To determine if a second approximation has to be done, one computes the error of this position: the angle of observation o = 243 - 108 = 135°.

N/N' is determined as follows:

N = $\mathbf{e}'\mathbf{a}$ where $\mathbf{a}$ lies at position 10N, 22°35'W and $\mathbf{e}'$ is at position 11°12.7'N, 26°21.6'W.

$\mathbf{e}'\mathbf{a}$ = 3°54'(N_o) or 234 miles

The result is easy to covert: $d$lat = 72.7miles; $d$lon = 3°46.6'; departure = 3.7° = 222miles.

N^2 = 72.7^2 + 222^2 N = 233.6.

N' = 3°25'4, or 205 miles. N' = $\mathbf{e}''\mathbf{a}'$ where $\mathbf{a}'$ = 10°00'18"N and 28°50'W and $\mathbf{e}''$ is 11°12'7N + 42'.5 x cos63 = 11°31'8N.

26°21'6W - 42.5' x sin63/cos11 = 26°21'6W - 38.6' = 25°43'W

N = 234, N' = 205. N/N' = 1.14 and $\mathbf{o}$ (135°) determine K = 0.9

Thus one obtains the value of E: 60.6^2 x 0.9/205 = 16. This value is not exact due to the errors of the azimuths. The actual error is only about 10 miles ($\mathbf{o}$ =12°10'3N, 26°02'5W and $\mathbf{x}$ = 12°N 26°W). Nevertheless, the value of E requires the computation of a second approximation as follows.

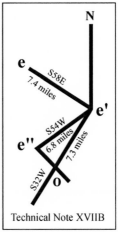

Technical Note XVIIB

D - L = 2°10.3' φ(D - L) = 148.1.

P = 26°02.5' - 22°35' = 3°27'5.

φP = 375.6. φP cosDcosL =.

375.6 x cos10 x cos12°10' = 361.7.

N$\mathbf{e}$ = 4°01.7' and the intercept is equal to 7.4 miles.

sinZ = 3.46° x cos10/4.03 = 0.845.

Z = S58°E(122).

This determines a new position $\mathbf{e}'$ at 12°06'4N, 25°56'W.

From $\mathbf{e}'$, one computes the second zenith distance:

φP cosD cosL = 264.2 x cos10 x cos12.1 = 361.7 and

φ(D - L) = 138.5.

N_e' = 3°32'2.

sinZ' = 2.9 x cos10/3.54 = 0.807 Z' = S54°W (234).

$\mathbf{e}'\mathbf{o}$, has the direction V_1, perpendicular to S58E (122°) is aligned in direction 212° (S32W).

$\mathbf{o}$, the angle between the azimuths, is equal to 234 - 122 = 112.

$\mathbf{eo}$ = 6.8/sin112 = 7.3 in the direction 212°.

END

Printed in the United States
202606BV00005B/1-33/A

9 781588 320681